ORGANIZATIONAL TIME MANAGEMENT HOW INFLUENCES

INFLUENCES

CONSUMER BEHAVIOR

JOHN LOK

Copyright © John Lok
All Rights Reserved.

Contents

Preface

Introduction

Whether can apply behavioral economic method to raise productivity, service performance in organizations and predict consumer individual emotion in consumption market. What factors cause organizational behavioral management pressure ? I write this book aims to explain whether behavioral economy methods can be attempted to solve how to raise productivities challenge in organizational situations as well as how to predict consumption behaviors challenges. This book divides two parts. Part one, I explain what behavioral economy mean and what behavioral economic methods can be applied to predict consumer emotions and raise staff productivities behaviors.

In part one, chapter one I shall explain how to apply behavioral economic method to predict normal basic income consumption client group's habitual spending behavior as well as how to apply behavioral economic method to predict how labor market changing behavior and predict when labor market changes will occur in order to solve shortage of labor or job supply shortage challenges, I shall explain how can apply behavioral economy method raises basic stable income consumer consumption desire, I shall explain behavioral economy method to explain what is the mean of basic stable income consumption great of small amount desire, how to apply life-cycle advertisement method to predict of consumer behavior, and explain how to apply behavioral economy method to raise electricity consumption from electricity user individual habit.

In part one, chapter two, I shall explain how to apply behavioral economic method to build consumer confidence is as a predictor of consumption spending. I shall also explain what confidence in consumption survey means and I shall apply behavioral economy method to explain how and why to apply survey to gather data in consumption market. It can measure how much degree of confidence of overall clients to the brand of product or service as well as how to build consumer confidence to buy the brand of product or consume the brand of service as well as I shall also explain what a confidence indicator means and how to apply confidence indicator to predict how many potential consumers will choose to buy the brand of product or consume the brand of service. I shall explain how to apply behavioral economy methods to influence employee individual psychology to achieve to raise productivity of long term incentive invention. I shall apply behavioral economy method to explain why increasing salary is short term incentive productivity method, how to improve the design of incentive structures to encourage productivities organizations, how to build employees and managers kindly co-operational relationship method, explain whether bonus method can encourage service performance to be raised as well as how to apply behavioral economy method to explain how to predict human motivation natural behaviors. I shall apply behavioral economic method to explain that why under-level productive efficiency is not represent low production number to the manufacturer as well as low-consumption desire is not represent less consumer demands or customers lose confidence to the product.
In part two, I shall indicate some large organization cases how to apply behavioral economy methods to predict consumer behaviors and solve consumer desire challenges as well as how to apply behavioral economic methods to raise staff productivities.

Prologue

contents

Bibliography

Behavioral economic method predicts stable basic income consumer individual spending behavior
● How to apply behavioral economic method to contribute to the stable basic income target consumer group's consumption prediction?
● How to apply behavioral economic method to predict labor market changing behavior ?

How can apply behavioral economy method raises basic stable income consumer consumption desire
1. Basic stable income consumption great of small amount desire
2. Life-cycle advertisement method prediction of consumer behavior
3. Raising electricity consumption from electricity user individual habit
    Consumer confidence is as a predictor of consumption spending
● What is confidence in consumption survey ?
● What is a confidence indicator ?
    How to apply behavioral economy methods influence employee individual psychology to achieve raise productivity of long term incentive intention?
● Increasing salary is short term incentive productivity method
● How to improve the design of incentive structures to encourage productivities organizations?
● Building employees and managers kindly co-operational relationship method
● Can bonus method encourage service performance to be raised ?
● Economic views of human motivation nature

Under-level productive efficiency and low-consumption desire behavioral economic influences

Time press how influences
video playing game consumer
purchase behavior

Time pressure consumption or
production situation explanation

Behavioral micro and macro economic concept

Behavioral economy method predicts organizational behavioral changes and marketing behavioral changes

Over the past 20 years, many researchers believe to apply behavioral economic macroeconomic models which can predict market behavioral change. The reasons are based on assumptions of optimizing behavior in many cases have difficulty accounting for key real-world observations. Hence, researchers have used behavioral economics assumptions with the aim of making their model predicting better fit the data. The reason for behavioral economics results into macroeconomics will be more accurate to predict market behavioral change in macro-economy view point, such as economic fluctuation prediction, the consumption, formation of expectations and determination of wages and employment how to aggregation supply and the possibility of consumer individual demand product or service number prediction more accurately.

● How to apply behavioral economy theory to predict marketing behavioral changes more accurate?
Anyway, economists aim to develop models of human behavior and interactions in market in order to build useful models. Economists make simplifying assumptions to analyze why the market will be changed by consumer individual consumption behavior changing.

Why do I assume consumers are as economic man ? In behavioral economy view point, how the perception of the economic man's behavior (including consumer choices) of economic models with the development of economics as a science. Economists explain the concept of economics as a science. It is the concept of consumer as an economic man, the essence and complexity of consumer behavior.

The consumer and consumer purchasing behavior are an important area of interest of many scientific disciplines. The process of economic decision making as well as consumption choices are connected with wider human activities. The terms of both consumer individual attitudes and group social behavior will influence group social behavior will influence consumer individual final consumption decision in every consumption choice process. Thus, behavioral economy method can predict consumer behavioral changing, it can apply these sciences to research, includes sociology, psychology, anthropology, operational research, decision theory etc. different literature research aspects. I assume that businessmen can apply behavioral economy method to predict market changing behaviors successfully if they own behavioral economy knowledge.

In this part, I shall concentrate on explain how the perception of the economic man's behavior (including consumer choice) is applied to predict market behaviors. After explaining the concept of consumer as an economic man, the nature and complexity of consumer behavior are discussed to below different industries' marketing behavioral changing every case studies in US or UK countries.

Why is consumer as an economic man? IN behavioral economy view point, the concept of answer is one of the fundamental concepts in economics because the consumer is the case market participant along with the producer. In general, lecturers define the consumer in various ways, but in behavioral economy view point, consumers mean economy man. Because who will compare cost and benefit to any product or service to decide to choose to buy the product or consume the service. Consumers are as "economic man", who will make own subjective preferences (tastes), habits and traditions and existing objective constraints (i.e. disposal income) market prices of products and services in order to satisfy whose needs to a maximum degree and in the most rational way.

Thus, economic man means consumers need to make psychological mind to decide whether who either prefer to buy this product or another product or prefer to consume this service or another service more suitable. Thus, any markets or industries need have themselves benefits and consumers must need to evaluate whether the product or service has more benefits to compare other products or services in the consumption market to satisfy whose needs. It means that if the product or service has more benefits to compare other similar products or services. Then the product or service will persuade many consumers to choose to but the product or consume the service.

Consequently, in first part, I shall indicate how to apply behavioral economy theory : economic man psychological method, benefits and costs benefits method, how to predict these US and UK enterprises marketing behavioral changing more accurate.

In the second part, I shall apply micro employee behavioral economy concept to explain how to solve these US and UK inter-organizational management challenge.

I believe that behavioral economy method can be applied to research organizational employee behaviors change, e.g. how any why the employee chooses to do this action in whose organization. Moreover, behavioral economy method can be applied to consumption market to predict how any why the consumer choose to buy the product or consume the service. So, any consumers and employees personal psychology and external environment economic factor will influence how to choose to do decision in any organizations or consumption environment.

Bibliography

Bandiera, O., I. Barankay, and I. Rasul (2005). Social preferences and the response to incentives: Evidence from personal data. The quarterly journal of economics 120 (3), 917-969.

Exadaktylos, F., A.M. Espin and P. Branas-Garza (2013). Experimental subjects are not different. Scientific reports 3, 1213.

Lazear, E.P. (1979). Why is there mandatory retirement? Journal of political economy 87(6), 1261-1284.

Behavioral economic method predicts stable basic income consumer individual spending behavior

Can apply behavioral economic method to predict that the consequences of a stable basic income consumer's consumption behavior? It may be significantly different than the ones are predicted by the standard economic model if more realistic assumptions of human consumption behavioral prediction success.

Behavioral economic method assumes that consumer will compare whether whose benefits are more than costs after they buy the product or consume the service. I assume the consumer is only the who have stable basic income source consumer target. This stable basic income target consumers who will evaluate or feel they will earn more benefits than costs to every product in their consumption process, after they will make final decision to choose to buy the product to use or consume the service. Otherwise, if they feel they won't earn more benefits after they buy the product or consume the service in the consumption process. Then, they won't choose to buy the product to use or consume the service. In behavioral economic view point, it indicates their consumption behaviors are depend on comparing the product or the service whether it can satisfy their desire benefits and their desire benefits to the product or service must be more than their consumption cost.

There are four points to apply behavioral economic method to predict each stable basic income individual income spending. They include: motivation, conspicuous consumption, social preferences and crowding theory.

Each stable basic income consumer individual spending amount will be different and it is represent that every high stable basic income consumer must decide to consume any high cost services or buy high cost products to use. Although some economic teachers assume general high income people will accept to spend more expenditures for enjoyment or buy high cost of products to satisfy basic high level necessary expenditures. But, applying behavioral economic analysis, it is not absolute true, some low income people also accept to spend more to buy high cost of products or increasing spending expenditures for enjoyment for their basic necessary expenditures.

The field of behavioral economic can be fined as a combination of economics and psychology that tries to capture human behavior in a more realistic. Understanding each consumer individual consumption behavior, we need to know how who does each decision to influence each consumption choice. Consequently, analysis reaches the conclusion. Every high or low level stable basic income consumer individual behavioral consumption that the microeconomic consequences of a stable basic income of individual consumer target consumption group could be efficiency enhancing, but at the same time incentives about positional concerns could lead to wasteful and inefficient spending to the stable low basic income consumer target group.

How to apply behavioral economic method to contribute to the stable basic income target consumer group's consumption prediction?

What is basic income mean? A basic income is an income paid by a political community to all its members on an individual basis, without means test or work requirement. How to apply behavioral economic method to contribute to the basic income consumption prediction?

I assume high income tax is charged to one high income tax payee , it will influence the high income tax payee individual consumption desires to be fallen, also extrinsic incentives will effort and intrinsic motivation and how the labor market change these variables under and big changes predicting, how income security changes social consumption preferences, e.g. how a big change affects the overall level of status -seeking behavior and this effect with income inequality to influence consumer individual consumption attitude or habit.

How can behavioral economic methods predict consumer's consumption decision, in special the stable basic income consumer target group? In any consumption decisions are involving risk and uncertainty, the standard economic model usually assumes that decisions are based on final condition, regardless of the changes are caused by the results of a consumer's decision.

An alterative mode of how consumers make decision and judgement under risk and uncertainty. This situation is often occurred in consumption market.

In behavioral economic view point, it explains how consumer's consumption, however, which excludes the stable basic income earn factor can influence the stable basic income earn target consumer group decides to make final consumption decision to compare to the non-stable basic income earn target consumer group. The reasons include as below:

(1) Consumers evaluate decisions over gains and losses with respect to some natural reference point, when they feel need to consume, which is assumed to be judgement about a sequence of outcomes are based on changes in wealth, rather than whether how much absolute basic income earn to influence whose consumption desires.

(2) Thus, behavioral economic theory assumes the consumer is the low level of income group in society, but when who feels that he is still gains more than losses when who decides to buy the expensive product or consumes the expensive service. Then, the low level of income consumer who will accept to buy the expensive product or consume the service easily. Due to whose gains feeling is more than losses feeling, when who buys the product or consumes the service.

(3) Behavioral economic theory also assumes the taxpayer will pay high income tax in this year. The, even the high income taxpayer can earn high basic income, but due to whom needs to pay high income tax in this year. Then, he/she will reduce much spending, even he/she reduces spending on cheap products or cheap service consumption for enjoyment. This is the taxpayer's economic decision to influence whose consumption behavior, due to the high income tax expenditure factor influences whose consumption behavior to change to be reduced spending expenditures in this year.

How to apply behavioral economic method to predict labor market changing behavior?

Instead of applying behavioral economic method to predict every consumer individual consumption effort. Behavioral economic method can be also be applied to predict every country's labor market changing behavior. Particularly, how salary clerical workers or low wage labor workers should move from one type of job to another based on these factors. They include as below:

Their intrinsic motivation and how their levels of effort would change after this movement, investigates the effects of income security on social preferences in labor market changing behavior, and how cooperation in social contribution is affected when income security is guaranteed, how to predict the role of positional externalities on conspicuous consumption and how would change the incentive to influence consumption. So, it seems that general labor market job changing behaviors will not influenced by external economic environment better or worse changing factor, or salary changing factor etc. different environmental condition changing factors influence to employees' job changing. Generally, employee's job changing behavior is more influenced to persuade who changes job by himself/herself intrinsic motivation negative emotion influence mainly.

How to apply motivation crowding theory to predict labor productivity? One of the main challenges of economic theory is to find what are the optimal incentives that increase productivity of labors. The standing point is usually extrinsic incentive be it is form of monetary compensations for high effort or fine for low effort.

It is a kind method of reward or punishment to increase or decrease number of productivity to every labor. But it can only raise short term number of productivity in possible and it can not guarantee high quality of productivity. So if one employer wants a labor to do more of an activity or with a higher quality, consider paying the labor for working hard on punishing whom if for providing a low level effort.

This idea is that people do not like to work, and therefore they used some sort of compensation for doing a specific activity, and that the more they are paid the harder, they will work. So, payment better compensation is only beneficial to encourage labors to do one specific task or activity in short term. This method can not be suitable to rise long term beneficial productivity and high level quality of production or excellent performance in long term and it can only keep in short term raising productivity and high level quality of production or excellent performance benefits.

Consider paying the labor for working hard on punishing whom if for providing a low level effort. This idea is that people do not like to work, and therefore they used some sort of compensation for doing a specific activity, and that the more they are paid the harder they will work. So, payment better compensation is only beneficial to encourage labors to do one specific task or activity in short term. This method can not be suitable to raise long them beneficial productivity and high quality of products.

However, economists would argue that, is a labor has high intrinsic motivative to perform a task, who will provide a high level of effort without compensation by himself/herself but an even higher level of effort of whom is compensated. If a labor does not have any intrinsic motivation to perform a task or an activity, who will provide no effort or a low effort of whom. There is no compensation, but who will increase this level of effort of an extrinsic incentive is implemented.

Hence, in behavioral economic view point, the labor individual high level effort is a main psychological factor to influence whose productivity to be raised or the qualities of products to be raised, when the products are manufactured by the high level effort labor. It means that high compensation is not the good method to encourage labor productivity or raise quality. Otherwise, how to influence the one low level of effort of labor to change to be one high level of effort labor. It is the best psychological method to influence the labor to raise productivity and quality and service performance to any products or services in manufacturing process or service process for any organizations in long term beneficial possible.

How can apply behavioral economy method raises basic stable income consumer consumption desire

Economists aim to develop models of human behavior and interactions in consumption markets. But consumers behave in complex ways, such as how to predict consumers to make rational decisions in consumption processes. Moreover, self-consumption control and motivation can vary significantly across different individual consumer.

In order to build useful consumption prediction models, economists make simplifying assumptions, aims to predict how to raise stable basic income consumer target group consumption more success. However, behavioral economy method is one kind of accurate consumption prediction method. It can be applied to predict economic decision-making to every consumer consumption choice more accurate raising whose consumption desire?

I shall indicate how to apply different behavioral economy methods to raise stable basic stable income target consumer group consumption desire in these different consumption situation (consumption environment) aspects as below:

1. Stable basic stable income consumer group consumption great or small amount desire

The consumption of products and services is a fundamental part of consumer's welfare. Basically, every one who has stable basic stable income, who will like to consume any products and services. Even, consumption great or small amount desire won't be depended on whether the person whose income is more or less. It means low income level of people will still like to consume great amount to buy expensive products or consume expensive services, because consumption is human's part of life and basic needs.

This stable basic income people will like to consume, because they have stable income source when they do not worry about unemployment occurrence to cause them have no enough money to support their life. Otherwise, non-stable basic stable income people won't like to consume because they feel they have no stable basic income source to support their life and they will worry about unemployment occurrence any time. Hence, stable basic income people will have more consumption desire to compare non-stable basic stable income people in any countries usually. Behavioral economic method indicates they feel their economic benefits will be loss if they planned to buy any products or consume any services easily. So, they prefer to save money in bank more than consumption.

1. Demand systems and micro-economic factor influence basic income people consumption attitude

Why stable basic income people will like to consume? Because who have more demand, a demand system shows the level of consumer demand for different products and services: e.g. one basic stable income person may refer to the demand for clothes, another the demand for food etc.

How the demand for that particular product varies with the prices and demographic factor will influence who to accept consumption. Such as stable basic income people who will not consider to decide to buy the cloth to wear or the food to eat if who feel the cloth or food price is even more expensive to compare other kind of cloth or food. Otherwise, non-stable basic income people who will consider to decide to buy the cloth to wear or the food to eat if they feel that they still have enough cloths to wear or enough food to eat at homes , even these food or cloth price are less expensive to compare others. Because they feel they lack stable income effort to support them to consume. Hence, basic stable income factor can influence the consumer's consumption decision.

2. Life-cycle advertisement method can influence consumer individual consumption behaviors to be increased

Consumer behavior makes strong assumptions about the informational and computational bases of consumer behavior. Generally, consumer behavior is reasonably characterized as the maximization of expected lifetime utility subject to budget constraint and conditional on the available information.

Generally, consumers prefer to buy any discounted products or it is reasonable that consumers accept to buy many attractions to persuade them to buy any kinds of bargain discount products. Hence, low bargain discount product is one good behavioral economic principle to encourage or persuade or attract any consumers to increase consumption. What is behavioral life-cycle model? This model explains consumer behavior can be persuaded to buy any discounted products by advertisement, e.g. television, radio, newspapers, magazine etc. promotion channels. Because frequent advertisement promotion method can let any consumers often remember the product's brand, discounted price, style, color and image from advertisement content.

So, advertisement can be one part of consumer behavioral life-cycle. For example, when the television audiences often watch TV. Hence, when the brand of product advertisement often makes fun image and discounted message to let TV audiences to remember this brand of product, when they are watching TV. Then, it has possible to persuade any potential consumers to choose to buy this brand of any products or consume this brand of any services, due to its advertisement of discounted sale message is very attractive to every one to let this advertisement audience's attention to remember this brand of products or services are selling or serving in market at this moment. So, it is advertisement image behavior influences audiences to buy the brand's any products attractively and persuasively.

3. Raising electricity consumption from electricity user individual habit

For electricity use market case example, how to analyze people's behavior in consuming electricity using a behavioral economic framework ? Electricity consumption is modeled by the means of consumer's individual useful habit, electricity price, consumer satisfaction level, willingness to invest in new technologies, social interactions, and marketing strategies by the power utility. Because electricity is necessary to every home or electric vehicle users needs or businessmen office etc. different needs every day.

Power companies supply electricity to a region's homes and industries. However, electricity needs modernization of power system companies expect to increase price. Due to competitive factor, such as other fuel resource choices, outdated kind of energy electricity supply, and renewable fuel energy source competition.

Hence, applying behavioral economic concept, I assume electricity consumers will compare to electricity and other kinds of energy choices to weigh up the costs and benefits of all alternatives, aiming to maximize their benefits, before making a decision to choose to use electricity for their house electricity demand or electric vehicle or shop or factory manufacturing etc. function of different aspects of electricity users.

For example, electricity business clients, they aim to reduce cost, such as energy expenditure, when they use any energy to manufacture their products in factories. If they feel electricity is expensive price to compare other kinds of energy power supply. When, they feel that they can not earn much beneficial advantages to use electricity to produce their products. Otherwise, if they feel other any kinds of energy supply can replace electricity to give more benefits to compare electricity energy. Then, many business electricity users will change to use other kinds of energies to consume to replace electricity power.

However, electricity can have competitive ability in electric vehicles market, if many drivers feel environment protection is more important to compare vehicles will be popular to be driven, due to many drivers don't want air pollution. They will like gas vehicles. Hence, the main attribute from the consumer side is one their habit electricity consumption behaviors, satisfaction level, energy efficient interaction with the power utility.

Consequently how to predict electricity consumer's demand. The important factor is how to let electricity users to feel power companies are changing a reasonable level to compare other similar energy supply products. When electricity users feel electricity which can bring more benefits to compare other kinds of energy products. Then, in energy supply market, if the demanding number of electricity consumers can increase more than other kinds of energy demanding number. Then, it is right time to raise electricity price to charge electricity consumers. Hence, how to persuade electricity consumers to feel that they can have more benefits to compare other kinds of energy products. It is the main successful factor to electricity power supply companies.

Consumer confidence is as a predictor of consumption spending

Behavioral economists believe it has link between confidence and economic decisions to cause consumers to choose spending, if the consumer has confidence to believe the product is worth to use, then who will accept to buy the product to use.

Concentrated on the conceptualization of confidence and its role in mode in theories of consumption. It also concerns on whether the confidence indicators contain any information beyond economic fundamentals. The concern is whether confidence can be explained by current and past value of variables, such as income, unemployment, inflation or consumption or in other way.

Whether confidence measures have any statistical significance in predicting economic outcomes once information from the above variables is used. Economic variable factor will also influence consumer confidence to decide consumption spending, e.g. real consumption expenditures (income, wealth or interest rate).

Finally, it will identify under which circumstances confidence indicates can be a good predictor of household consumption. Hence, survey is one good measurement method to predict whether how much every household has confidence to spend to consume the brand of products to use. Why is survey a good confidence consumption measurement prediction to every household in every country?

The reasons include survey can gather every household consumption habit history data to evaluate whether every survey person has how much confidence to consume the brand of products. Which in most cases correspond to periods where there are large changes in household survey indicators, liking during financial crises or geopolitical tensions to measure or predict whether the country's future good or bad economic condition factor will influence every household consumption desire in the year.

This modelling approach assumes that there is a certain (unknown) in confidence index changes beyond which confidence starts impacting consumption behaviors. So, sample household surveys can show the contribution of confidence in explaining consumption expenditures increases when household survey indicators feature large changes. So that confidence indicators can have some increasing predictive power during the survey investigation period in the year.

Other view point, surveys have been concerned on whether the confidence indicators contain any information beyond economic fundamentals. The concern is whether confidence can be explained by current and past values of variables, such as income, unemployment, inflation or consumption or the other way. Whether confidence measures have any statistical significance in predicting economic outcomes once information from different external variable factors to influence the survey household group.

What is confidence in consumption survey ?

Confidence in consumption. For example, to measure whether how much degree of strong inflation in the economy, such as recessions and recoveries will influence the country's household confident consumption in the year.

The surveys consumers' questions usually concern on major expenditures and changes in the respondent's financial situation, focus on job availability and current business conditions etc. questions. It is then possible that about consumer confidence depending on the relative performance of the variables that may be more relevant balances, with respect to the factors that determine unemployment and other labor market related issues. It aims to investigate whether those any one of variable factors will influence consumers general loss confident consumption desire in this year.

What is a confidence indicator ?

A confidence indicator is considered as an explanatory variable for consumption together with standard variables used on predicting consumption expenditure. However, the natural real personal consumption expenditure is unexpected and unpredicted easily.

In conclusion, consumption expenditure depends the consumer individual confidence. If the consumer has much confidence to feel this year economic change will be better and he/she is easily to find job, then he/she will accept consumption easily in this year. It seems financial wealth and unemployment etc. economic factors will influence every household consumption desire. So, survey is one kind of good psychological consumption prediction method to predict consumption spending for any country in the year. I recommend manufacturers may choose to apply survey method to attempt to enquire sample survey people to gather data to predict whether what degree of consumption desire to them and find solution methods to solve low degree of consumption desire challenge.

How to apply behavioral economy methods to influence employee individual psychology to achieve raise productivity of long term incentive intention?

Increasing salary is short term incentive productivity method. Behavioral economy assumes labors will choose to do beneficial behaviors to themselves when they feel their work behaviors can earn more benefits to themselves more than their employers in the organizations. Otherwise, if they feel their work behaviors can earn more benefits to their employers more than themselves. Then, they won't choose to do their work behaviors, e.g. raising productivities or work hard. Due to they feel work hard or raise productivities behaviors that only give more benefits to their employers more themselves.

Whether does cheap product price incentive consumption desire to influence effective consumption behavior? Whether is monetary increasing salary payment incentive labors might be willing to work on task? I feel raising labors productivities is similar to raise incentive consumption, which both have similar point, such as increasing salary payment or cheap product price is the main factor to influence incentive consumption or raising productivities. Hence, it seems monetary factor is not the main effort to encourage labors to work hard.

In labor's behavioral economic view point, for example, if an employer pays an employee more doing a task, who might be less willing to work on it, who might be less productive given whose efforts and who may enjoy the task less. If you want your employees to save more for retirement. You may want to give them fewer investment options. If you want them to engage more in a task, you might want offer them an additional alternative, instead of increasing salary to that task. Thus, increasing salary is not only method to encourage productivities of incentives.

How to improve the design of incentive structures to encourage productivities in any organizations?

Any monetary incentive can only encourage productivities in short term. It can not only encourage productivities in long term in any organizations. It is similar to cheap or discount product price can only attractive consumers to buy the product in short term, it can not attract consumers to choose to buy the product in long term, it prefers to have more options to encourage labors to incentive productivities, e.g. investing good beneficial retirement plans. Suggesting that employees do not have free disposal of their investment options. These standard incentives seem irrelevant raising salary monetary factor, they can be quite effective in inducing labors to take particular actions to incentive productivities in long term. Due to when they can hard work, then they have more beneficial retirement plans or investing plans for their retirement. It means when they can achieve the most effective or efficient productivities to the employer for long term. It will give better retirement benefits and investment benefits to the better or even the best performance of employees. Otherwise, the worst performance employees won't earn good retirement benefits and investment benefits, when their employers feel their perform very poor in the organizations in long term.

Hence, increasing salary level method is not one successful long term incentive method to persuade every employee to raise productivities or encourage excellent performance optional method. Increasing salary level is only similar to reduce product price and it is only short term encouragement to consumption or productivities method.

In conclusion, extrinsic monetary factor can not incentive labor's raising productivities more than every employee themselves intrinsic motivation to raise productivities as excellent performance in any organizations. Thus, organizations need to let employees to feel that they can give long term economic benefits to encourage their intrinsic motivation effort to be raised their productivities or performance more effective or efficient in order to achieve long term both win-win economic benefits to employees and employers both.

Building employees and managers kindly co-operational relationship method

If you are an economist, your employer has no without any financial incentive to encourage your economic research tasks in your organization. It is equally difficult to certify that such activity will contribute to your growth of human capital and increased productivity in research or teaching.

The standard model, which explains employee's effort only through the way (determined by productivity), is therefore incomplete. In particular, it doesn't consider that incentives to work do not have to be monetary in other words, that there are other things besides the disutility of labor (Kamenica, 2012) and section 1.3 have.

Why will short term wage increasing method only influence short term labor supply to raise productivities? The effect of reference raising wage can be most easily identified on short term labor supply to raise productivities. For US, New York city taxi drivers case, they have to decide every day for low long they are going to offer their services, given the day-to-day variable ability of demand they face (peaking during bad weather and/or when big conferences and public events are taking place in the city).

In the standard model, houses worked should grow with any growth in demand for New York taxi drivers' services. (one day's earning will have only a negligible income effect in the longer run). And yet actual cabbies work less on a demand heavy day. One of possible explanations suggests that New York city taxi drivers expect a certain income, they have set themselves a specific target income, who expect to achieve every day. During low demand for their taxi services, then they work longer hours to reach the target, when during peak demand, their referential income is achieved quickly and they only work short hours. Elasticity of hours worked with respect to their earnings is therefore negative (Lamerer, Babcock, Loewenstein, & Thaler, 1997).

However, taxi driver is either one self employment business or one taxi company employment driving service occupation. It is similar to other kinds of service jobs in societies. Servicing employees, such as waiters, salespeople, securities, customer services, bus drivers etc. different kinds of service occupations. They are not similar to manufacturing occupation to be applied how many amount of piece of products production to evaluate their productivities efforts. Thus these any one of service job nature is depended on their service performance to clients to feel their service performances are excellent to compare general service performance effort of service employees. Considerably, respectively, I assume that if these service employees' managers can build kindly working environment, e.g. manager individual attitude and behavior can let their employees to feel happy to work together in their teams. Then, the managers' kindly as enthusiastic behaviors or attitudes will let every employee more positive encouragement of service attitude to serve their clients in their teams. Then, the client complaining number will be possible reduced, even none of any complains. Hence, building kindly relationship between managers and employees will raise excellent service performance to any organization service nature employees.

Can bonus method encourage service performance to be raised ?

In service job nature of bonus method can also raise employees' overall productivities or service performance. For example, when employees got a provisional bonus before the start of the workweek, but were warned that they would lose it on payday, unless they achieve the productivities or excellent service performance norm, they worked more productivities or let many clients to satisfy their service performance. Hence, managers can achieve bonus plan to compensate any excellent productivity or excellent services to them. Then, they can let clients to feel their service performance more satisfactory than employees of a control group who were merely given the standard promise to receive a bonus upon achieving the norm.

The effort was relatively small, however, productivity grew 1%. Interestingly, the effect of a loss was stronger when how teams were rewarded this way, social pressure came to bear on the less productivity team members. When the team members won't earn any bonus. So, long-term productivity gains were achieved through bonuses paid by excellent performance compensation method to compare to low service performance employees receiving no bonuses at all.

Economic views of human motivation nature

There are only two main types of economic actors and by making simplifying assumptions about how these types of actors behave and interact. The two basic sets of actors in this model are firms, which are assumed in this model are firms, which are assumed to maximize their profits from producing and selling products and services, households, which are assumed to maximize their utility (or satisfaction) from consuming products and services.

It seems any employees will choose to do behaviors to achieve to earn much benefits from their organizations. The models of economic behaviors that consider considerate employees' choice of goals, the actions they take to achieve these goals and the limitations and influences that affect their choices and actions.

For university students choose which universities to study case, suppose that any college enrollment students are deciding which courses to study. Thus, it implies that if the university can provide many different kinds of suitable or right courses to any college enrollment students to choose to study. It means that if the university can provide many different kinds of courses to enrollment students to choose to study. Then, it will have much chance to attract enrollment students to choose this university to study. It's competition can be raised by many courses choice factor. but, in fact, it is not absolute right, although the university can provide many courses to provide to enrollment students to choose to study. But, it is not guarantee to represent it must attract many students to enroll this university to study.

For example, suppose that college enrollment students are deciding which courses to choose to study. Although, it has right course to prepare to these enrollment students to choose to study. But, they see a summary of evaluations from hundreds of other students indicating that a certain course is very good in this university. Then, suppose that they match a video interview of just one student to give a negative review of this university of the course. Even when students were told in advance that such a negative review was worse to this university of the course. They tended to be more influenced by the negative review than the summary of hundreds of evaluations, even although such behavior seems irrational. Hence, although many right courses choice has much chance to attract students to enroll this university to study. But, if its bad educational quality from this course from negative review factor, which will influence the enrollment students number to be reduced.

It implies that students will compare this university's the course educational quality whether is better or worse to compare other universities' similar course educational quality, even this university's this course fee whether is reasonable in educational market. This is cost and beneficial comparison behavioral economy principle to all enrollment students before they decide to choose which universities.

Hence, this case implies that universities how to train teachers' teaching skills to let students to feel that they can learn new knowledge from their teaching staffs absolutely. It means how to raise education training skills to raise teachers' teaching performance. It is very important factor to influence the university's teaching development success. So, many courses choice is not important factor to attract many students to enroll the university. Otherwise, although the university can not provide many courses to let students to enroll, but it's teachers can provide excellent teaching service to teach whose students. This is important factor to attract many students to choose to enroll this university to study.

Under-level productive efficiency and low-consumption desire behavioral economic influences

In behavioral economic influence view point, I feel that under-level productive efficiency is the represent low production number to the manufacturer as well as low-consumption desire is not represent less consumers demands or customers lose confidence to the product.

On the one hand, I shall apply behavioral economic method to analyze why under productive efficiency is not represent low production number influence. Otherwise, I feel under-productive efficiency will have possible to increase production number after the manufacturer can review what factor(s) to influence under-productive efficiency.

I shall give reasons to explain as below:

As Jim, P. & Brendan. M. (2013) indicated who had ever been experiencing failure to do their businesses. Although, they had lost a million dollars, but they felt that they can be taught to learn undiscovered knowledge to know how to do their businesses successful by their wrong judgement and decision learning experience. They explained that " in ll risk taking, speculation, business ventures, entrepreneurial activities, it is the loss side on which you must focus first. This is even true for gambling, the gambler determines how much he's willing to bet, and loss, before the game is played. He doesn't wait for the game to end and then let the croupier or dealer assign his wager for him. How do you determine the downside, and how do you control or minimize it? With objective decision making and a plan that has as its starting point the stop-loss parameters"

Hence, it explains any business will have under-level productive efficiencies and low consumption desire business risk. However, to any one entrepreneur, who needs to know it is one game between the himself/herself and whose clients. They also need to know with objective decision making and a plan that has as its starting point.

Hence, I assume that if the entrepreneur has wrong decision to cause under-level productive efficiency, it is possible that, due to there is no enough employee number to manufacture the product or many employees are not skillful to manufacture all product in normal time or many employees are lazy etc. different factors to cause under-level productivities. However, when they discover their productivities are very low to compare similar competitors their employees' productivities and efficiencies. Then, they can attempt to find what factor(s) to cause low productivities and low efficiencies. it is possible that any one among of these factors case. They include many employees' lazy to influence low productivities or there is no enough employee number or many employees are not skillful to manufacture their products in production process.

Hence, wrong decision or plan is not represent failure. Otherwise, it can give chance to let the entrepreneur to learn whether what the factor(s) is (are) to cause low productivities and low efficiencies in whose product manufacturing process. As I feel that under-level productive efficiency is not represent low production number. Because I assume that if one worker lacks enough skills and manufacturing experiences to manufacture the product, but who can spend less time to manufacture the product and whose spending manufacturing time is same to the another owning enough skillful worker's time to do the product. Hence, I believe that the product quality from the low-skillful worker's manufacturing skill, it's quality will be worse to compare to the product quality from the high skillful worker's manufacturing skill. Hence, if the low skillful worker needs to spend much time to produce the product, but the product quality can be same to the high skillful worker's product quality. It means that it is sure because the low skillful worker has no excellent skill to compare to the high skillful worker to produce the product. Hence, his manufacturing spending time must be longer than the high skillful worker's time. It implies that the low skillful worker spends less time to raises high production number, but his product must be poor quality to sell. Then, his fast and efficient manufacturing speed that is not achieve economic beneficial to the organization's manufacturing process, e.g. less electricity spends to manufacture the product. Otherwise, the low skillful worker's fast and efficient manufacturing speed of behavior will raise the organization's cost in manufacturing process because consumers would not like to choose to buy any low quality product when they can choose which similar products to compare which one has the best quality and cheap price to buy.

Hence, efficient production is not the main factor to influence the business's success. Otherwise, good quality of the product factor is more important to compare it to influence the business's success.

On the other hand, I shall apply behavioral economic theory to analyze why low-consumption desire is not represent consumer demand lose to the business. As Jim. P. & Brendan. M. (2013) also identified " rather than looking for success to follow, who explained the formula for failure to avoid. As an Wang, founder of Wang laboratories said " it is my belief that there are no secret to success." The formula for failure is not lack of knowledge, brains, skills or hard work and it's not lack of luck, it's personalizing losses, especially of preceded by a string of wins or profits. It's refusing to acknowledge and accept the reality of a loss when it starts to occur because to so so would reflect negatively on you."

Thus, as whose feeling to explain why low-consumption desire is not represent less consumers demands or customers lose confidence to the product. The reasons include the causes of low-consumption desire are possible due to worse economic environment factor influences consumption desire to be reduced. It is not due to whether the product price is too high or quality is worse to compare others. Hence, as Jim & Brendan indicated the formula for business failure is not lack of knowledge, brains, skills or hard work and it's not lack of luck. It's not lack of luck. It's personalizing losses, means its reflecting to knowledge and accept the reality of a loss when it starts to occur. As it is applied to explain why low-consumption desire is not represent less consumers demands or customers lose confidence to the product. It's possible that external economic environment changing worse factor to cause the business personalizing losses, it is not reflect who lacks knowledge, skill, hard work factors to cause failure. Hence, ho to predict when and how and why economic environment changes worse will be important factor to predict when and how and why consumption behavioral changes to cause business's success.

Reference

Camerer, C.F. Babrocks, Loewenstein, G., & Thaler, R. (1997). Labor supply of New York city candrivers: One day of a time. The Quacterly Jounrnal of economics, 112 (2), 407-441. doi: 10.1162/003355399555244.

How do you view the outlook for consumer confidence in your key markets next year? Source from : http://www.Just-food.com Confidence survey, Nov.2015

Jim. P. & Brendan. M. (2013) . What I learned losing a million dollars, p.160. Colimbia University, Columbia business school press, New York, US.

Kamenica, E. (2012). Behavioral economics and psychology of incentives. Annual review of economics, 4 (1), 427-452. doi: 10.1146/annurev-economics-080511-110909.

Maselli, 2012 Technology driven job polarization in
EU , 2000-2010. % change in labor supply
skilled/upgrade (ISCED) and labor demand for
skills/tasks (ISOD).

Behavioral economy method Predictive marketing behavioral changes

CHAPTER II

Walt Mark Supermarket sale management pressure

Apply behavioral economy method critically assess the extent to which whether Body Shop to be a truly marketing oriented organization throughout its 30 years history. Is body shop daily product is one truly marketing oriented organization? I shall apply behavioral economy method to analyze whether consumers will be influenced by economic environment change to influence their consumption desire to choose to buy Body shop products. If consumers won't be influenced to reduce to buy body shop products by economic environment influence, then it will be one truly marketing oriented organization.

● Body Shop Background

The body shop international power line carrier (the body shop) was founded by Dame Anita Roddick in the England in 1976. It sold personal beauty care products, such as baby and child specific products, bath and shower and color cosmetics, deodorants, skin care, hair care, fragrances, sun care etc. skin health products to provide human body benefits. Nowadays, the body shop was skin and body care manufacturer and retailer operating in 55 countries with over 2,100 stores. It had 42 exclusive outlets in Hong Kong. It's missions were to dedicate to pursuit of social and environment change to meaningfully contribute to local, national and international communities in which trade to passionately campaign for the protection of the environment, human and civil rights and against animal testing and to make fun, passion and care part of our daily lives (Adrian, P. 2012).

● What is the difference between production orientation and societal marketing orientation and sales orientation

In behavioral economy analysis, Body shop consumers' consumption behaviors are trend to satisfy needs more than cheap product price. It means that Body shop had built famous brand. It doesn't consider whether its skin health products are cheaper price to compare competitors' price. It needs to concentrate on researching to manufacture many attractive skin health products to let consumers who feel it can give more skin health beneficial advantages to let them to feel why who need to use Body shop any skin health products. Thus, its consumer consumption behaviors are not influence by its price, they are influenced by their skin health function.

There are five main marketing orientations of which a company will adopt one. This will determine the way it interacts with the customer. Such as product orientation suggests that a company focuses inwards looking at what it is capable of, rather than the needs and wants of the client; sales orientation is based upon selling existing products with a turnover sale numbers relationship marketing orientation recognizes the value of repeat business over, not only with customers but suppliers as well; societal marketing orientation is relatively new in the scheme of things but suggests on top of meeting the needs and wants of the customer and the organization there is the societies interests to be looked and marketing orientation is based around the needs and wants of a customer to meet business objectives and it assumes that a sale depends on a customer's decision to purchase a product or provide a service.

● What is marketing two levels meaning ?

Marketing can be seen at two levels, the first level is such as a business philosophy, marketing puts customers at the center of an organization's consideration and which is reflected in basic values , such as the requirement to understand and respond to customers' needs and the necessary to search constantly for new market opportunity. In a truly marketing oriented organization, these values are instilled in all employees and should influence their behavior without any need for prompting. The personnel manager would have a selection policy that recruited staff who could fulfil the needs of customers rather than simply minimizing the wage bill in any marketing oriented organization. The other level is techniques of marketing also include pricing, the design of channels of distribution and new product development.

● What are the three components of market orientation ?

The assessing the nature and importance of market orientation for large firms, such as body shop. The three components of market orientation could be analytically separated. The components of market orientation organization include the first component is the customer orientation, it means an organization must have a thorough understanding of its target buyers, so that it can create a product of superior value to give client benefits ; the second component is the competitor orientation, it means any firm should look at how well its competitors are able to satisfy buyers' needs. It should understand the short term strengths and weaknesses and long term capabilities and strategies of current and potential competitors as well as the third component is to develop marketing plans that are not acted upon by people who are capable of delivering promises made to customers and a marketing orientation organization requires that the organization draws upon and integrates its human and physical resources effectively and adapts them to meet client's needs. Otherwise, a production and sales orientation may be appropriate to firms at certain stages in the evolution of markets. Where the dominant business environment is based on the need for good production planning above all, the company that does this best will achieve the greatest overall business success. It is either production orientation, it means organizations that produce what they imagined consumers wanted, rather than what they actually wanted. Planning for full utilization of capital equipment are often seen as more important than ensuring that equipment is used to provide goods and services that people actually wants. Production-oriented firms generally aim for efficiency in production rather than effectiveness in meeting customer's needs . It is either or selling orientation, it means advertising, sales promotion and personal selling techniques are used to emphasize product differentiation and brands and it does not focus on satisfying client needs or desire new product offerings and production led. Hence, one market orientation organization needs to focus on satisfying clients' needs profitably by these marketing mix, such as product, price, place, physical evidence, processed, people and promotion. Anyway ,Market orientation implied that body shop , which ought seek information about clients, such as current and future needs and took action based this information (client orientation); it ought seek information about competitors' current strengths and weaknesses and their long term strategies and took actions based on these information (competitor orientation) ; it ought coordinate the actions taken by sharing clients and competitors information internally (intra-firm communication).

● What is the three components of market orientation ?

The three components of market orientation meant social marketing and understanding boarder concerns and ethical environmental, legal and social context of marketing activities and programs. The cause and effects of marketing clearly beyond the company and the consumer to society as whole. New terms humanistic marketing and ecological marketing were suggested to societal marketing concept.

● What is the social marketing concept ?

The social marketing concept holds that the organization's task is to determine the needs, wants and interests of target markets and to deliver the desired satisfactions more effectively and
efficiently than competitors and the society's welling being, such as body shop had achieved sales and profit gains by adopting and practicing a form of the societal marketing concept called cause related marketing.

● DISCUSSION
Body Shop is marketing orientation organization in 30 years.
Critically assess the extent to which I consider Body Shop to be a truly marketing oriented organization throughout its 30 years history . It seemed body shop had achieved cause-related marketing as an opportunity to enhance their corporate reputation, raised brand awareness, increased customer loyalty and built sales.
It's corporate values were composed of five core values. The first one was to oppose animal testing. The opposing animal testing for both cosmetic products and ingredients began in 1976 years.
In the 1980 year and 1990 year, who successfully campaigned with animal protection groups to change the UK and European laws to support the development products were tried on human
volunteers. Along with the development of technology testing had played a leading role to protect the rights of both human and animals . The second one was to support community trade, it initiated the trade not aid objective of creating trade to help people in the third world utilizing their resources to their own needs. This reflects communities needed a fair price for natural ingredients who purchased from these often marginalized countries. The third one was to activate self esteem. Women were the main customers and employees in the body shop. The fourth one was

to defend human rights. The body shop had long campaign on human rights, highlighting abuses and increasing the global awareness of issues by making full use of the geographic advantages of their shops and supporting other human rights organizations. The last one was protect our plant. In 2001 year, huge campaign against global warming was hosted by the body shop and green peace, who advocated the use of recyclable source and materials (Adrian, P. 2012). Although profits were an essential element of long run survival in body shop and it was likely to be overall corporate and marketing objectives, but body shop seemed more to be required level of profits rather than profit that there were many other objectives, which might pursue through its pricing strategies . For example, if body shop wanted to maximize market share or simply survive, a different set of prices would be delivered than if the objectives were to maximize profits. Hence, body shop ought to see viewpoint the marketing side of pricing and it ought not to see viewpoint the production / supply side of pricing if it was a truly marketing oriented organization. The key inputs for body shop to make pricing decision whether it was marketing oriented or productive / supply oriented included production objectives or marketing objectives, demand or supply numbers were considered cost or sale price and competitors or clients consideration factors, such as beauty skin care products in competitive markets demand, i.e. To decide the price whether customers are willing and able to pay is a major consideration in the selection of pricing strategies and levels of demands . Hence, body shop ought to consider demand numbers , it ought not consider production / supply numbers if it was a truly marketing oriented organization. For example, since most of the body shop's factories were still located in the UK, where wages and salaries were much higher than in Asia, so UK itself sale product prices were higher than that from Asia itself sale product prices.

I think Body Shop was a truly marketing oriented organization more than production/supply oriented organization throughout its 30 years history. In fact, Body Shop was experiencing market level growth. It could expand its sales market in Europe, America, Middle East, Asia and Africa etc. different countries. It seemed that it had attempted to carry on marketing research to decide to choose which countries would have more client numbers to demand to buy its personal care products, then it would follow the countries' estimated client numbers to produce its products to sell to the countries. So, it was why some Asia countries sold its bath and shower and skin and hair care and colour cosmetics products more than its fragrances products, such as Hong Kong young people were more acceptable to use bath and show and color cosmetic and skin and hair care products more than fragrances products . It seemed that Hong Kong Body Shop sold fragrance products numbers were less than bath and shower and color cosmetics etc. products. Nowadays, I think the personal beauty care products new businesses which planned to entry this market was more difficult. It was possible than Body Shop was a famous personal beauty care products sale company, it had owned many clients too many years. So , it caused barriers to any new personal beauty care product competitors felt difficult to entry this market .Furthermore, Body Shop had build strong buyer and seller power to increase clients had more confident to use its products, it was possible that who felt its different kind of products could give more health to their skin or body more than other similar personal beauty care products. Moreover, I believe Body Shop had attempted to carry on technological experimenting to aim to build different countries' clients had more confident to use its products forever.
In conclusion, it seemed that Body Shop was truly marketing oriented organization more than productive/ supply oriented organization oriented organization throughout its 30 years history.

2. To what extent are the pursuits of profit and meeting the needs of wider groups of stakeholders incompatible? Whether Body shop pursuits social responsibility aim or profit aim more.

Any companies need to consider the social responsibility during which are the pursuits of profit and meeting the needs of wider group of stakeholders incompatible. Without this self interest, there will be little motivation for firms to provide better services, workers couldn't earn better salaries and clients couldn't aspire for a high level of consumption. Hence, self interest which helps markets work more effectively for the benefits of all. Hence, companies should adopt a code of behavior and conduct and ethical behavior which would not influence any stakeholders groups' benefits to pursuit their profit honestly. Corporate social responsibility is a form of corporate self regulation integrated into a business model. It aims to give responsibility for corporate actions and to encourage a positive impact on the environment and stakeholders including consumers, employees, investors, communities and others and it is titled to aid an organization's mission as well as guide to what the company can give the best benefits to serve its customers.

I shall use body shop company as one example to judge whether what extent are the pursuits of profit and meeting the needs of wider groups of stakeholders will be incompatible. Factually, body shop could adopt a code of behavior and conduct and ethical behavior which would not influence any stakeholders groups' benefits to pursuit their profit honestly. Such as, one of the major and most successful initiatives which body shop used an effective supply chain for their products and body shop made use of their sustainable chain supply strategy to ensure that there was the promotion and the maintenance of the social ethical behavior in its business. Hence, it seemed that body shop could be compatible to achieve an effective supply chain to deliver to different countries' stores to meet clients who had more need to buy different kinds of skin care products to provide them to choose to buy in the reasonable price choices in the short time. It is therefore in the best practices and interests for body shop to reach out to the communities in their businesses to provide raw materials to help the manufacturers of the beauty products. It also partook in the development of the market for such small scale suppliers. In many cases the body shop tried to outsource its raw materials to its customers. This had ensured the sustainability of its customer base this included it's sensitivity to its environment and the required standards of the labor practices of its partners. Hence, it seemed that body shop could be compatible to help its partners to earn profits and any countries' partners could provide more job chances to unemployed people to work from body shop's outsourcing strategy. Hence, this had been developed by the body shop by including strategies, such as third party logistic providers and intermediaries in which who had no ownership. The body shop was a multinational company also adopted trading to purchasing approach where it shifted from short term where focus of buying articles to long term focus of fewer suppliers. This was an attempt of it to develop quality products where prices were also fair and affordable to sell to different countries' clients.

It seemed that body shop could be compatible to sell reasonable prices of products to it's clients. Moreover, it had included in its strategies the aspect of business promotion using catalogues. For the same reason, it had been involved in printing of catalogues which were given out to the clients with their purchases. It was important to note that it' catalogues always contained all it's information descriptions and any person who purchased it's products was bound to receive the explanation of all it's product. This was an attempt of it to develop quality products where prices were also fair and affordable to sell to different countries' clients. It seemed that body shop could be compatible to provide clear information description in catalogues to let whose clients to know what it's different kinds of style body skin care products ingredients and benefits were , then who could compare it's products to other competitors to decide to buy or not buy fairly.

In Oct. 2007 the campaign for safe cosmetic products, in which 25 multinational companies participated, tested 33 brand name lipsticks and found one-third of the sampled exceeded the limit of lead allowed in confectionery. The affected brands included L'Oreal and Christian Dior. A definite effect would be that consumers would be more concerned regarded the ingredients of products who used, which was likely to have an effect on cosmetics and skin care products were released to capture share. It seemed body shop needed to consider its beauty personal care products were the most ensure to own organic ingredients to let any countries clients (stakeholder) to meet their body health care needs (Adrian, P. 2012).

On the health and natural aspect, body shop had health and safe responsibility to consumers. Although, I felt who had considered this issue because it had 30 years history to operate this business and it had not received any serious negative complaints damage its health product image from clients before. However, with consumers were increasingly informed and were educated, who were now more demanding for more information regarding products and were becoming more aware of health issue. Products with organic ingredients and natural ingredients, such as tea and plants were gaining popular. Furthermore, consumers were looking for healthier substitutes to seemingly unhealthy products, such as color cosmetics. Hence, body shop began to sell the reducing numbers, it was possible due to clients compared it's body care products quality to the other competitors and who felt it's product's ingredients existed some poor ingredients to cause every one's body to be unhealthy. Hence, it's productive processing was very important. It seemed that body shop could be compatible to consider its individual client body skin health issue whether after who had used it's body skin care products to have skin hurt or skin pain feeling. In conclusion, to judge what extent are the pursuits of profit and meeting the needs of wider groups of stakeholders incompatible for any individual business, it is depended on whether the company's any stakeholders, such as employees, clients, suppliers, partners, society (communities) etc. who will have positive or negative influence from it. I feel that it will be incompatible if the company give negative influence to any one of its stakeholder. Hence, if any one company's at least one stakeholder who felt who had negative influence due to it did business to relate to whom unwillingly, then it's pursuit of profits aim would be incompatible to meet it's needs of its any one of stakeholder. Such as body shop will give positive influence to its all stakeholders. Hence, I feel it is compatible extent to pursuit of profit and meeting the needs of its wider groups of stakeholders definitely.

3. What companies, if any have managed to sustainable reconcile these two aims?

I feel that Nestle company has managed to sustainable reconcile to pursuit profits and meeting the needs of its wider groups of stakeholders two aims compatibly. Nestle was the world's largest food and beverage company. Nestle in the United States, which represented seven operating across the USA country and it was the first expanded effort in USA and achievement tied to Nestle 's global sustainability principle and commitment. Nowadays, It served 97% of American householders and Nestle 's mission was to lead the industry in nutrition, health and wellness and to create a more sustainable future. Instead of it's mission was to pursuit of profits aim, it had also achieved specific sustainability commitment and progress in the categories of nutrition, environmental impact and water use, social impact, rural development and responsible sourcing to meet the needs of it's wider of groups of stakeholders' aim. On the nutrition, health and wellness aspect, Nestle met the needs to its stakeholder (clients), such as, Nestle rolled out new portion guidance tools and launched an educational campaign and balance your plate to help consumers build nutritious and delicious and convenient meals that met the dietary guidelines for Americans; Nestle also reduced sodium content in many of its most popular brands, such as Stouffer's and DiGiorno and committed to further reduce sodium content by 10 percent in products that did not meet the Nestle; Nestle also reduced sugar content, such as ninety six percent of Nestle 's children's products met the Nestle criteria for low sugar and by the end of 2014 year, 100 percent of children's products would meet these criteria as well as Nestle also removed trans-fat content, such as Nestle committed to reach zero food and beverage products with trans-fat originating to use as functional ingredients by 2016 year. It seemed that Nestle had considered its food and beverage production content whether these content would have negative influence to its stakeholder (clients) nowadays (Adrian, P. 2012).

On the environmental impact aspect, Nestle reduced waste during it's food and beverage products were producing. As part of its commitment to eliminate all forms of waste, Nestle reduced 44 percent of waste per ton of product since 2010 year in the USA five factory locations reached zero waste to landfill status by the end of 2013 year; Nestle also considered responsible packaging responsibility, such as Nestle Waters North America led the USA bottled water industry in light weighting packaging, in part by reducing the plastic content of its 1/2 liter bottles by 60 percent since 1994 year. Since 2003 year alone, more than 3.3 billion pounds of plastic had been saved by Nestle as well as Nestle also adopted responsible sourcing, such as Nestle Purina Pet Care implemented responsible sourcing guidelines for seafood that align with Nestle 's global responsible sourcing guidelines, working with experts to track suppliers and contribute to healthier ecosystem. In 2013 year, Nestle also reached an important target for palm oil, with 100 percent of palm oil now Round table on sustainable palm oil certified. It seemed that Nestle also considerate whether environment would have negative influence occurrence during it's production (Adrian, P. 2012). On social impact aspect, Nestle supported local communities, such as Nestle in USA donated more than $2.3 million dollars to support local United Way organizations; It also provided disaster relief, such as Nestle waters donated more than 685,000 bottled of water and Nestle Purina contributed more than 60,000 pounds of pet food and 41,000 pounds of cat little to local shelters across the USA for disaster relief as well as it grew supplier diversity, such as Nestle works with over 4,100 small, minority, women and veteran owned businesses to help to spur local economies. It seemed that Nestle also considerate social needs. Thus, it is seemed Nestle company have managed to sustainable reconcile these two aims to pursuit profit as well as it also could gave positive influence to its stakeholders. Such as consumer could feel safe to enjoy to eat Nestle company's health foods; societies could be reduced unemployment from its outsourced assistance job to partners; natural environment could be reduced pollution from its productive protection. Hence, it was not actually neglect its shareholders' benefits during it was doing business as the same time

(Adrian, P. 2012).

4. What are basic lessons in marketing that the Body Shop might have taken on board in its early years in order to improve its chances of long term success?

The body shop is a global manufacturer and retailer of naturally inspired , ethically produced beauty and cosmetics products. Founded in the UK in 1976 year by Dame Anita Roddick, who now have 2,133 stores in 55 countries with a range of over 1,200 products in Europe, America, Middle East, Asia and Africa. However, the body shop has not entered the China market. It takes a strong position on activism, ethical business, human rights and environmentalism in a global perspective. The body shop is banned in China because cosmetics sold there have to be tested on animals, according to Roddick. In, 2006 when it was bought by the French cosmetics company L'Oreal which is a big player in China. China has launched scientific developing strategy for future the current policies of advocating. Hence, it is the perfect time for the body shop to enter China market. However, prior to that, as an independent member of the L'Oreal family, the body shop has to make decisions on differentiation marketing strategies, market segmentation and marketing position (Adrian, P. 2012). It might have taken two purposes to body shop marketing in its early years in order to improve its chances from short term to long term success. The short term objective was to generate more sales for the body shop. Through, the introduction of a new service, the market up class, it was hoped that clients could try and experience the body shop cosmetic products. Positive experience of using its products could then be developed through their trial using the market up class. It was estimated that this positive experience could push up the sales.

The long term objective was to educate the belief of the body shop to the young potential clients, so that who would become those who preferred natural cosmetic products and were loyal to the body shop in the future. Objectives could provide the starting point for marketing plans and strategies and should be specific targets that are obtained but also challenging. Specific, measurable, agreed, realistic and time related objectives might be taken to body shop to improve early years in chances in long term success. It seemed that Hong Kong was one good market for body shop to satisfy an unfulfilled customers needs to pursue body shop investment chance. Therefore, the objective were to push up sales and built a loyal customer basis for the future. For example, Hong Kong was one young student clients growth market to body shop. In the past, one cosmetic products market statistic was indicated that the colour cosmetic retail value had been increasing from 2002 year, HK$938.3 million dollars to 2007 year, HK$1,132,3 million dollars, so percentage was increased to 5.12% . (Adrian, P. 2012). It seemed Hong Kong might be one good skin cosmetic care products developed market to this body shop in early years. The another factor might improve body shop long term success factor was whether body shop had attempted to analyze direct competition. The body shop's direct competition was not from the name brand like Dior, Chanel or Olay, but rather the less well known brands, from Japan or Korea. Along with the great impact of Korean fashion, many Korean cosmetics brands like Missha and the Face shop had already established shops in China. These two brands also promoted their natural ingredients and target the young customer segment as what the body shop products competition concept could be offered to a market to satisfy a want or need and offered five levels, which were the core benefits, basic product, expected product, augmented product and potential product. Each level added more customer value and the five constitute client value hierarchy products of these three brands were all using natural ingredients and simple and natural in packaging. The body shop , however, differentiated itself at the top levels of the five product and transformations the products might undergo in the future.

Marketing management and planning was essential to body shop, it was the implementation of strategies to achieve long run profitability to body shop and growth. When body shop was looking at how it would achieve this in early years in order to improve the chances long term success, its two keys points to consider are: What was body shop man activity at a particular time? And how it would reach its goals? It might design a strategy that insured a consistent approach to offer its skin care products to raise competition in mind the skin care products changing market. These included product line, distribution methods, marketing communication and pricing. For example, achieving marketing research to Hong Kong and China skin care products market to analyze what were these factors to influence these country people who felt needs to buy its skin care products: Such as internal factors include personality, motivation, learning, perception and attitude; external factors included culture, social class, reference groups , family and personal influences and situational factors included time, income, mobility and availability. The reason was because due to consumers bought skin care products to protect whose skin (core benefits) and their expectations if who were willing to pay more basic product. To enhance the product level, body shop skin health product needed emphasize that skin products were natural. Products of the body shop offered the same effective and natural and flavor and unique corporate values. Body shop was mostly natural (augmented level). Far more than the visible products, the shop shop's unique corporate values create the potential value to fulfil customer's desire of making a better health world. It's good corporate desire citizenship went beyond supplying rational and emotional benefits. Body shop might enter China market to improve long term success. The body shop divided its markets to include overseas Pacific Europe, America , Australia and New Zealand, Middle East, Africa and local UK countries. Adrian, P.(2012) indicated that a sampling questionnaire survey was conducted among 200 consumers, ranging from 18 to 50 ages in May 2006, a total of 170 valid responses that were used for analysis. Among the 170 responses, 66% were females. The findings were:

(1) About 60 % hoped that cosmetics could be a symbol of being environmental friendly.

(2) 90% would choose products made of natural ingredients.

(3) 90% spent less than 300 RMB on cosmetics and skin care products quarterly.

(4) 83% Chinese youth (age range from 18 to 25 ages) were innovators and conscious of environment.

Hence, the body shop might take a share of potential market in China. It should launch its products among younger cosmetic industry were young females who chased beauty and were willing to spend money on it. So, packaging was one of the vital factors in attracting client. The body shop took a unique approach by choosing simple packaging. The package was not made for mature women. It was made for young female students, who could enjoy on international brand at an inexpensive cost. The body shop was not only to meet young people's demand for beauty , but the demand of being responsible to environment and human rights. Hence, the target market of the body shop should focus on young people ageing from 15 ages to 30 ages. Hence, body shop might take marketing research in Hong Kong and China market to have more confident to invest in these market to improve more success. Next, Whether body shop might achieve price strategy to improve to raise success chance. An assumption is when the individual client is considering the price of any a body shop's beauty skin health product. Economic theory suggests that the customer will act in a totally rational economic manner, such that body shop's every client total utility (or satisfaction) is maximized. In deciding whether try or not try body shop's product, which totally rational consumer will carefully equate whether ought to buy or ought not buy body shop's product at the asking price set will maximizing whose utility. In making judgment, the economist assumes that the consumer has perfect information about both the prices and utility of all the other competitive products in the market and that price is the only consideration in choice. Clearly there are unrealistic assumptions. Price could be determined easily when a target market was identified.

(Adrian, P. 2012) From survey indicated 64% of the 170 responses spent less than 1000 RMB on cosmetics and skin care every quarter and 24% of their expenditure was between 100 RMB and 300 RMB on cosmetics an skin care. This number could not be ignored if a cosmetics company wanted to enter this large market and be a leader. For the younger generation, the prices of the products could not be high. The price of these main competitors ranges from 10RMB to 200 RMB. The prices in Hong Kong have higher than that in the USA or the UK. And the consumer's purchasing power in mainland China is much lower than that of Hong Kong . Hence, body shop should adopt a price range in China which was similar to that of the USA or the UK rather than of Hong Kong. Once the body shop established greatly reduced and the capability of price adjustment would be achieved accordingly.

Further, body shop might have chain stores selling channel strategy to attempt to achieve long term success. Sample survey revealed that supermarket was for Chinese to purchase skin care and cosmetics. 120 out of the 170 responses hoped that who could choose products from the chain stores in the future, which suggested that the body shop should build up its own stores was regarded as cares about corporate culture and corporate image. It insisted on selling in its own stores rather than setting up counters in a shopping mall. The stores of body shop could be found easily worldwide because of stores were importance in this competitive buyer. Hence, in China, its appearance should be same as worldwide. Some housewives joined the body shop as sales agent and hold sales parties for other housewives. The sales channel allowed the body shop to reach out to more clients by bringing the store directly into client's homes. This would be a totally new method of marketing in China, but it offered a good opportunity for women to choose products and share feedback in a relaxed atmosphere. This fresh concept could attract female consumers. Nowadays, students in China could only obtain famous skin care products and cosmetics brands from campus agents, as who could not afford the products sold over the counters. It was a major problem that agents could not guarantee the ingredients and the quality of the goods. If the body shop could hold small parties to share products and opinions, that would be a good way to boost sales among students. Hence, body shop might take price strategy to Hong Kong and china market to predict whether what price who could accept to raise more confident to invest to this market to improve more success. Further, body shop might also have promotion strategy to attempt to achieve long term success.

The body shop adopted environmental friendly manufacturing, opposed abuses of human rights and was accountable for its actions. The unique values attracted numbers of media groups in many countries. This results in its establishing a good reputation without any advertisements. The body shop also joined numerous social causes, which substitute advertisements. In China, however, it was totally different. In this brand new market, most people were out aware of this company. If it carried on a marketing promotion of no commercials it was impossible to reach a high market share. Hence, commercial advertisements were needed in China. The body shop could use this advertisement to give on impression that women should care about their well being both mentally and physically and it had created a sexy grand with simple packaging and without objectifying women. Many brands reach customers directly by colorful commercials and show their products in movies and TV play series. For the sakes of brand image, some movies about human rights , environmental protection and animal protection could be chosen by the body shop as carriers for particular commercial as most of the audiences were well educated, well paid and environmentally concerned. The target consumers of the body shop aged from 20 to 40 ages were energetic , knowledgeable and environmentally concerned. The body shop could give some lectures on makeup or skin care on campuses to raise feeling among students. To reach brand awareness and high brand loyalty , some samples should be given to students by experience marketing approach. Hence, body shop might take promotion to Hong Kong and China schools to let many young people to know why who needed to buy skin care products to protect their body skin to persuade who felt more needs. In conclusion, the body shop was famous for creating a niche market sector for naturally inspired skin care and cosmetic products through it's unique corporate values worldwide. The significance of the body shop's early entry into China market were strongly proposed. Once the body shop decided to enter the China market, the relevant marketing strategies and management should be implemented, such as the market segmentation and market positioning with the proper consideration of Chinese consumers should be studied in order to win the mind share of potential Chinese customers with the right marketing strategies. Overall, the findings of market survey and theoretical analysis strategy support the feasibility of the body shop's early entry into China market.

Consequently, cheap price is not the main successful factor influences Body shop success. The guaranteed skin health critical is the main successful factor to influence Body Shop success. So, Body shop seems a truly marketing oriented organization. Consumers won't be influenced to reduce its products by bad economic change factor.

CHAPTER III

Walt Mark Supermarket sale management pressure

Case study change in the marketing environment on sales of ready meals to supermarket, such as Walt Mark

1. Using an appropriate framework of behavioral economic method analysis, briefly summarize the effects of change in the marketing environment on sales of ready meals.

In behavioral economy analysis, consumers prefer to buy ready meals to supermarket acceptance factor which will influence Walt Mark wholesale business success. Because consumers' eating habits had been changing. Many housewives don't like to cook at home generally. They like to go to supermarkets to buy ready cooked meals to eat, who feel it is more economic behavioral consumption model when they often buy ready cooked meals in order to reducing cooking time and food expenditure more than who buy uncooked meal to cook at home from food stores. Although, previously dismissed and a poor substitute for real cooking and ready meal sales have grown rapidly in recent years in many western developed countries, such as UK, France or Germany. But, Ready meal manufacturers ready to respond to a changing marketing environment. Due to one big change in recent year has been growing demand for ready prepared meals bought from a supermarket. An analysis of the reasons for the growth in the ready prepared meals markets indicates the effects of boards factors in the marketing environment on the size of a particular market. In fact, this food market is changing to drive the growth in the ready meals market, but there are differences in the food market potential between countries. The effect of change in the marketing environment on sales of ready meals, such as technology has played a big role in the growing take up of ready meals and new technologies have allowed companies to develop ready meals which preserve taste and texture, which still making them easy to use by the consumer. Furthermore, great advances in distribution management, in particular the use of information technology to control inventories, has allowed fresh, chilled ready meals to be effectively and efficiently distributed without the need for freezing or added preservatives. Ready meals particularly appeal to single householders, which individual family members tend to eat at different times, so family meals together remains stronger in many continental European countries than in the UK individual ready meals. Young people have lost the ability to cook creatively, as cookery has been reduced in importance in the school, so young clients group will rise to buy ready meals from supermarket. Marketing can be seen as a system that must respond to environmental change. A food market can be defined as a meeting place for stakeholder (consumers) and sellers. Food market can be set up in a supermarket or restaurants. A food market consists of the individual's target taste, such as older group, family group, young group or business clients who are actual or potential caters of a restaurant meals or supermarket package of foods. Grocery stores (supermarkets) have an influence of meals (fast cooked food) outlets in low income urban areas, which has contributed to the income in access to healthy foods. An organization's marketing environment means the individuals, organizations, and forces external to the marketing management's ability to develop and maintain successful exchanges with its customers. The marketing environment to ready meal manufacturers had three levels.

Firstly, it includes the micro environment, it describes those elements that impinge directly on the ready meal manufacturers themselves, so the micro environment of ready meal manufacturers which include business clients who have direct contact, such as restaurants, supermarkets and individual clients who have direct contact. Otherwise, supermarket shoppers, restaurant clients and food supply competitors who have no direct contract to ready meal manufacturers, so who won't include in food market micro environment to ready meal manufacturers. Secondly, it includes the macro environment, it describes things that are beyond the immediate environment but can nevertheless affect an organization, so the macro environment of ready meal manufacturers which include the export countries' economies forces, such as unemployment ratio, GDP; technological forces, such as the export countries' factories food productive technology; social/ cultural forces, such as the export countries' people taste acceptance; political/legal forces, such as the export countries' import food quota numbers. Thirdly, it includes the internal environment, it describes ready meal manufacturers' employees and equipment and finance and functional responsibilities. Environment means everything outside influences the person, in contrast with individual or personal variables . The effects of change in the marketing environment on sales of ready meals can be analyzed by creating healthy food and eating environment changing factor and supermarket technological changing factor as below:

The ready meal manufacturers could not ignore threats to the natural ecological environment change Due to the food companies could have technology to manufacture good taste cooked ready meals to provide to supermarkets to sell. Thus, it might influence the consumers to decide whether restaurants or supermarkets or ready meals suppliers who could provide the most reasonable price and taste to satisfy whose eating needs every day. Thus, it caused the growing demand for ready prepared cooked meals bought from supermarkets. Due to it was possible that consumers felt to eat ready cooked meals in expensive restaurants or who did not like to buy foods to cook from food suppliers or who could not feel which could supply more good food taste and health food quality to compare supermarkets specially. Otherwise, although, supermarkets could provide cheaper ready cooked meals to satisfy who to feel good food taste and health food quality. Due to ready meal manufacturers had new techniques to develop ready meals which preserve taste and texture, which still making them easy to use to eat by the consumers. Furthermore, great advances in distribution management, in particular the use of information technology to control inventories, has allowed fresh , chilled ready meals to be effectively and efficiently distributed to supermarkets or restaurants without the need for freezing or added preservatives. Creating healthy food and eating environments view describes an ecological framework for conceptualizing the many food environments and conditions that influence food choices, with an emphasis on current knowledge was been regarding the home, child care, school, work site, retail store and restaurant settings.

The status of measurement and evaluation of nutrition environment and the need of action to improve health are highlighted in marketing environment. More processed and convenience foods are available in large portion sizes and which were supplied at relatively low prices at supermarkets. Parents are working larger hours, there are fewer family meals and more meals are eaten away from home. The school food environment is remarkably different. It seemed that it would be changed in the marketing environment on sales of ready cooked meals to supermarket more easily. Due to supermarkets' cooked meals should focus on selling high calorie and low nutrition foods are available in multiple venues throughout the school student client group target because it was possible that supermarkets could sell ready cooked ready meals prices were more cheaper to compare to restaurants or school canters' cooked meals provided prices.

The effects of change in the marketing environment on sales of ready meals which indicated that consumers chose prefer to buy ready cooked meals from supermarkets. It seemed that a restaurant market failure could be caused to arise. For example, there was poor information on the part of food (ready cooked meals) to provide to the restaurant about the foods that consumers in a location(place) would demand for a given price to compare to the supermarket sale prices. The restaurant would lose clients if which cooked the kind of meals to sell higher price to compare to the supermarket sale of the kind of cooked ready meals price possibly.

Large size supermarkets could sell cheaper ready cooked meals to low income group clients. It could cause competition to constitute a market failure to small size supermarkets. If the small size supermarkets lacked good information on the true food (ready cooked meals) with concentrations to sell cheaper prices, then this ready cooked meal market failure was one potential reason why small size supermarkets did not locate to close to the large supermarkets. Due to supermarkets grew in size would influence clients' choice to buy the numbers of cooked foods (ready meals) products. Moreover, The advent of computerized logistics and inventory systems were integrated with the large size supermarkets themselves occurred between the 1980 years and 1990 years .

So large size supermarkets were reliance on their own distribution and cooked food (ready meals) inventory systems along with larger supermarket sizes to allow super center to change to sell ready cooked meals at lower prices. Supermarkets marketing can promote healthful eating by increasing availability, affordability or restricting / de-marketing unhealthy foods to sell cooked Food (ready meals) marketing strategy at supermarkets, including labelling, packaging, pricing and point of sale advertising. Consumers' cost saving efforts and income and ready cooked meals prices increasing or decreasing factors can drive the choice of supermarkets as well as cooked meal products use of coupons and loyalty cards bargain shopping is another factor to influence their choice. Private label or store (supermarket) brands are taking an increasing share of consumers shopping dollars as the importance of brands. Supermarket shoppers stated priorities are cooked food (ready meals) quality or taste and price and healthy cooked food (ready meals) choices. However, supermarket shoppers' buying behaviors don't always reflect on favor healthful foods. Due to demand for locally grown cooked food is increasing. Anyway, restaurant meals are changed to supermarket to sell, which decide what kinds of meals to stock and how many of different kinds of meals to stock and how much variety of kinds of meals to offer to any one supermarket as well as supermarket shoppers prefer fewer options, provided that their preferred brand or cooked food (ready meals) products are available. The designs of supermarket ready cooked meal products and packaging to supermarket to sell is the focus of unusual colors or shape which can be used to increase interest and is specially pervasive among fun foods to compare to restaurant meals. Package design, including where text and images are placed, which can influences cooked foods (supermarket ready meals repurchasing again).The influence of design differs by the type of display consumer segments seek (convenience, information or images) and ready cooked meals package sizes have a relatively strong influence on consumption; larger ready cooked meals packages might increase per-use consumption ,but smaller packages might not improve self regulation and might not actually increase total consumption. In conclusion, I suggest that this ready meal manufacturers need to give more attention to be paid to food sellers, such as supermarkets' competitive differentiation and understanding the way in which customers attribute value to its ready meal products choice. Moreover, many consumers have become increasingly concerned about the health implication of the food they eat, so ready meal manufacturers will need to continue responding to such concerns. For example, who have responded with a range of low calorie meals, and addressed specific, sometimes transient, health fads, with respect to trans-fatty acids and omega 3 supplements of these cooked meal ingredients. Many consumers have also become concerned about the ecological environment and some supermarket suppliers, such as Marks and Spencer have incorporated sustainability agendas into their ready meals, for example by reducing packaging and sourcing supplies from sustainable sources. Thus, it caused ready meal manufacturers why who needed to give more attention to concern how supermarkets helped them to sell cooked ready meals in this foods market.

2. Critically discuss the link between the economic environment and consumer consumption behavior of ready meals in supermarket

The macro environment, it describes things that are beyond the immediate environment but can nevertheless affect the organization. Such as the ready meal manufacturers in its macro environment, including the economic environment which can cause the manufacturers sell ready meal numbers whether which can sell more or less to different exported countries due to the exported countries' unemployment ratios, GDP and Government policies etc factors influence. Economic theory can help to explain why it can influence consumer behavior. In food sale market, it can include consumer behavior and demand side as well as retailer behavior and supply side two issues. Consumer behavior and demand side issue, such as the exported countries' consumer whose knowledge of the nutritional benefits of foods whether which prices were raised to choose to buy reasonably as well as retailer behavior and supply side issues, such as investing for developing a restaurant or supermarket in an underserved area whether the types of meals choices which are valued or which are not valued to buy to offer to clients from imports. On the other hand, economic environment factor, individual income can influence who chooses the type, quantity and quality of food that is purchased for a house holder and it also influenced the cooking and storage facilities available in a household to influence food choice.

On the other way, economic environment variation factor can also influence food access across areas. It is important to understand the economic conditions that may contribute to food deserts, that is the costs that food retail businesses face and the choice available to consumers who want to buy foods. Economic environment factor considers the consumer and demand factors, business and supply factors and the market conditions that interact to create differences in the food retail environment across areas and subpopulations. In general, high income meal client group can accept to choose to go to supermarkets or restaurants to spend than low income meal client group. The impact of the economic environment on sales of ready meals is such as an individual get richer, who can afford to buy ready prepared foods, rather than spend time and effort to prepare to cook them at home. It seemed that low income consumers were decreasing to eat meals at expensive restaurant to the alternative of relatively cheap ready prepared meals at home. Research could also consider how consumer knowledge and preferences and the time cost tradeoffs affect consumer decisions of which foods to eat and whether to make or to buy prepared foods from supermarkets or to eat at restaurant meals . Travel costs and time costs of acquiring foods as well as the time costs of preparing foods (meals) are also likely to affect demand for particular foods. Research on price variation at the local level and demand models could also be used to help determine which factors contribute to differences in access to food retailers. Price is also major determinant of food (meal) demand. The higher, the price of a food(meal), the lower the meal quantity demanded. On the other hand, the higher the price of a substitute food (meal), the higher demand will be for that food (meal) item. Given the budget constraints of low income consumers and the price of some specific foods (meals), low income consumers may substitute higher priced foods (meals) with lower priced foods(e.g. hamburger for steak or canned fruits for fresh fruits). Considering restaurants foods purchasing choice, such as economies of scale, which is when the costs of operating a restaurant decreases as restaurant size increases and economies of scope, which is when the costs decrease as more meals variety increases, suggests that larger restaurants that offer greater variety can offer lower meal prices. Both factors may account for the ability of larger restaurants to survive more easily than smaller restaurants. Considering supermarkets foods purchasing choice, it is possible that food retailers (supermarkets) actually have some market power, especially in setting where there are few competitors to close. It would have an incentive to increase food (ready meal) price and restrict foods(ready meals) supply quantities to increase profit. Supply side conditions, such as economies of scale, it could lead to (ready meal) food retailers (supermarkets) to have more market power, if it was not close between supermarkets. Individual behavior to make healthy choices can occur only in a supportive economic environment with accessible and affordable healthy food choices. Hence, food environment and sale strategies is needed to consider to adopt the exported countries' economic change.

Food marketing client target groups can include home parents, students and working people groups mainly and marketing and economic environment factors would cause food choices and these factors impact health and nutrition and the focus on the connections between people and their environments.

In conclusion, macro level economic environmental factors play a more indirect role but have a substantial and powerful effect on what people eat. Macro level factors operate within the larger society, include food marketing, social norms, food production and distribution systems, agriculture policies and economic price structures as well as social environmental to influence within the home, such as model of healthful dietary intake by parents feeding style, frequent family meals may promote healthful food consumption among children.

3. Discuss economic changing factors that might affect sales of ready meals in your country over the next five years.

Hong Kong people can choose to go to restaurants to eat or go to supermarkets to buy foods to cook to eat. Although, ready meal manufacturers had increased the sale numbers of the ready prepared meals in many western countries in recent years. However, there still had any factors to limit it's sale numbers to Hong Kong market over the next five years, so it needed to aware of what was changing in Hong Kong food market environment and appreciated how change in this Hong Kong food environment to lead to change patterns of eating cooked ready meals demand to attempt to win its similar food competitors in Hong Kong market next five years. Hong Kong food environment related to Hong Kong people eating behaviors, include social environments and physical environments and macro level environment. The cooked meal quality and quantity of available can influence food numbers to produce meal to supply to Hong Kong food market. Hence, Hong Kong natural climatic change can influence the overseas food supply numbers to be imported to cause meals prices to go up or go down. If next five years, Hong Kong climate was good to grow plants and feed animals e.g. pigs and cows etc. meats. The restaurant meals or supermarket meals sale prices can be cheaper due to farmers who have much foods and vegetables to supply , so who can sell cheaper price to these restaurants or supermarkets to cause whose production cost to be decreased next five years in my country. Hence, ready meals prices could not sell more higher than Hong Kong meals prices. Hong Kong people eating behaviors are often changed over a lifetime. In general, Hong Kong people want to eat to satisfy physical hunger and psychological desires and yet want to be healthy, which may enquire adopting eating patterns that conflict with these desires.

My country people make decisions about food several times a day: when to eat, what to eat, with where to eat and how much per meal prices and how much per meal numbers . In general, Hong Kong people like to eat Chinese foods , but who also like to go to restaurants to eat or supermarkets to buy western foods, such as liking of specific tastes are important influences. However, these can be modified by experience with food from various intrapersonal and interpersonal factors to influence Hong Kong people to choose to buy uncooked or cooked meals from Hong Kong supermarkets. The next five year, food retailer behavior and supply factors of food access might affect overseas sales of ready meals numbers imported to my country. In general, supply is driven by the costs of input foods. The land, materials, machines and labor costs are needed to build and operate a restaurant or supermarkets. If these costs are increased to these food suppliers in my county next five years, overseas food demand shall be caused to be decreased if Hong Kong economy had changed to be worse and the new restaurants and supermarkets which costs were changed to be higher to much as well as Hong Kong unemployment was caused to be raised and many people lost jobs to have efforts to go to supermarkets to buy higher prices ready meals or go to restaurants to eat higher price ready meals.

My country's social environment and physical environment which also might affect sales of ready meals numbers next five years. Social environment includes interactions, with family, friends, peers and others in the community to impact food choices through mechanisms as well as physical environment includes the different places where people eat or buy food, such as whether the supermarkets or restaurants locations which are close to the buyers, e.g. schools, offices, houses. Hence, food suppliers' locations choice can influence who (target client groups) choose to buy more or less ready meals numbers. Foods prepared at home factor there may be relatively greater time costs than those to buy cooked foods(ready meals) from supermarkets or takeout foods. Hong Kong consumers may value the convenience of a fast food or takeout cooked meal more because it doesn't require spending much time to prepare to cook at home. Hence, Hong Kong people whose taste is for different kind of cooked foods (ready meals) and who feel the food suppliers' locations whether are convenient and Hong Kong economy whether is better or worse to cause unemployment numbers next five years, these factors can affect sales of imported ready cooked or uncooked meal numbers to my country Hong Kong next five year.

Consequently, Walt Mark needs to distributed many ready cooked meals to sell itself if it expects to compete in this global wholesale market, due to economic changing will influence consumer behaviors.

CHAPTER IV

Ryanair airline & Easy Jet airline & budget airline air pollution social responsibility control pressure

1. If you are the marketing manager of an airline, such as Ryanair, how would you address the ecological concerns? Does this ecological non-economic factor influence passengers choose to catch Ryanair air plane?

In behavioral economy analysis, Ryanair airline needs to consider the air pollution issue if it expects air passengers choose to catch its air planes because travelers consider how airplanes cause air pollution to bring global warmth negative effect. So, if travelers still feel Ryanair is one airline company, which neglects social responsibility to consider how its airplanes cause air pollution when they are often flying. Then they won't choose to catch Ryanair airplanes and choose other any airlines to catch when they feel other airlines can consider air pollution issue.

In recent years, social, economic and environment pressures have pushed airlines to accept their social responsibility. Closely tied to this acceptance is a corporate policy that aims at

raising social and environmental standards on a voluntary basis and that means beyond legal and contractual requirement. It means that corporate social responsibility is not just an optional

consideration to core airline business activities, such as airlines industry fuel consumption pollutes sky air to cause global warming problem. Rather, Ryanair airline needs to concern social responsibility because it's fuel emissions would cause negative influence to stakeholders. e.g. causing bad negative climate to influence farmers to grow rice and vegetables etc. foods successfully, so global warming will make farmers stakeholder can not earn more income and food buyers stakeholder won't eat rice and vegetables etc. foods easily, even global warming will damage natural environment to cause strong wind or strong raining or water natural hazard to damage any countries' houses to make house owners stakeholder who lose their houses to live. Hence, in the long term, if Ryanair airline still continue consume too much fuels to use to fly to cause emissions to pollute air to any countries as well as other airlines do not achieve any actions to reduce to consume to use more fuels together efficiently. I believe that global warming will become very serious to influence human living and eating problem occurrence in our earth as soon as possibly. Hence, such as Ryanair airline is among of global airlines, which have responsibility to consider how to reduce fuel consumption to cause too much emissions to pollute air in our earth. Such as, I was Ryanair airline marketing manager , I ought need to let Ryanair airline to measure whether it ought only concern how to sell cheaper air fares and buy many airplanes and consume much fuels to fly to raise income or it ought concern it's fuel emissions to pollute environment to cause global warming to influence global human stakeholders encounter living and eating problem to face natural foods resource shortage to supply in the future.

The ecological concerns global warming problem is serious nowadays, it brings the possible long term harmful consequences of executive emissions to the atmosphere. The developed countries, such as Northern Europe and United States people needed often to play travel entertainment by airlines transportation choice. However, scientists proved airlines used fossil fuels to harm excessive emissions to natural environment which would cause global warming problem to cause devastation of low lying areas to influence natural environment danger, even the developing countries people life and their houses would also encountered to be hazarded in the long term. If I was the marketing manager of an airline, such as Ryanair, I must concern socially responsible needs to Ryanair airline. Although, Ryanair aircraft had become more efficient in use of fuel during 1990 years, but Ryanair airline's passengers were booming demand to cause to increase airplanes numbers to supply to satisfy passengers' travel needs and to pursue raising profit aim every year.

In fact, Ryanair airline used fuels to give energy to push airplanes to fly and it also polluted sky air during it's airplanes often were flying to cause global warming. For example, Ryanair airline marketing strategy was low fare prices to attract to increase many passengers to choose to attract to increase many passengers to choose to sit it's airplanes and it designed a cheap weekend break by Mediterranean travel to increase the unknown and remote possibilities of global warming. Hence, Ryanair would increased many new airplanes to increase to use fossil fuels of excessive emissions to the atmosphere to cause the effects of aid rain, poor climate change , destructive winds, rising sea levels and devastation of low lying areas by global warming bad consequences. Hence, it seemed that Ryanair airline had responsibility to concern how to protect natural environment due to its airplanes numbers and passengers were increasing to cause to increase to use more fossil fuels to cause the possible long term harmful consequences of excessive emissions to the sky to bring global warming occurrence nowadays. As I was this Ryanair airline marketing manager, I shall recommend Ryanair airline needed to consider this global warming socially responsible issue due to its airplanes spent too much fossil fuels to cause harmful consequences of excessive emissions to the sky. It would bring threats to developing countries people life and houses by global warming, so it concerned only how to raise itself interest marketing behavior of performance, but it neglect the serious global warming to cause bad influence to any developing countries people life danger, it was possible that passengers would feel it was not a socially responsible airline company, so it could not build a good image to whom in this airline industry and its further passengers would choose its other competitors (socially responsible airline companies) to substitute its airline service provision.

● Discussion

I should suggest Ryanair airline needed to control fossil fuel numbers to reduce to harm excessive emissions to natural environment seriously and it could spend much expenditure to buy good quality of fossil fuels to active the reduction of too much emissions to damage natural environment aim and it could shorten the sky flying distance to fly to other countries' airports from its airport to aim to attempt to reduce to use much fuel to pollute sky air per day and it could cancel some long flight flying routes and increased short flight flying routes to reduce flight spending hours to attempt to reduce to use fossil fuels to provide every airplanes to fly to pollute sky air every day.

Although, these marketing strategies would be possible to reduce airline income, but it would also attract many further passengers to choose to sit to its airplanes to go to travel if it could build good image to prove it was a socially responsible airline to serve passengers to let them to like to choose to use its flying service to go to travel willingly, even it could lead other airlines to follow it to use its marketing strategic methods to reduce to spend too much fossil fuels to pollute sky air to raise global warming problem seriously together. Hence, if Ryanair airline could attempt to achieve to reduce the fossil fuel numbers to use to airplanes to fly , it was possible that the other airline companies should follow it to do the same behaviors to aim to do social responsible organizations to concern how to reduce the global warming problem to cause to harm to our natural environment seriously for long term in the future.

2. The case study refers to apparent hypocrisy of clients who may claim to be concerned about the environment, but nevertheless continue to fly what might bring about a narrowing of this gap between what consumers think and what they actually do?

In fact, some apparent hypocrisy of consumers who may claim to be concerned about the global warming harmful natural environment problem due to airline companies, e.g. Easy Jet,
Ryanair etc. western countries' airlines which allowed fossil fuels produced harmful consequences of excessive emissions to atmosphere, but nevertheless continue to fly. However, I might recommend these methods to bring about a narrowing of this gap between what consumers think and what they actually do.
I think to bring a narrowing of this gap between consumers were happy to carry on airplanes to fly and it would not influence them to concern about climate change problem at the same time.
There was certainly a possible that governments would intervene. Such as the UK government and European commission had floated the idea of taxing aviation fuel and brought aircraft emissions within scope of the European emission trading scheme. Thus, if these western countries governments raised to charge aviation fuel taxing, it would possible to threaten any western airlines to shorten any flight routes hours and flight flying distance to fly to destination of the countries' airports from these airline companies' every country's airport, so which would not need to use more fuels for its airplanes to use if it had shorten flight flying routes distance to arrive other countries' airports. Hence, the airlines did not want to pay higher aviation tax to government, so which would attempt to shorten some flight flying routes from long distance to be short distance when their airplanes needed to fly to some other countries' airport to aim to buy less fuel numbers or which would not buy more airplanes.

Due to they needed to pay high aviation tax expenditure to their countries governments every year. Thus, it was possible that high fuel tax expenditure would cause airlines to shorten flight routes time. The most important, when some airlines decided to buy less fuels. These airlines might bring about a narrowing of this gap between what consumers think and what they actually do and these airlines were possible to raise their competitive ability, due to which would possible to persuade the concerned environment protective passengers who would choose to buy these airlines air tickets to more than to buy the other airlines' air tickets. Due to some airlines could not reduce to buy more fuel numbers to provide their airplanes to fly and which would increase air pollution to sky seriously, those airlines' spending excessive long hours (time) of every flight flying routes to fly to different countries' airports which would use more fuel to fly to cause air pollution to harm natural environment seriously and which would let these clients to feel unhappy to choose to buy air tickets to sit their airplanes possibly. Hence, different governments raised aviation tax would cause many airlines to reduce to buy too much fuel numbers to use possibly. It seemed that airlines needed have a social responsible duty to concern they needed to buy more fuels if they increased airplanes numbers, then they would raise air pollution to cause global warming problem seriously. Hence, I think passengers would not buy air tickets to fly to travel by airplanes when who would have long days of holidays. Otherwise, who would choose to stay at home or who would choose to go to travel by cruises on water transportation on their holidays. However, in western developed economies, legislation to enforce environmentally sensitive methods of productive is increasing, so airlines might adopt environmentally sensitive flight service processes to gain a competitive advantages. The challenges of using fuels resources in more efficient and less polluting way has achieved research and development, e.g. wind power research, solar panels, heat pumps and carbon capture technology have presented opportunities for airlines to improve the efficiency of fuels and airline marketing to business and individual group passengers.

Legal actions to place control over the emission of air pollutants have been instituted in several ways, such as the form of a public nuisance low. This is when conditions cause discomfort, inconvenience, damage to property or injury from airlines fuels to cause air pollution. The governments have also intervened in the protection of the public to threaten the airlines' fuels emissions pollute air in the sky. As a result of much research, devices for pollution control have been developed, guidelines for air quality were established fuels tax increasing incentives were introduced to enforce ordinances for restricting the emission from airplanes' fuels. For example, governments can pass the clean air act, legislation to reduce air pollution in their countries. In conclusion, airlines can co-operate environmentally friendly management to prevent global warming, it is as a part of its corporate social responsibility and makes company wide efforts to do by saving energy and reducing aircraft fuel emissions. Hence, global airlines ought plan to achieve to reduce to consume excessive fuel emissions to reduce a narrowing of this gap between what consumers think and what they actually do concerned about the environment pollution was caused by airlines if which still wanted to make travelers who prefer to choose to go to travel by flying more than other water or ground transportation etc. methods.

3. How would a company , such as Easy Jet airline measure and monitor consumer's attitudes?

Easy Jet airline has created environment problems, e.g. harmful chemicals sift down from smoky trails of low-flying jets. The scream of Easy Jet airline engines is constantly heard by
people who love near big city airports. It's aircrafts produce air pollution with consequent changes in climate.
It is a fact that many people prefer air travel rather than ground or water transportation, This has promoted a critical look at safety and quality control. Contributions to air pollution is a chief concern because of this revolutionary change in public transportation in the United States and around the world. The government must also establish standards for exhaust emissions. Thus, Easy Jet airline measure and monitor consumer's attitudes which needs to indicate to let them to believe that which suggests which airplane manufacturers are forced to develop low pollutant engines. Due to the problem of air pollution from its airplanes involve a complex set of interactions among technical, social and economic factors. Hence, it also needs to measure it's emission from Easy Jet aircrafts, particularly on landing and take offs, are a source of bitter complaints from nearby residents. In a few airports visibility has been dangerously restricted by particulate emissions and photo chemical smog. Easy Jet airline also needed to have energy savings activities to its operations, ranging from procedural and flight plan improvement to reduce flight distance

and attitude and weight management and it also needed to create energy through maintenance to achieve to continue to reduce co2 emissions by introducing high efficiency aircraft and through other measures to monitor consumers' attitudes . In line with its aim to be an environmentally friendly airline that harmonizes the needs of natural , humans and airline businesses. It aims to be respected by society , live up to its social responsibilities and make a contribution to society. Although emissions from aircraft are not included among greenhouse gas reduction targets, but it also needed to make systematic efforts to improve energy efficiency and reduce emissions by creating a road map to actively participate .

Furthermore, Easy Jet airline also needed continually to pursue a management style that concerns nature, people and fellow corporations, even under the most severe conditions as a major practice toward implementing its environmental policy. Easy jet airline achieves environment goals to measure and monitor consumer's attitudes, such as minimizes energy and resource consumption and introduces up to date and fuel efficient fleet and engines and develops and apply energy efficient operation technique, it establish strict internal environmental standards to set internal standards that are stricter than general environment laws applied worldwide and minimize pollutants through systematic management and observance of standards. It systematically analyses the airlines' environmental impact and make the outcome to carry out reductions and evaluates the environmental impact of its aviation operations, maintenance and service and improves environmentally friendly processes and it continually improves environmental systems through feedback .

In conclusion, Easy Jet airline can increase the recycling of waste to reduce fuel consumption of resources and it can make systematic efforts to reduce emissions by creating a roadmap and actively participating in global warming by saving energy and reducing aircraft emissions through engine washing to aim to consume fuels efficiency and reduce emission to pollute air.

4. What might be the consequences for the marketing of a budget airline of Government policy measures which have the effect of doubling air fares in real terms?

If the country Government decided to raise higher flight fuel tax charge policy to budget airline. Due to the country Government hoped budget airline to reduce fuels consumption to provide to airplanes to use to reduce sky air pollution to cause global warning problem. In fact, budget airline needed to increase to use much fuels to provide to many flights to carry on passengers travel needs. Generally, budget airline would not like to choose to reduce to consume much fuels due to it's passenger numbers had been increasing. If budget airline decided to buy less fuels to reduce much fuels to consume for its flight needs. It would lose many passengers if it had not enough times of flights to provide airplanes to fly to different countries' airports to satisfy passengers' different flight route choices. However, the consequences for budget airline would also be passengers to choose to buy budget airline air tickets possibly if it decided to raise doubling air fares in real terms. Due to budget airline hoped to compensate its loss if it's country Government raised higher fuels tax to cause budget airline needed to pay high cost expenditure every year. Hence, budget airline needed to raise to spend two kinds of expenditure every year, such as purchasing more fuels expenditure and paying more fuels expenditure both. For long term, budget airline would choose to raise doubling or more air fairs in real terms in order to reduce to need to pay too much feel tax expenditure to compensate it's loss every year. In result, it's passengers would feel it's air tickets fares were not reasonable raised to compare it's other airline competitors, but it's flight services were not excellent to compare it's airline competitors specially. Hence, it's increasing air fares would cause many passengers to choose other airline competitors possibly.

5. Critically discuss how the marketing manager of a budget airline might respond.

Marketing manger might use cost benefit analysis to let budget airline to know how to invest in intangible asset, such as corporate social responsibility to give long term benefit to itself budget airline. I suggest this marketing manager needs to explain the reason why reducing fuel consumption is an investment in intangible asset to budget airline as below:

Airline transport has increasingly become a global technologically and dynamic growth industry. However, airline companies need to remain committed to satisfy the clients' growing demands in a sustainable manner when at the same time maintaining an optimal balance between economic progress, social development and environmental responsibility. The concept of corporate social responsibility is a challenge for who to face today's risky, competitive and complex airline business environment. There has been a need for airlines in the airline industry to develop an environment agenda and take measures to minimize the ever increasing environmental impacts created by their activities. The forms of corporate social responsibility in the airline sector includes working in partnership with local communities, socially sensitive investment as well as involvement in activities for conservation of the environment. The fact, airlines are spewing 20% more co2 into the environment then previously estimated and there is a tendency for amount to increase to 1.5 billion tons a year by 2025 year. So, airline industry must need to innovative, environmentally responsible industry that drives economic and social progress. It has risks (social, environmental, operational, threat, strategic and financial risks) that they have to deal with marketing managers airlines, such as budget airline marketing manager is responsible for the optional decision making about corporate risks in its daily business. Adrian, (P. 2012) indicated that the marketing manager of budget airline needs to indicate the benefits can be categorized into three namely to let budget airline to feel as below:

(a) Regarding the economic view, budget airline is essential for facilitating world business and tourism, it needs to create jobs and enables the expansion of trade across the global by opening
up new market opportunities. It also attracts businesses to locations all over the world, hence satisfying the mobility requirement of a growing portion of the world's population. It also aids in the movement of products and services quickly over long distance facilities economies and social participation by remote communities.

(b) From the social perspective, budget airline forms an unique global transport network that links people in different countries safely and efficiently. Air transport is increasingly accessible to a large number of people who can now afford to travel by air for pleasure and its business purpose.

(c) Lastly, in terms of the environmental perspective, there is a need for budget airline to minimize or contain the impact in its environment through the continuous improvement of its
fuel consumption, noise reduction and the introduction of new technologies. Budget airline marketing manager can enquire this question to whose company, such as how budget airline can quantify the benefits derived from such investments to do with how to quantify the benefits, so budget airline can be compared to the cost of investments. Through budget airline has be different over the years to value many intangibles, such as corporate social responsibilities. Budget airline marketing manager needs to make choices among several alternatives: it is important to adopt a tool that with allow choices to clearly weigh and distinguish between the options available. So, budget airline marketing manager needs to persuade whose company to believe to maximize the gain, which may be either economic or social and may be beneficial to an individual, a group or society at large, e.g. reducing fuel cost can maximize economic or social benefits for long term. The measurement of benefits from corporate social responsibility policy includes gains from additional income to an increased quality of life or a cleaner environment. On the other hand, the costs are made up of the opportunities forgone, internal and external costs and externalities. For instance, increasing the flying route for budget airline, the noise and air pollution are the externality when the secondary effect could be an increase in the cost operations. In this case, the pollution creates the new cost (externality). The budge airline business cost is the increase in the cost of operating the additional route. The budget airline's fuel consumption causes air pollution will influence whose client stakeholders' powers of seeing and thinking, cultural setting, experience is from the past and motivation at the time of sensing to the airline image to be poor due to who will feel the budget airline is not a social responsible organization. It aims to earn profits from passengers, but it neglects to take care other stakeholders benefits due to its fuel consumption to pollute environment to cause global warming problem. It seems that budget airline needs to considerate to use more fuel consumption to cause global warming problem more than doubling air fares in real terms if Government decided to raise more fuel tax charging to it to reduce its income.

I suggest marketing manager of a budget airline to reduce to use more fuels to pollute air, so budget airline does not decide to increase double air fairs charges to clients due to Government raises fuel taxation expenditure. Because it will cause clients to cancel its air tickets if who feel its air fairs are not reasonable to raise prices to compare other airline competitors. The marketing manager of a budget airline might respond to promote this navigation system to persuade budget airline does not choose to double air fares if Government raised fuel taxing charge. Innovation of flight operation on the optimum routes using (RNAV) Area navigation, as conventional airways and routes between airports were built by connecting ground navigation aids to the destination, the budget airline often became rather inefficient. On the other hand, RNAV can build routes connected any points with almost straight line by confirming aircraft position by means of global positioning system etc. in addition to radio navigation destination of fuel consumption and CO2 emission through shortened flight time and distance. Other reducing fuel consumption include reduction of aircraft weight, use of new type point for aircraft painting to reduce emission of polluted to air . Hence, budget airline will spend less fuels to avoid to pay high fuels taxation expenditure to its Government and it does not need to charge double air fairs in real terms to cause many passengers who will choose to find other airlines to buy cheaper air tickets or who will cancel their budget airline air tickets due to who feel budget airline charges unreasonable air fairs. So, if budget airline did not achieve as above any methods to attempt to reduce fuel consumption, I believe that it will lose many passengers due to it decide to charge doubling air fares in real terms to compensate its fuel tax increasing expenditure .

Consequently, global airlines need to consider air pollution issue from their airplanes cause if they expects travelers choose to catch themselves airplanes. So, ecological non-economic factor will influence passengers choose to catch any airline places.

CHAPTER V

Ethnographic research (non-behavioral economy method) predicts consumer behavioral how and why change methods

1. How can (non-behavioral economy method) ethnographic research predict consumer emotion ?

Ethnographic research is one preferable consumer behavioral psychology method to predict consumers' general shopping model. Because any businessmen can install one video record camera to record the consumers' life habit at home. It aims to watch every video record camera observers whose life habits or life behaviors to evaluate the reasons why who choose to buy the product to make shopping desire more accurate.

Critically assess the role of ethnographic research as a means of learning More about buyer behavior. To critically assess whether the role of ethnographic research as a means of learning more about buyer behavior. I shall indicate what the marketers who use general methods to learn more about buyer behavior to compare to ethnographic research difference. In general, marketers learn buyer behavior who shall follow the simplified stages in the buyer decision process , such as the beginning is from need recognition to information search to evaluate to decision to the end of post purchase evaluation stage. Hence, the any buyers behavior shall be cycle stage to decide whether who shall repeat to choose to buy the company's product or use it's service if who feel the product or service had achieved their satisfaction after who spent. The marketers shall use questionnaires or marketing researches to enquire consumers to gather their ideas to analysis to get evaluation to assess whether how whose companies need to produce what kinds of new products style, design, color, price level and sale channels to achieve the most suitable marketing strategy to raise their sale competition. Otherwise, the role of ethnographic search is one different method to learn more about buyer behavior. In general, companies shall not need to arrange questionnaires to enquire participants to fill to answer questions to gather data to carry on evaluation and which do not need to follow the simplified stages to assess target client groups purchase decision process to carry on the sale and post purchase evaluation cycle to evaluate whether what are their product criteria or weaknesses which need to improve to raise their sale competition in their market. I think ethnographic research can get closer to the truth about consumer behavior. On behalf of companies' clients, which can seek to uncover hidden truths about the way their clients' lead their lives, by paying volunteers to be followed for days on end, being filmed and having their every more recorded.

Companies will pay their target householder participant group to carry on an observational survey by digital cameras to be filmed record at home. One essential feature of ethnographic research is that it must not have any predetermined agenda. There is little value in undertaking this type of research if the mind set of the researcher is expecting to see preconceived phenomena, it is the unexpected that is often of most interest, and which is so difficult to pick up through more structured forms of survey. In fact, participants in a survey may feel self conscious when who are being filmed, and the more interesting insights are likely to be observed when participants are feeling relaxed and off their guard .It is not just what people actually do that can be interesting, but what they almost do, and the body language used when members of the household are discussing an issue. It can take several hours of filming to yield just a few moments of true insights into participants' true attitudes and behavior.

One example of the company's ethnographic research in action was provided by a project commissioned by the footwear brand Dr Martens. It wanted to understand how young people used fashion brands in their every lives . Why for example, did some brands, such as Nike trainers or baseball caps become popular in youth culture? The researchers identified groups of young people around the world who responded to Dr Martens' target market. In return for a payment, volunteers were followed for several days and their daily routines filmed with a handheld digital camera. In total, 180 hours of captured film was edited to just one hour of highlights showing the key drivers of youth culture which are relevant to the Dr Martens brand. It seemed that young people preferred fashions that allowed them to customize an item of clothing and in some way take ownership of it. The research drew the conclusion that iconic fashion items for young people had to have a distinctive label or style that made their wearers stand out as part of a tribe. Hence, ethnographic research seems to help this company to know why the young clients choose to buy other brand sport shoes, it is possible that they the other brands sport shoes' color or design can be accepted more to than to buy Dr Marten brand's sport shoes when they wear different style of clothing.

Hence, it can use digital camera to observe the worldwide choice of paying target youth volunteers whose daily individual behaviors at homes to get the more actual evidence to evaluate what factors influence youth clients choose to buy other brands of sport shoes. Otherwise, if it use structured questionnaire surveys to enquire youth clients , it is possible that who can not give their feedbacks honestly. Otherwise, observable youth people whose daily activities can help this company to know it is possible that their design and color of clothing are one factor to influence their choice to buy preferable brands of sport shoes to wear if who felt the brand of sport shoe was suitable to wear to influence their clothing to be felt more smart in appearance. However, I suggest companies to avoid to tell householders what the research project is about, until it is over. That way, the chances of participants deliberately playing to the camera can be reduced. Hence, ethnographic researcher ought not tell to participants why who needs to record their daily activities at home till to the end of observable survey finishing due to it is possible that the participants will not perform their actual behaviors if who knew the researcher's observable intention. However, if marketers need to understand how whose companies clients actually make purchase decisions to their products, who shall use structured questionnaire surveys for collecting large scale factual data, but it will have major weaknesses when companies can not understand individual's attitude. Complex sets of factors that influence their buying decisions can only rarely be captured by a questionnaire.

Qualitative approaches such as those using focus groups can get closer to the truth, but participants often still find themselves inhibited from telling the full story to the companies to know.

Ethnography is one of many approaches that can be found within social research.

Ethnography was a descriptive account of a community or culture. Ethnography usually involves the researcher participating in people's daily lives for an extended

period of time, watching what happens, listening to what is said, and/or asking questions through informal and formal interviews collecting documents. In more detailed terms, ethnographic work usually has most of the following features: People actions are studied in every contexts rather than under conditions created by the researcher, such as in experimental setups or highly structured interview situations as well as data are gathered from a range of sources including documentary evidence of various kinds, but participant observation and/or relatively informal conversations are usually the main ones as well as data collection is for the most past relatively unstructured in two senses and it doesn't involve following through detailed research design at the start and the categories that are used for interpreting what people say or do are not built into the data collection process through the use of observation schedules or questionnaire to analysis.

Generally, fairly small scale, perhaps a single setting or group of people. This is a facilitate in depth study and the analysis of data involves interpretation of the meanings, functions and consequences of human actions and how these are implicated in local and perhaps also wider contexts what are produced for the most part are verbal descriptions, explanations and theories and statistical analysis play a subordinate role at most. How ethnography can learn more about buyer behavior. It means collection of data to pursue an answers to these questions more effectively and to test these against evidence. Collecting data in natural settings, in other words in those that have not been specially set up for research purposes (such as experiments or formal interviews). Where participant observation is involved the researcher must have some role in the studied and this

will usually have to be done at least through implicit and probably also through explicit, negotiation with people.

The methodological model for social research is physical science conceived in terms of the logic of the experiment. Ethnography was sometimes dismissed as quite inappropriate to social science on the grounds that the data and findings it produces are subjective. Hence, ethnographic research is the role to learn more about buyer behavior through marketers may have been listening more to consumers (e.g. through qualitative research), efforts have almost always been directed at controlling consumers; ranges of products or services pre determined by producers have been pushed through with little real involvement of consumers in the process at a time in which consumers are ever more aware of what is being done to marketers. Ethnographic field research involves the study of groups and people as who go about every day lives. There has two distinct activities. First, the ethnographer enter into a social setting and gets to know the people involved in it; who participates in the daily routines; develops ongoing relations with the people in it and observes all the approach. But second the ethnographer writes down in regular systematic ways what who observes and learns when participating in the daily rounds of life of others. Thus, the researcher creates an accumulating written record of these observations and experiences. These two interconnected activities comprise the core of ethnographic search: firsthand participation in some initially unfamiliar social world and the production of written accounts of that world by drawing upon such participation. Hence, ethnographers are committed to get close to the activities and everyday people.

Getting close minimally requires physical and social proximity to the daily rounds of people's lives and activities, the field researcher must be able to take up positions in the midst of the key sites and scenes of other's lives in order observe and understand whom. In learning about others through active participation in their lives and activities. Finally, close continuing participation in the lives of others encourages appreciation of social life as ongoing processes. Through participation the field researcher sees how people do uncertainty and confusion, how meaning is through talk and collective action, how understandings change over time.

Consumer behavior refers to the behavior that consumers display in searching for purchasing, using, evaluating and disposing of products and services that who expect will satisfy their needs and it's behaviors that are directly involved in the action of obtaining, consuming and spending products/services, including the decision processes that precede and follow these actions. The knowledge of consumer behavior helps the marketer to understand how consumer think, feel and select from alternative like products, brands and the like and how the consumers' buying behaviors are influenced by their environment, the reference groups, family and salespersons. Most of the factors are uncontrollable and beyond the controls of marketers, but who have to be considered when trying to understand the complex behavior of the consumers. Consumers buying cycle processes involved when individuals or groups select, purchase, use or dispose of products or services or ideas or experiences to satisfy needs and desires.

In the marketing context, the term consumer refers not only to the act of purchase itself, but also to patterns of aggregate buying which include pre-purchase and post purchase activities.

Pre-purchase activity might consist of the growing awareness of a need or wants and a search for and evaluate of information about the products and brands that might satisfy it. Post purchase activities include the evaluation of the purchased item in use and the reduction of any anxiety which accompanies the purchase of expensive and infrequently bought items. The various factors include lifestyles and its impact on the consumer behavior. On the first hand, ethnographic research can learn more about buyer behavior as below: ethnographic research described the dominant, positivistic consumer perspectives and methodological and analytical overview of the traditional perspectives. There are two factors mainly influencing the consumers for decision making. Risk aversion and innovativeness. Risk aversion is a measure of how much consumers need to be certain and sure of what who are purchasing. Highly risk adverse consumers need to be very certain about what who are buying. Whereas less risk adverse consumers on tolerate some risk and uncertainty in their purchasing. The second variable, innovativeness is a global measure which captures the degree to which consumers are willing to take chances and experiment with new ways of doing things. Hence, ethnographic research can learn whether the buyer's shopping motivation is abound with which various measures of individual characteristics, e.g. innovative, variety seeking etc. different factors to the buyer behavior.

On the second hand, perception is a mental process, whereby an individual selects data or information from the environment organizes it and then draws significance or meaning from it. Perceived fit is an attitudinal measure of how appropriate a certain channel of distribution is for a specific product. Consumer's perception of the fit between a service/product and channel is very influential in determining whether who will consider using that channel for a specific service. In fact, perceived fit was found to be more important than consumer's preference for the distribution method or service. Product quality and packaging and brand awareness familiarity with a channel is a measure of the general experience who have with purchasing products through special channels , e.g. internets, newspapers advertisement factors let consumers to decide to choose to buy or not buy the specific product. Shopping motives are defined as consumer's wants and needs as who relate to outlets at which to shop. Two groups of motives, functions and non functional have been proposed with time, place and possession needs and refer to rational aspects of

channel choice. The functional motives included convenience, price comparison. Otherwise, the non functional motives entailed recreation and it related to social and emotional reasons. Hence, ethnographic research can assess whether the product or service is the functional motive or non functional motive to cause the buyer's choice.

On the third hand, economic theory holds that of largely rational and conscious economic calculations. Thus, the individual buyer seeks to spend whose income on those products that will deliver the most utility (satisfaction) according to his tastes and relative prices. It aimed to simplify assumptions and examine the effects of changes in single variables (e.g. price) holding all other variables constant. (e.g. low price of product is the higher the sales. The identified the impact of price differentials on consumers' brand preferences; changes in produces on demand variations; changes in price on demand sensitivity and scarcity on consumer choice behavior amongst many others. The consumer behavioral perspective in contrast to the economic view which underscores the importance of internal processes in consumer decision making, the behavioral perspective emphasizes the role of external environmental factors in the process of learning, when which it is argued causes behavior. The behavioral perspective therefore focuses on external environmental, such as advertisement that stimulate consumer response through learning. Consumers must be exposed to information, e.g. advertisement of it is to influence their behavior. Hence, ethnographic research can assess whether the product/service is consumer behavioral perspective or behavioral perspective to cause the buyer's choice.

On the fourth hand, consumers were suggest that high involvement with a product results in an extended problem followed by an information search, alternative evaluation, purchase and post purchase activities. The process is aided by an active information processing sequence involving exposure, attention, comprehension, acceptance and retention. The choice is determined by the outcome of the information process aided decision sequence may have satisfying or dissatisfying outcomes. Consumer's motivation and intention and that unpredictable factors (such as non availability brand or insufficient funds) may result in modification of the actual choice made by a consumer. This model assumes that observed consumer behavior is preceded by intrapersonal psychological states and events (attitude intention-purchase sequence). Hence, the events are as outputs of the processing of information, taking for granted that consumers seek and use information as part of their rational problem solving and decision making processes. Hence, ethnographic research can learn why the buyer doesn't choose to buy the product whether it is unpredictable or predictable psychological factors.

On the fifth hand, personality perspective means some purchases have more personal relevance than others. When this partly reflects on factors, such as price, it also bears on the way in which some products enhance the consumer's self concept , e.g. possessions are considered to reflect on a consumer's image of whom. Personality in general is understood as a concept. Personality has also been understood as the unique way in which traits, attitudes, when individuals might not always be uniform and predictable in their patterns of choice in different situations, it might be possible to make sense of and to forecast the general reactions of broadly defined groups and classes of purchasers.

It is the concept of consumer general behavioral response patterns that forms the basis for marketing's personality based segmentation strategies. The possibility of using measures of personality to guide marketing action, for example in segmenting markets , tailoring new brands of innovative consumers and repositioning mature brands has encouraged a large volume of research. Attitude itself is a learning experience and can lead to a change in attitudes before buyers enter the buying process. Thus, attitudes don't automatically guarantee all types of behavior. They are really the product of social forces interacting with the individual's unique temperament and abilities and social influences are not all of the behavioral variations in people. Two individuals subject to the same influences are not likely to have identical attitudes, although those attitudes will probably more points than those of two and cognition.

Affect refers to the way a consumer feel about an attitude object, behavior involves the person's intentions to do something with regard to an attitude object and finally cognition refers to the beliefs a consumer has about an attitude object. Thus, ethnographic research can learn whether it is from external social factors more or internal personality factors more to cause the buyer's choice. The theory of cognitive information processing , attitudes are formed in the order of beliefs, affect and behavior. Attitudes based on behavioral learning follow the beliefs, behaviors and affect sequence and finally attitudes formed based on the experiential hierarchy follow the affect, behavior and beliefs route. A consumer who is highly involved with a product / service category and who perceives a high level of product/service differentiation between alternatives will follow the cognitive hierarchy (beliefs affect behavior). From the ethnographic research marketers perspective the sequence of attitude formation is from a communication point of views from a strategic point of view, such as it has proved useful in specifying the different elements that work together to influence buyers' evaluations of attitudes ; products or services may be composed of many attributes or qualities, some of which may be more important than others to particular people. So consumer's decision is to act on whose attitude is affected by other factors, such as whether it is felt other factors, such as whether it is felt that buying a product/ service would be met with approval by friends and family. The complexity of attitudes is underscored by multi attribute attitude models, in which sets of beliefs and evaluations are identified and combined to predict an overall attitude.

On the final hand, the situational influence perspective, a situation is defined by factors over and above the characteristics of a person and product or service. For example, situational affects may be behavioral (e.g. entertaining friends), experiential or perceptual (e.g. being depressed or being pressed for time). According to the behavioral influence perspective of low involvement decision situation, consumer decision making is a learned response to environmental cues, as when a person decided to buy something on impulse that is prompted as a surprise special in a store.

According to this approach, then ethnographic research marketers must concentrate on assessing the characteristics of the environment, such as the physical surroundings and product/service placement, that influence members of that target market. For example, point of purchase (such as product/ service samples) are particularly useful in inducing impulse purchases. Ethnographic research marketers focus on measuring consumers' effective responses to products or services and develop offerings that elicit appropriate subjective reactions and employ effective symbolism. Situational effects can also be perceptive, e.g. there could be a number of ways in which mood can influence purchase decisions. For example, stress can impact information processing and problem solving abilities. In addition, time poverty can impact buying decisions. An individual's priorities determine whose time style. According, consumer buying change is not something which consumers do for themselves, rather it is a result of something that is done to them by some internal ,e.g. trait or external ,e.g. environment force over which they have little or no control. Thus, ethnographic research can assess what is the situational influence factors to cause the buyer to choose to buy the product or consume the service. In conclusion, conditions of competition are changing rapidly today and companies need strategies to react to those changes promptly to raise competition. Due to technological developments, physical differences of products/ services have decreased. Differentiation should be on the meanings products/
services bear instead of on their physical features and a successful brand differentiation can be possible by building personality. Hence, understanding consumer behaviors are related to marketing natures in the product sale or service provision to every marketer who needs to considerate to win whose competitors.

2. Discuss the ethical issues that are raised by ethnographic research.

Consumer research has been important to the development of marketing theory and practice. Consumers are seldom, if ever, involved in the research design and analysis processes which raises issues that go beyond ethics. Particularly, problematic when participant observation is employed , as little is and little could be addressed by research guidelines and codes of ethics relevant to marketing research. Some of the relevant ethical issues to participant observation that arise from the lack of the consumer in the research process as well as the potential issues that may be involved in participatory research designs, the shortcomings of the available ethnographic marketing research guidelines and codes of ethics as for as participant observation is concerned. Some argument regards the real time and nature of ethical circumstances at the field where the ethnographic researcher must often respond to unexpected situations immediately.

3. Why ethical ways of thinking it is important to recognize that are raised by ethnographic research.

It is possible that the issues of power that can arise ethnographic research as well as it is from the consequences of simply doing research , even if the intentions are good and it is from the fact that ethnographic research marketers' knowledge system is necessarily linked to other forms of structural power (e.g. gender, race, development, the system). The ethnographic research marketers whose emotional and power issues present in ethnographic research relationships are also acknowledged to influence ethnographic results, and this is where the key issues of using research participants for data collection comes in. Ethnographic research designs that objectify and don't include research participants in the conceptualization of the research study through to data analysis have been widely criticized by ethnographic researchers and these issues must be considered within the scope of the ethics of care.

Researchers (ethnographers) need have moral responsibilities toward research, included informed consent, confidentiality, reliability and validity. In sum, ethical guidelines and codes of conduct can be beneficial in alerting consumer researchers of ethical ways of conducting research. However, participants needed rules to be aided by researchers' own ethical reasoning in the field. The ethnographic researchers need to highlight the importance of constant negotiation of participation in the different stages of research, how participants may not be willing (due to lack of time or even personal circumstances) to help ethnographic researchers in the data analysis process and how researchers' own deadlines and academic constraints may get in the way of the idealized research process of involvement between ethnographic research participants and researchers are well to their discussed topic. In general, ethnographic researchers need to know what who need to understand about ethics, such as harm, consent, data protection etc. recap of ethical approval what it is and what ethnographic researchers need to do and what further sources of information and support need. In ethic principles, ethnographic research should be designed, reviewed and undertaken to ensure integrity and quality.

Participants must normally be informed fully about the purpose, methods and intends possible uses of research, what their participation entails and what risks, the confidentiality must be respected research participants must take part voluntarily, harm to research participants must be avoided in all instances and the independence of research must be clear and any conflicts to interest or partiality must be explicit and increasing stakeholder demands. The mature of the ethical consumer is educated, middle class or over emotional to decide what kind products who needs to buy and how many numbers are enough to buy. For example, with the environment dropping out of media attention, ethic provided new moral ground and campaigns or opening of a chain of ethical supermarkets, ethical image became a desirable commodity for the big retailers. Some ethical customers need to satisfy with fair trade marked products to buy from the ethical supermarkets. How morality may play a significant role in the performance of buyers' actions. It is concerned specifically with how rules, responsibilities and values centering on right or wrong influence the character of consumption. The idea that morality (ethicality) can have a considerable impact upon the consumption. Hence, I think business moral performance is needed to satisfy every buyer's decision of consumption and it is linked to the ethnographic research growing literature on ethical consumer behavior. Within psychology, for instance, morality can be seen as a process of cognitive learning where systematic punishment and reward help to educate individuals of their actions.

Whether consumption is informed by at least some of the available moral perspectives to some of the available moral perspectives, so it caused ethical issues that are raised by ethnographic research. Ethical consumption is concerned with predicting market behavior, it included some kind of relationship between the attitudes, values and behaviors of a defined ethical consumer group. For example, ethnographic researchers have been interested in the effects of environmental concern on environmentally friendly consumer behavior. Depending on how ethical consumption is defined, it recognizes alternative forms of what are essentially moral values, attitudes and buyer individual behavior. Consumer behavior has been changed by external elements, such as economy, technology, cultures, religion etc. factors. It would be unfortunate to be great importance for an understanding of ethical consumption issues.

In conclusion, consumption behavior is the art of need for desire to, it could be thought of as directly influenced by certain core values held as sacred within society. For example, ethical buyer behavior may concerns about animal protection, environmental protection, human protection etc. life rights issue. Facts, knowledge and truth about morality in consumption are seen as being raised by ethnographic research. According, the relationship between morality and consumers behavior could be better through of as the products of a continued process of political, social, technological and religious re-organization of life. For example, capabilities of new digital , microchip technology enhanced many consumers with the delights of efficient, task-saving, small and shiny products. Simultaneously, and not unrelated turbo-charges cars, mobile phones, cock tail parties etc. high technological products are arguably reflected power, success and good living to influence buyer behavior ethically daily in our society. Hence, I believe ethical issues that are needed to consider by ethnographic research.

4. Discuss possible alternative approaches by which marketers may learn more about youth culture.

` Market based trading -selling, buying and consuming has existed in our society. Human action and interaction and behaving in different roles in exchange markets and various trading situations which is a typical of consumers and market trading interplays of several actors in economic, societal and cultural contexts as well as consumer behavior and consumer culture and consumption which have close relationship. Individual youth consumer or a group of youth consumers who is described as humanistic economics where people, their values and culture are primarily analyzed. In general, research on brands and organizational issues of the marketing function defined the questions of how to sell more products or provide more services to speed up the general level of consumption in order to better the economic situation of a firm or a nation. Basically, individual youth buyer seeks to speed whose income on those products/services what will deliver the most utility, typically satisfaction, according to whose tastes and budget. In economic, consumer behavior is identified with rational decision making. Decisions are automatically translated into purchasing and consuming,

The price and income constraints are generally accepted factors in an economic analysis of consumer behavior. Consequently, consumers are seen as rational actors that purposefully optimize the production of their utility.
Sociological and macro and cultural perspective which focuses on consuming , emphasizes on emotions, multicultural new consumers aspects, cultural studies and the meaning of culture for consumer research surfaced also in the late 1980 years. For example, consumption symbolism, different aspects to property and possessions, political consumption, research and cultures and subcultures. In consumer studies can be traced to the mid 1990 years, when consumer culture was recognized as a distinct cultural entity. Consumption was seen as a society activity which above all others, unities economy and culture. The one alternative approach is that learning more about youth culture, there is a clear common sense about its influence on social youth consumption changes, and the importance of its analysis in order to understand modern youth consumption. For example, marketers may learn more how to make youth to cause excessive consumption nowadays. The influence of the means of mass communication and oriented medias has contributed to send promotion messages to different youth audiences, e.g. from children and teen ages to youths. To see themselves in real conditions why who need to buy products or need services before beyond their possibilities have been planned to buy electronics, cars and even a house etc. products.

The another alternative approach is that marketers may also learn what are youth consumer modern culture how to make them, such as symbol status and power how become habituated to consume familiar products/ services able to reinforce familiar image in youth cultural different target groups. The final alternative approach is that culture is sociological influence on client's needs, it is based on the individual's physiological and psychological needs, such as food choice. Maslow recognized that once individual have satisfied these basic physiological needs, such as foods and drinks, who may seek to satisfy social needs by cultural influence, for example, the need to have meaningful interaction with peers. More complex still, western cultures see increasing numbers of people seeking to satisfy essentially internal needs for self satisfaction, products therefore satisfy increasing complex needs. Moreover, food is no longer seen as a basic necessary to be purchased and cooked for self consumption with growing prosperity, youth people have sought to satisfy social needs by eating out with friend or family. Youth peoples' satisfaction of such social needs may influences on their foods sating basic needs. Hence, if the youth clients had afford to go to

restaurant to eat more expensive and good taste foods. The high class food culture can change the youth client's food necessity to influence whose food choice. A young child is often considered society unacceptable, so such youth behavior is socialized out before the child reaches adulthood. The faculty cultural influences a child's perception of the world and the family cultural influences lasts into adulthood. For example of this effect on buying processes can be found in youth adults selection of a particular brand breakfast cereal because it is the one that who were brought up with youth individuals are surrounded by peer group/or reference groups with act as a guide for youth consumption of behavior peer groups can be primary and direct to influence their youth culture (e.g. colleagues at work and school), popular movie actors can secondary and indirect to influence to their youth culture (e.g. guideline or behavior provided by popular movie actors or media figures) ; youth individuals culture can also
identify with a social class and the values of this class can influence youth behavior, e.g. school culture or working class. However, culture in its widest sense influences youth buying behavior and deference to suppliers can differ significantly between different countries' youth culture to choose to sell their products or provide their services to the countries' youth markets. Youth needs are also influenced by the situation in which youth currently find themselves in their countries. The subjects of age and socio-economic status can have profound effects on youth buying behavior at different youth age market segmentation, such as youth client groups can divided to any companies to concentrate on selling, e.g. between 20 ages to 40 ages or between 10 ages to 20 ages etc. different age groups.

In conclusion, marketer may learn more about youth culture from different countries' family life cycle stages of change which have sought to take account of their increasing complexity to influence to estimate the countries' youth buyer numbers. The family relationships can include single parent family, married parent family, no children family youth buyer groups of family life cycle youth buyer changing numbers in marketers' target countries. Due to all different countries family life cycle youth buyer numbers can indicate the countries' youth individual needs changing numbers and the target countries' youth buyer numbers are likely to change their purchase tastes and needs as youth culture goes through life. Hence, marketers can measure the target countries youth age segmentation estimate numbers to decide how many products or how much services to supply to them to satisfy their needs accurately. Consequently, video record camera observation at home is one good behavioral psychological method to be used to predict consumer individual shopping desire. So, it is not only behavioral economy method can predicts consumer behavior.

CHAPTER VI

Quantitative and qualitative approaches (Non-behavioral economy marketing research method) predicts consumer behavioral how and why change methods

● Critically evaluate the relative merits of quantitative and qualitative approaches to data collection for a large retailer.

Survey is one good marketing research method to predict consumer individual shopping desire. Because it can gather any consumer individual shopping habit and consumption attitude or trend or reason to predict the kind of product overall consumption market trend and change more accurate.

The marketing research process needs to follow these steps: defining the problem and research objectives, developing the research plan, collecting the data, analyzing the data, then presenting the findings. In general, the specific marketing research major activities include: Research into customer needs and expectation and a variety of qualitative techniques are used to study the often complex sets of expectations that customers have with respect to a purchase. For example, when buying a personal computer, what are customers' expectation with respect to reliability, after -sales support, design etc? Customer satisfaction surveys indicate customer areas of satisfaction or dissatisfaction; how spending money on various forms of communication, such as advertising, sales promotion, and public relations; researching similar industry studies about competitors in completely unrelated business sectors how to improve own marketing effectiveness; researching key client studies about number of customers how to make special efforts to ensure that these customers are satisfied with its standards of service and prices; researching into intermediaries, such as agents dealers are close to consumers to gather information about consumers' needs and expectation. For example in relation to reliability, delivery times and after sales services; researching front line employees their attitude towards the company and researching environmental scanning changing on trends to influence the company development in the future. Structure of market research includes spending on market research, types of market research and potential problem. Market research means researching the the immediate competitive environment of the marketplace, including customers, competitors, suppliers, distributors and retailer. Otherwise, marketing research includes all the above and companies and their strategies and markets of whose products sale or services provision and the wider environment within which operates (e.g. political, social, economic etc factor influences).

Hence, marketing research means the systematic design, collection, analysis and reporting of data and finding relevant to a specific marketing situation facing the organization. In general, the ten most common market research activities for a large retailer data collection, include determination of market characteristics, measurement of market potential, market share analysis, sales analysis, studies of business trends, short range forecasting, competitive product studies, long range forecasting, pricing studies and testing existing products.

The reasons why a large retailer needs to conduct that research in new product development include the product must appeal to the customer, timely market research can help the large retailer to predict its client's needs/wants, market research tends to point out success and failure before its product is launched for real and it can save its money and time. A large retailer's market research can be sources by either primary or secondary or both and it can use either qualitative or quantitative or both methodologies and it can achieve objectives either exploratory or descriptive or causal experimental.

The primary source is collection of data specifically for the problem or project in hand and the secondary source is based on data previously collected for purposes other than the research in hand. e.g. published articles, governments etc.

On the quantitative benefits hand, it is cheaper to sample

size ; probabilities in depth motivations and feelings, it allows managers to observe real client reaction to the issue, e.g. comments and associations regard a new product fresh from the laboratory. It often used precursor to quantitative research, it can give the research department a low cost and timely sense of which issues in quantitative research. Quantitative research is designed to gather information from statistically representative samples of target population. The sample size is related to the size of the total population being studied, the variability within it, and the degree of statistically reliability required, balanced against time and cost constraints. It includes these skillful analyses such as below:

Correlation analysis means two phenomena are associated with each other. For example, whether change in household income is associated with the amount that a household spends on eating out of or firm's advertising expenditure on a product and sale revenue for it's relationship. Regression analysis means to use to build a model of causes (independent variables), which lead to an effect (the dependent variable). Companies shall use a historical database to test models that are assessed for the amount of variance in the dataset that they explain. Analysis of variance is used to test hypotheses about differences between two or more means. It is widely used in experimental frameworks where the researcher wished to examine the effects of two or more treatments on customers.

Conjoint analysis can provide valuable information for market segmentation, new product development, forecasting and pricing decisions and it can analyze the real life trade off that shoppers make when evaluating a range of features that are present in a range of product. Cluster analysis is frequently used in segmentation studies, but does not provide the marketer with a unique solutions.Neural network analysis splits a dataset into a training set and a testing set. However, quantitative analysis techniques can suffer from a number of weakness , such as sampling error, measurement error, significant estimation of sample population error, inappropriate estimation of population may be validated statistical tests and inappropriate interpretation of results can highly subjective.

On the qualitative merits hand, large retailer can get merits, such as many sample size and questions and information per respondent and much application of questioner's skill, analyst's skill and type of analysis. Qualitative techniques essentially seek to recreate the listening ear and interpretative mind that so many entrepreneurs use so well. Qualitative marketing research involves the exploration and interpretation of the perceptions and behavior of small samples of individuals and the study of the motivators behind observed actions. It can be highly focused, exploring in depth, for example, the attitudes that buyers have towards particular brand names. The techniques used to encourage respondents to speak and behave honestly. However, it is difficult to assess the validity of qualitative research techniques, and the tests for significance that are available for most quantitative techniques are largely lacking for qualitative techniques.

The quantitative and qualitative approaches to data collection for a large retailer its merits can achieve objective is either by exploratory, it means preliminary data needed to develop an idea further, e.g. outline concepts, gather insights, formulate hypotheses; it is either by descriptive, it means to describe an element of an ideas precisely, e.g. who is the target market, how large is it, how will it develops ; it is either by causal, it means to test a cause and effect relationship, e.g. price elasticity is by experiment.

Moreover, the quantitative and qualitative approaches to data collection can help a large retailer to find methods how to solve problems to raise competition confidently. In the beginning, of the market research process step, it needs to define the problem and objectives, such as it needs to distinguish between it's research type needed, e.g. exploratory descriptive or causal . Then, it needs to develop the research plan, such as deciding on budget, data sources, research approaches and instruments, sampling plan and contact methods. Next, it needs to collect information, such as information is collected according to the plan. Following step, it needs to analyze the information , such as statistical manipulation of the data collected, e.g. regression or subjective analysis of focus group. Final step, it needs to present the findings, such as overall conclusion to be presented rather than statistical methodologies.

Data collection gathers for a large retailer, it can gather syndicated data from householders, it is gathered either by psychographics and lifestyle, advertising, evaluation etc. styles of surveys and use panels or both sources. Primary data is originated by a researcher for the specific purpose of addressing the problem at hand, the collection of primary data involves all six steps of the marketing research process as well as secondary data has already been collected for purposes other than the problem at hand. These data can be located quickly and inexpensively. The intention to uses of secondary data for a large retailer, it aims to identify the problem and better defines the problem, develops an approach to the problem, formulates an appropriates research design, for example by identifying the key variables, answers certain research questions and test some hypotheses and interprets primary data more insightfully.

On qualitative merits to secondary data collection for a large retailer. The criteria aspect, this data collection method can give merits of response rate, quality and analysis data, sampling technique and size, questionnaire design, fieldwork benefits to a large retailer, so it's data should be reliable, valid to the problem; on error and errors in approach, research design, sampling , data collection and analysis and reporting, so it can assess accuracy by comparing data from different sources. On currency aspect, this data collection method can assess time lag between collection and publication, frequency of updates, so census data are updated by syndicated large retailer; on objective aspect, secondary data collection method can help large retailer to judge whether the data collected were needed to used for which parts of market strategies benefits for consumer research, so the objective determines the relevance of data; on nature aspect, this data collection method can define key variables, units of measurement, categories used, relationships examined, so it can reconfigure the data to increase a large retailer market strategies benefits usefulness and on dependability aspect, this data collection method provides expertise, credibility, reputation and trustworthiness of the source, so it's data should be obtained from an original source to raise market research benefits to a large retailer. Hence, internal secondary data collection can help large retailer department project to store project to analyze sales by product line, by major department, e.g. men's wear, by specific stores by geographical region, by cash versus credit purchased, sales in specific time periods, by size of purchase and trends in many of these classifications were also examined.

Secondary data collection can include demographic data, which is type of individual household level data available from consumers, such as identification, e.g. name, address, telephone , sex, marital status, age, income, occupation etc. as well as psychographic lifestyle data, such as consumer personal interest. Hence, a large retailer can get this quantitative and qualitative data to judge whether who is segmentation target to compete in its business market. For example, market research demands cooperation and trust between the client commissioning a study and the company carrying it out.

The reputation that a market research agency has built for itself
is particularly important where qualitative research is involved as well as qualitative research techniques are utilizing quasi quantitative technique in order to enhance their credibility.
In conclusion, large retailers are reliance on customer's view due to many experienced larger retailers are relying more on interactive development with lead clients. Because traditional market research for truly innovative new products have frequently proved misleading. Hence, quantitative and qualitative approaches must need to use to gather to assess how to achieve marketing strategies timely and objectively and relevant to win whose competitors nowadays.

2. Discuss the limitation of statistically based consumer databases of the type discussed here. Do qualitative approaches based on small groups offer any advantages?

Any large retailers need to follow this process to use marketing information system to gather data from consumer databases. First step, which need to gather data either from internal data or external data source or both. The internal data includes enquires, orders, customer complaints etc. as well as the external data is from customer panels, intermediaries etc. Next step, the marketing information system will carry on processes as data collection and analyzing internal data. Final step, the marketing information system will produce outcomes, such as input to decision support system and data for decision makers to evaluate and storage of data in a data warehouse outcomes. A large retailer can collect consumer data computerized database, from online bibliographic database or from internet numeric databases, full text database or offline directory databases, special purpose databases.

Hence, computerized published external secondary sources can help large retailers to identify individuals or organizations to collect specific data, for example, consultants and consulting organization directory, directory of market research reports, studies and surveys and research services directory and gather indices to help in locating information on a particular topic in several different publications. Hence, large retailer can collect classification of computerized databases include bibliographic databases are composed of citations to articles, numeric databases contain numerical and statistical information , full -text databases contain the complete text of the source documents comprising the database, directory databases provide information on individuals or organizations and services and special purpose database provide specialized information. Hence, large retailer can get syndicated service to collect and sell common pools of data of known commercial value designed to serve a number of clients and syndicated sources can be classified based on the unit of measurement (households/consumers) and institutions two groups. Syndicated services of householders/ consumers include surveys, data collection is from psychographic and lifestyles, general and advertising evaluation as well as it also include panels data collection is from purchase and media of volume tracking data and scanner diary panels as well as it also include electronic scanner services is from scanner diary panels with cable television.

Potential problems to limitation with market research of statistically based customer data bases include, small groups do not know when and how to do research from database and problems exist with research buyers and suppliers and it needs frequent techniques and small groups exist problems with traditional market research effort. On limitation of when and how not to conduct market research issue, it includes lack of resources, closed mindset, poor timing arrangement in marketplace, research results are not actionable, late timing is process, unclear objectives and cost outweighs benefits limitation. On the lack of resources occasion issue, if quantitative research is needed, it is not worth doing unless a statistically significant sample can be used, On the research results, small groups' clients are difficult to get psychographic data from statistically based consumer databases to analyze to carry on market research.

On the closed mindset limitation issue, when research is used as a preconceived idea. The statistically based consumer databases needs long time to gather data to analyze to carry on marketing research in its process. It cause poor timing to give clients to find marketing research result, if the client wants to know whether who ought to invest to develop the new product to promote to the marketing to sell from statistically based consumer database in the short time.

On cost outweighs benefits limitation, the statistically based consumer databases expected value of the information gathering time and resources spending cost should outweigh the cost of gathering the data from normal marketing research method.

On the limitation of problems with research statistically based customer databases , qualitative limitations include narrow concept of research, unrealistic view of timeframe, as well as variable quality of market researchers and it is possible that market researchers have not own sufficient technical to apply statistically based customer data bases. For example, market researchers will feel difficult to find facts from statistically customer data bases and who will spend much time to define research result from finding.

The qualitative approaches based on small groups offer any advantages from statistically marketing research customer databases only, but small groups can not offer any advantages from statistically market research customer databases. The reason is due to market research is about determining the characteristics of a market, for example, in terms of its size, requirements, growth rate, market segments and competitor positioning. Otherwise, marketing research is broader and is about researching the whole of a company's marketing activities. In most organizations, such search would probably include monitoring the effectiveness of its advertising, intermediates, and pricing position. Hence, small groups need to focus on marketing researching its company's internal marketing activities, such as pricing strategy, advertising method. Due to small groups are not large organizations, which did not focus on market research to external marketing environment, such as growth rate, market segment etc. influences. However, statistically based customer databases also have these qualitative approaches to small groups offer advantages include, easy of completion, realism, comprehensive, per-testing, questioner training, respondent motivation, repetition, cultural issues, bias in formulation and sensitivity of question etc. qualitative approaches.

3. What effects do you expect the development of interactive electronic media to have on retailers' collection of marketing research information from consumers?

The effects that I expect the development of interactive electronic media to have on retailer's collection of marketing research information from consumers. Limited use of market research indicated formal market analyses continue to be

useful for extending product lines, but they are often misleading when applied to radical innovations. Problems, with traditional market research has allowed prominent product failures and wrong predictions; markets are increasingly becoming micro-segmented, e.g. sports shoes aimed at fashion conscious women specifically for aerobic, so mass market research becomes correspondingly irrelevant; it is helpful for improvements, but traditional market research method is less for radical innovations and is less for more accurate targeting.

Thus, I expect the development of interactive electronic media effects to have on retailers collection of marketing research in formation from consumers. It may be advantageous to analyze continue to be useful for expanding product lines in the most short time and it will not mislead to businessmen when who applied this electronic media on retailers collection of marketing research method to get radical innovations accurately. For example, predicting whether who are major targeting segments for the sport shoe company to sell in the short time accurately, such as between 10 ages and 30 ages young male client group or young female client group or between 31 ages to 50 ages adult male client group or adult female client group.

On the evaluating internet resources for retailer's collection of marketing research legal hand, it needs to indicate the content of a resource must be reflective. If there is change, the resource must promptly reflect that change; if a law has been amended, any discussion on the web must reflect the law as amended. Otherwise, the internet resource is not qualified for citation in legal marketing research; research specialization and achievement, institutional and professional affiliation, medium of communication, e.g. professional journal and publishers are all useful criteria to evaluate credibility; questions to ask include: Is it a reviewed articles? Is it a law review journal? And does the author exhibit critical assessment of a resource? ; Copyrighted work means that an individual or an institution could claim ownership, responsibility and liability for the resource. It also publication and therefore users may have to comply with the principle of fair value; resources with citations journalistic ones. Researchers should therefore accord higher preference to resources with citations; many web resources disappear with the resources who contain. For instance, an electronically published law report must not only be current but also be continuous for it to be a dependable source for consultation, it is important to examine whether a resource reflects the attributed of misinformation half truths prejudice; a marketing researcher needs resources that can be connected to individual retailer or company's resources. In general, online market researchers know that search engineers vary in how who select ranking of results. With the advent of search engine optimization and the role of online marketing search engines, results are impacted by things other than returning results that are customized to rank higher sponsored links, with the page owner paying advertising dollars to get their site ranked higher. General search engines can be helpful when getting started or determining the scope of a particular question. Search engines like Google, Yahoo can be powerful tools. It is good practice to not rely on only one general search engine. General research engines, like Google, also have power helpful in narrowing large search results.

An old librarian advertisement page is that customers can have something quick, cheap and accurate but who can only pick two out three.

Therefore, choosing the top two most important factors will help consumers decide between conducting an open web marketing search and using specialized commercial databases. However, law firm librarians need to play important roles in helping their firms and staff members locate, manage and use internet resources efficiently and cost effectively and who need to understand not only the needs of their firms and clients, but also the specific types of information available online as well as offline to meet clients' unique needs and who also need to help business firms grow and strength their client services by taking advantage of the rich information online. For instance, law librarians need to lead the form in creating the best and most comprehensive combination of knowledge and information re-sources, including capturing and preserving reliable free and low cost internet resources, that accommodates the firm's budget and user needs, maintain the firm's intranet, further enabling cost effective online legal research, promote free and low cost online resources and research techniques, whenever, feasible to help attorneys and staffs improve research efficiency and cost effectiveness, manage electronic subscriptions which now generally account for a large annual spending than books and newsletters, educate users and conduct training sessions on online research skills, provide tailored content for individual users or groups to facilitate intelligent filtering of the abundance of available information online, provide guideline on the usefulness and reliability of legal resources, guide attorneys as well as consumers in finding information from the internet efficiently.

On evaluating internet research surveys marketing research hand, there have advantages of internet research surveys, rather than mailing a paper survey, a respondent can be given a hyperlink to a web site containing the survey or in an email survey, a questionnaire is sent to a respondent via electronic mail, possibly as an attachment . Electronic media survey is as an alternative to conventional survey modes , e.g. the telephone, mail and face to face interviewing. For example, a web survey can relatively simply incorporate multi-media graphics and sound into the survey instrument, automatic branching and real time randomization of survey questions and/or answers into self administered web surveys. However, unlike when phone and mail surveys were first introduced, concerned exist about whether these internet based surveys are scientifically valid and how they are the best conducted. Because internet can offer possibility of multimedia and interactive surveys containing audio and video, convenience samples to respondents email address. As a result, quick polls and other types of entertainment surveys have become increasingly popular and widespread on the web marketing research.

On the web marketing based surveys had particular three of benefit assumptions to attract companies to choose to do marketing research: (a) internet based surveys are much cheaper to conduct, (b) internet based surveys are faster, (c) when combined with other survey modes, internet based surveys yield higher response rates than conventional survey modes by themselves. In general, companies shall consider the following key characteristics of surveys choices: Response rate, timeliness, data quality and cost .

(Adrian, P. 2012) indicated that in response rate hand, web surveys respondents that can or will answer via the web may not be sufficiently large to compare mail surveys possibly. However, a company AT& T employees surveys experiment indicated to report a 63% response rate via email (63 returned not of 100 sent by email) compared to a 38% response rate for postal mail (14 returned out of 40 sent by mail). Interestingly, it indicated the response rates to the fast that, at the time, At& T employees received a lot of corporate paper junk mail yet over the internal email system, they received little to no electronic junk mail. I expect the development of interactive electronic media market research survey can achieve responses from a convenience sample might be useful in developing research hypotheses. Responses from convenience samples might also be useful for identifying issues, defining ranges of alternatives or collecting other sorts of non inferential data.

On timeliness hand, survey timeliness is increasingly stressed. The length of time it takes to field a survey is a function of the contact, response and follow up modes. the relevant measure is not average response time, but maximum response time (or perhaps some large percentage of the response time distribution) since survey analysis generally does not begin until all of the responses are in. However, simply concluding that internet based surveys are faster than mail surveys ignores the reality that the total amount of time for survey fielding time is more than just the survey response time. A complete comparison must take into account the mode of contact and how long that process will take and the made of follow up allowing for multiple follow up contact periods. For example, if email address of respondents are unavailable and a probability sample is desired than respondents may have to be contacted by mail. In this case a web survey only saves time for the return delivery of the completed questionnaire and not for the contact and follow up, so that the resulting time savings may only be a fraction of the total survey fielding time. For example, a internet survey company, knowledge networks has indicated that to achieve 70 to 80 % response rates they must leave a survey in the field for about 10 days. This period comprises one workweek with two weekends because they find that most respondents complete their surveys on the weekend (Adrian, P. 2012).

In conclusion, the delivery time of an internet based survey is faster than the delivery of a survey by mail, it does not necessarily follow that the increased delivery speed will translate into a significantly shorter survey fielding period. Two points are relevant: dramatic possible for specialized populations and even for populations in which all electronic surveys are possible.

On the quality hand, the primary purpose of a survey is to gather information about a population , the information is useless unless it is accurate and representative of the population. When survey error is commonly characterized in terms of the precision of statistical estimated, a good survey designing seeks to reduce all types of errors, including coverage, sampling, non response and measurement errors. Data quality includes unit and item non response, honesty of responses , particularly for questions of a sensitive nature, completeness of responses particularly for open ended questions and quality of data transcription into an electronic format for analysis of requires by the survey made. Data quality is usually measured by the number of respondents with missing items or the questions, longer answered are usually considered more informative and of higher quality email surveys may incur a higher percentage of items missing than mail surveys. Other quality issues for internet based surveys resulting from some sort of sampling errors are generally the same as for conventional surveys. However, such accuracy may be misleading if non response biases are not accounted for and researchers need to carefully consider the trade offs between smaller samples that allow for careful non response follow up and larger samples with less or no follow up. Web surveys can be programmed to conduct input validation as a logical check of the respondent's answers. These types of checks improve data quality and subsequently save time in the preparation of the analysis file. This will eliminate errors and from the respondent's point of view, simplify the process of taking the survey.

On cost hand, designing a survey fundamentally involves making trade off between the quality and quantity of data and cost. For smaller research surveys that are not subsidized in any way, a major component of total survey cost is frequently the researcher's time for survey design and subsequent data analysis. The labor cost of the personnel who actually execute the survey. It depends on the size of the survey and the complexity of the design either researcher labor cost, survey personnel labor costs or a combination of the two will likely dominate the survey budget. When lower costs are often of the benefits, of internet based surveys, Couper et al. (1999) found no cost benefit in email compared to postal mail surveys in their work. In a large and comprehensive survey effort of different government agencies. Couper et al. compared an all email survey (contract, response and follow up) versus an all mail survey. They found that evaluating and testing the email software took over 150 hours almost 4 times as much as they budgeted.

For the mail survey, costs for printing and posting were $1.6 per reply and data editing and entry cost about $1.81 . For the mail survey , managing the email cost $1.74 per completed case. In addition, they handled over 900 toll free call of a technical nature when the printing and mailing costs were eliminated for the email survey. Couper et al.(1999) found that the cost of evaluating and testing the email software, additional post collection processing and the cost of maintaining a toll free phone line which was largely dedicated to responding to technical questions related to the email surveys offset any savings. For example, email survey was designed so that respondents would use the reply function of their email program so the resulting replies could be automatically read into a database upon receipt.

I expect web marketing based surveys can reduce errors to avoid to mislead companies to find the wrong marketing strategy to compare paper surveys from every time of individual group customer questionnaires researches from internet. Moreover, I also expect web marketing based surveys can reduce cost to compare paper surveys from every time of group customer questionnaires researches from internet. In conclusion, I expect the development of interactive electronic media to have on retailers collection of marketing research information from consumers, the internet companies need to consider the electronic surveys response rate and time and quality and cost and legal responsibilities issues to let any companies to use their electronic media to carry on marketing research from customers to feel more satisfactory to compare to traditional questionnaires market research media if internet companies still hoped business companies still chose to use whose service to do marketing research in the future. So, marketing research method (non behavioral economy method) can be applied to predict consumer behaviors.

CHAPTER VII

England wine bar drinking customers age segmentation sale method

1. Can behavioral economy method can critically evaluate the bases that bars may use to segment their markets.

Behavioral economy analysis, UK wine bar businesses need to arrange their bar location to close to their target wine consumers. For example, the wine bar location ought need to be located to close sport centers or entertainment places or gardens if the bar target wine consumers are sport entertainers; or the wine bar location ought need to be located to close any transportation tool places if the bar target wine consumers are office consumers; or the wine bar location ought need to be located to close schools if the wine bar target wine consumers are students.

The United Kingdom bars market is a mass marketing, it means a strategy that presumes these is one undifferentiated market and that the bars wine drinking service provision will appeal to all consumers in that similar bar market. Marketing matching strategy divides segmentation, it means act of dissecting the marketplace into submarkets (segments) that require different marketing mixes, then targeting, it is the process of reviewing market segments and deciding which one(s) to pursue finally positioning, it needs to establish a differentiating image for a product or service in relation to its competition. segmentation variables may divide geographic, demographic, psychographic and behavioral variables.

In general, marketers may use a single variable or two or more variables. Geographic segmentation is based on the location of the target market, people living in the same area have similar needs that differ from living in other areas, climate, population, taste and micromarketing. Demographic segmentation is based on factors, such as age, gender, marital status, income, occupation, education, ethnicity. Psychographic segmentation is based on lifestyle and personality characteristics. Behavioral segmentation is based on attitudes toward or reactions to a product/ service and to its promotional appeals, usage rate, benefits sought from a product/ a service and loyalty to a brand or a store.

There are three basic market targeting strategies, such as undifferentiated, differentiated and concentration. Undifferentiated strategy ignores differences between groups within a market and offers a single market mix to the entire market and it works when a product/service is new to the market and there is minimal or no competition. Differentiated strategy means targeting two or more segments with different marketing mixes for each, concentration strategy focuses on one sub-market. Most British towns would had many small bars, all looking fairly similar to each other, with relatively few point of differentiation. Thus, if the UK bars do not use to segment their markets. I believe these UK bars will face much competition between themselves. In general, the market for drinking in pubs was fairly homogenous, comprising mostly male, who went to the pub mainly to drink and only very rarely to eat.

Now, UK pubs, clubs and bars continues to be a popular leisure activity in UK and pubs have benefits from a growth in eating out.

But, pub operators face challenges , including taxes on alcohol, growing competition from supermarkets for off sales, a smoking bad introduced. Pub operators have had to focus the design of bars on meeting the needs of smaller and smaller market segments. No longer is the pub market dominated by males going out to drink-professional women and families are among many segments and the professional and families segments, who seems dislike loud music or big screen television, who like to drink good quality coffee served more than beer, who like to enjoy bright and airy decorative in bars, who like to drink served to the table rather than queuing at the bar. These may have been design features that were unsought or unwanted by the traditional male heavy drinker segment.

Hence, it seems that UK female professionals and families shall be the popular segment in this UK bars market. However, segmentation can not be based simply on where people live, and must recognize their mobility and movement patterns. Therefore, for some sites located in town centers or on busy roads, an understanding of people's work patterns and commuting habits can be crucial. Being near a train station may be crucial for attracting a target market or urban professionals who want somewhere to stop off to meet friends before catching a train home. I think the UK bars may use to segment their market. Segmentation is essentially about identifying groups of buyers within a marketplace who have needs that are distinctive in the way who deviate from the average consumer. Some consumers may treat satisfaction of one particular needs as a seek to satisfy any of needs from a car purchase total market, the possible factor that might influence and individual's choice of car, car market segment targeted includes status, safety for families, a particular image, a cost effective transport, seeking environment by buying a green car and a company buyer saves tax client groups. Hence, British bars are fairly similar to each other, with relatively few points of differentiation. The market for drinking in bars was fairly homogenous and British supermarkets can sell wines and the comprising mostly males who went to the bar mainly to drink and only very rarely to eat. Today, the bar scene in any British town center is much complex. Hence, I think British bars ought to segment their markets if which wanted raise their competition.

On the first hand , the UK bar owner can choose professional women and family segment, in upmarket local, low density housing areas, it is likely to offer high quality food, no loud music or big screen television, good quality coffee served more than beer, bright and airy bar environment, drinks served to the table, rather than queuing at the bar, due to the proportion of women using these bars is higher than most of the locals.

On the second hand, the UK bar owner can choose male segment, in basic or mid market locals, that were unsought or unwanted by the traditional male areas; trade is focused on regular drinkers and tend to be met lead with little food. Beer, cider and spirits are the big sellers. Most show televised most offer some sort of food. There may also be themed evenings, quizzes, darts or pool. Customers tend to use the bar to meet friend and relax.

On the third hand, the bar can choose young local customers aged 18 to 30 secondary and university students segment. Amusements including pool tables and machines with feature and chart music and video screen will be prevalent.

On the fourth hand, the bar owner can choose city local to workers and shoppers segment, such as non office labors and supermarket buyers clients, it will offer basic bar food and snacks as well as centrally located in town centers but offering high levels of food, city dry led bars target the same customers as city locals, but focus on office labor clients mainly and it tends to be large and it may have function rooms and restaurant areas.

On the fifth hand, the bar owner can choose office workers and shoppers both segments. It may locate in centrally city location, but it needs to change from day to night to attract different types of customers. It can provide coffee bar attract in the day serving office workers and shoppers, but provide wine attract to young people's bar with loud music by might.

On the sixth hand, the bar owner can choose bar is located on or near the young non student people's circuit. Expect loud music, possibly a dress code and door staff and food is less important.

On the seventh hand, the bar owner can choose adults no children targets, in more upmarket areas. Restaurant quality food served for whose premium dining aim.

On the eight hand, the bar owner can choose family with children target, it again focuses on food these bar offers good value for money dining during the weekend and early evening.

On the final hand, the bar owner can choose to meet point for a specific customer group for example bikers, sport client segment in bicycle areas. It may be live music or entertainers to drink whose wine after who ride bicycle to need to find restaurant to sit down to relax and eat food needs. Hence, UK bar market is such as car sale market to follow family life cycle, gender and household composition, age, ethnic group, social class, individual income, lifestyles, individual attitudes, values benefits sought, the bar loyalty, the bar geographic location etc. the client internal psychological factors or the external environmental factors to divide different segments to sell in the market. However, I suggest the UK bars market segment ought to analyze to target young adult wine drinkers mainly. Bar consumer segmentation in the wine industry takes on many forms: demographic, geographic, behavioral and others.

For the bar wine industry, this group currently fits the legal drinking age range of 21 to 28 ages. With the recent oversupply of wine bars on the UK local market, so UK wine bars competitions are very high. Due to this situation, I recommend who need to focus efforts on finding new populations of wine existing consumers, rather than just redoubling efforts with existing clients.

I think wine bar marketers in the United Kingdom have primarily focused on the existing population of wine bar old consumers, which are the very large baby boomer young generation. This was an effective strategy for many years, when the wine supply and economic conditions were stable. Now, however, one of the most promising of the new wine bar consumer segments in the UK is that of the boomer generation. Generally viewed as children of the baby boomers. This segments group is considered whose consuming power and represented the future bars market for most wine brands drinking in UK bars. The children of the boomers who are young and who ought like to meet friends to go to bars to drink different kinds taste of wines and play entertainment in bars during who have school holidays. UK bars market segmentation means the process of dividing which different drinking wines taste into meaningful, relatively similar and identifiable segments or groups.

In general, UK bars market segmentation is useful for two major reasons. First, it assists bars marketing searchers in analyzing the needs of a specific customer segment. Second, the resulting data, it allows bars marketing campaigns to be focused on these identifies needs. In the long run, this allows bars to spend their marketing and advertising budgets wisely when at the same time meeting the needs of the drinking wine customer. Ideally, this should result in efficient, effective and profitable bars marketing and sales efforts. There are multiple types and levels of segmentation used in various industries, but those used most frequently by the wine bar industry are those that also fall into for four classic marketing segmentation bases. There are geographic, which is based on where the customer lives, such as big cities or small cities, demographic, which is based on age, gender, income, social class, psychographic, which is based on lifestyle and personality and behavioral which is based on occasions, benefits, usage rate , readiness to purchase stage.

In bars business, the wine taste is main factor to influence the clients choose to come to the bar again. In general, there are five consumer segments, such as conservative, knowledgeable wine drinkers; image oriented, knowledge seeking wine drinkers, basic wine drinkers, experimental, highly knowledge wine drinkers and enjoyment oriented, social wine drinkers. Anyway, psychographic factor can influence people choose to go to bars, the psychographic wine segments identify five major wine lifestyle, such as relaxed lifestyle, dining ambience, fun and entertainment, social aspiration and travel lifestyle. Hence, psychographic factor and wine taste knowledge factor are reasons why people choose to go to bars to drink wines instead of who choose to go to supermarkets to buy wines to drink. Regarding geographic segments in the wine industry, it includes individual wine bars or organizational wine bars or supermarkets or stores wine sale methods in UK country. Regarding wine consumption behavior is another factor, it includes five segments: Super-core, who consume wine daily; core, who consume wine at least two or three times per month; marginal, who consume wine at least two or three times per quarter ; non adopters, who don't drink wine, but drink other alcoholic beverages and non drinkers who don't on the areas where are not close to supermarkets or stores and the living people who are super core to consume wine daily in the areas. The bar has more chance to increase client numbers, it is unconsidered whether the bar's wine taste can satisfy its clients needs.

However, the young age market segment has very high consuming power. They don't only have a lot of money, but who influence family purchase. Many perform the grocery shopping for their families and have been given parent co-signed credit cards at a young age.

A key question in market segment analysis for this group is: What drives their purchasing behavior regarding wine? Young people can spend on average of 16.7 hours per week on the internet, excluding e-mail. They use it for shopping, in chat rooms, for research and to keep up is their primary source of information and who trust it. Because of this focus, wine bar marketers are urged to use integrated media to reach young people and not use only traditional channels. Online technology is a critical part of this,, but also offline locations where, such as music clubs, wine bars magazines, cable television and outdoor posters. E-mails targets at online interest groups and cell phone marketing are also useful.

However, wine bars advertising that ought includes diversity of race and gender. In addition, young people are highly influenced by minority cultures in terms of music, sport, dress and language. The wine bars marketing implication is that advertising should show a variety of diversity in terms of race and gender. Another consideration is to emphasize values and focus on cultural values when targeting specific ethno-centric segments of young people population in UK. I believe why wine bars can attract more young people, it is due to their focus on wine brands and who like to attempt different new or old wine taste, young people are very wine brand conscious and seek wine brands that provide quality, but at a fair price. Anyway, young people market segment characteristics is their belief in fun and responsibility, who tend to believe that life should be fun and enjoyable, but at the same time who do want responsibility and challenge on the job, who want to make sure that who take time out to enjoy life and believe that certain activities, so I feel young people accept to drink wine in base , the possibility is more than old people or adult ages people.

In conclusion, I think this UK bar market is an undifferentiated mass marketing, due to any bars characteristics can only give places to provide similar tastes of wines or coffees drinking or foods and entertainment for clients to enjoy to single formulation of its food provided services, to bars have traditionally offer one standard of food service delivery to all of their domestic or foreign customers. Due to UK small, middle and large size bars and supermarkets and restaurants are increasing to cause competition seriously. Overtime, however, bar consumers' needs tend to fragment into segments of different needs. Where UK bar markets are competitive, a bar may no longer to able to ignore the bar clients whose special needs of small groups of its customers, because if bar owner sold similar taste of wines, coffees drinking and foods to its competitors of bars and restaurants and supermarkets, I believe the non segment bar will lose many clients to compare the segment bar in UK bar drinking wine restaurant industry.

2. In the context of bars, discuss the relative merits of quantitative and qualitative approaches to market segmentation.

In UK bars market, I think it had the relative merits of quantitative and qualitative approaches to bars market segmentation. As UK bars market segmentation, the UK bar owners need to identify groups of bar customers who have similar needs and respond in a similar way to a given marketing stimulus to raise their bar competition. Hence, UK bar owner may use segmentation to measure whether whose bar ought to choose to locate where location (areas) to provide which kinds taste of wines, coffees, foods and entertainment to attract which kind of bar client group mainly, e.g. if the bar target client group is professional office female, it can locate at upmarket location in low density housing areas. It is likely to offer high quality food because there are many professional office female clients are in these low density housing living. However, bars market segmentation should be regarded as the bar wines and coffees drinking and entertainment service provision of critical thinking rather than as some pre-determined set of procedures. It shall follow that to let the bar owner to know what is an appropriate basis for the bar segment and one client group market may not be appropriate to all bar client groups in the UK bars market. To aware of the criteria by which the effectiveness of any UK bars segmentation basis can be assessed. I shall indicate those four important criteria to measure the relative merits of quantitative and qualitative approaches to UK bar market segmentation which can earn. The four important criteria include the usefulness to the UK bars marketing planning; the size of the resulting to the UK bar segment; the UK bar measurability and the UK bar accessibility four criteria.

On the usefulness to the UK bar's marketing planning criteria hand, it needs to ask this question before which chooses who is whose bar target client group and location and wine and food taste. Is the basis of bar market segmentation useful to the bar owner? It is easy to develop bases for market segmentation when losing sight of the purpose of the exercise. Essentially, the exercise is worthwhile only bar segmentation allows the UK bar owner profitably to penetrate a greater proportion of UK bars market then would have been the UK bar market case if the exercise had not been undertaken. UK bar market client groups identified as homogeneous bar market segments must be just that: Similar in terms of the needs of tastes of wines or coffees drinking and entertainment consumption behavior of the domestic or foreign individual client who contain. The UK bar shall fail in whose segmentation exercise because its assumptions about homogeneity within a bar segment, e.g. male or female or young student or young non student or family with children or family without children or bicycle sport client or office of non office segment, who overlooks some critical differences within the bar segment which leads to varied responses to the bar service offering that has been specifically targeted at the bar client segment. For example, a bar segment for the office workers target client group, instead of the bar owner needs to consider the location whether it is located to close to whose office, who also needs to consider these factors such as, what kinds of foods , wines, coffees drink taste and what kind of entertainment and service price charge and their habit consumption time. To be more effective, bar market segmentation must recognize the diversity of needs within this bar target client group. Hence, the bar can measure to quantify and quality its bar target client group to produce its bar market planning effectively.

On the size of the resulting to the UK bar segment criteria hand, the UK bar owner ought need to ask this question: Are the segments of an economic size to whose bar business? Any basic for bar segmentation should yield segments that are of a size that the bar can profitably exploit, because as the bar segments
get smaller who get closer to achieving the marketing philosophy of satisfying each bar client's needs as though each one were the center of the bar's attention. The problem for the uneconomic to provide for what a reasonable size of bar segment is varies from one UK bar market to another and is constantly changing over time. In the bar market , it is possible to provide quite unique tastes of wines or foods to target very small segments of the UK bar market. For example, if the bar target client group is professional female office worker clients. I think it ought need to locate its bar in the office areas location and the office and the office can not be close to supermarkets because supermarkets will have different style of wines and coffees to sell and its provision of cup of wines and coffees drinking and foods tastes must be different to supermarkets wines and coffees and foods tastes and the bar needs to consider what the entertainment is the professional female worker clients who need to enjoy in the quiet or noise bar environment. Because this factors will influence the bar's female professional workers' psychological needs and satisfactory needs. If who feel the bar's drinking and food and entertainment service provision which can't satisfy whose demand, who can choose another bars to close to office areas to cause the bar female client numbers will reduce. On the UK bar measurability criteria hand, the UK bar owner needs to ask this question: Can the bar market segment be measured? Ideally UK bar should be able to know the precise size of its identified bar market segment(s).

This is imported in order that the bar segment(s) can be compared and its profit potentials assessed. Unfortunately, UK bars clients data are often not available to the UK bar quantity market segments. So the UK bar owner should believe the areas of bar clients exist but can't measure or the bar client numbers should define bar segments only on the basic of what it can accurately be measured, but the different areas (location) bar clients may have litter bearing on the homogeneity of bar consumers' needs and consumption aims or reasons. The UK bar market segments information have include, e.g. the age profile of an area, number of people per household etc. However, bar owner also needs to assess of individuals psychological subjectively factor, such as whose attitude and lifestyles, e.g. if the professional female worker who does not like to drink coffee or wine drinking, even the bar location is close to the professional female worker office client, it will not persuade who to enter the bar.

Hence, the UK bar owner needs to find the areas where people whose lifestyles and attitudes to bar enjoyable feeling, then it may decide to measure whether the area (location) may have which bar target group(s) is/are the largest numbers to choose which kind taste of wines, coffees drinking and foods provision and which kind of entertainment to satisfy the bar's identified target client group(s) needs. Finally, on the UK bar accessibility criteria hand, the bar owner ought to ask this question: Are the segment(s) accessible to where bar business? There is little points to define the UK bar owner segment(s) of the UK bar market whose those bar segments are not accessible to the bar segments are not accessible to the bar owner or ever likely to be inaccessibility can come about for a number of reasons. Such as the UK bar owner may be prohibited by law from opening to locate whose bar in certain areas in UK geographic location (areas) or the UK law prohibits UK bar to sell some kind of taste of wines in whose country. Hence, the UK bar owner needs to know UK law prohibition to which kind of taste of wines drinking sold and where location (areas) to open its bars before who decides where to open its bar to sell wine to whose target clients segment(s) in British country. In conclusion, the UK bar owners can earn the relative merits of quantitative and qualitative approaches to market segmentation from these four criteria consideration.
Consequently, UK wine bar customers who are serious considerable wine bar location and wine price to influence they choose which wine bars to drink wines. So, their wine consumption is influenced by economic environment changing.

CHAPTER VIII

P&G body and skin product marketing advertisement strategy

● How would you explain the success of the fairly brand?
● Can economic changing factor influence consumers choose to buy R&G products?

Behavioral economy analysis, P&G does not need to consider whether its skin and health product price is cheaper than its competitors because it had built confidence to consumers to use its skin health products. Otherwise, it ought consider to manufacture more different skin health products to give its traditional and potential consumers who have more skin health product choices.

P&G fairly brand which mainly sold low value consumer goods, such a household detergents from bar of soap washing products to sell in UK country supermarkets in the beginning. Then, it innovated to produce liquid soap washing products to sell in UK country supermarkets. Further, it continued to innovate to produce soap products, such as the power of four for price of one, launched this low bulk, high concentration soap product to sell more cost effective to sell in supermarkets, even overseas supermarkets. P&G predicted domestic dishwashing machines instead of liquid of soaps , so it innovated to produce dishwasher cleaning fluid detergents products to let housewives to clean their dishwasher after every family used dishwashers to clean their plates to aim to keep their dishwashers to feel more clean to compare to clean by hand washing. Even, P&G will continue to innovate to produce potential anti-bacterial food washes to satisfy consumers' increasing concern over resides on the surface of fruit and vegetables.

In fact, P&G can predict what the new washing products will sell in this washing market, who will be its direct competitors, which are generally similar in form and satisfy customers' needs in a similar way as well as who will be its indirect competitors, which may appear different in form, but satisfy a fundamentally similar need. Such as P&G sold bar soap washing products in the beginning, it aim to satisfy families wash body to feel more clean needs. But, P&G felt it's direct competitors can sell similar bar soap products, so it innovated to produce new liquid soap washing products to raise its washing unique products and was different to its body washing product competitors. On the other hand, P&G also predicted domestic dish washing machines instead of liquid of soaps , so dish washing machines shall be which indirect competitors. Due to housewives can use dish washing machines to wash plates, so who will not use hands to wash plates after eating, it will cause who reduce to use bar or liquid washing soaps to wash their hands. So, P&G innovated to produce dishwasher cleaning fluid detergents products to let housewives to clean their dishwashers after every family used dishwashers to clean their plates to aim to keep their dishwashers to feel more clean to compare to clean by hand washing.

Even, P&G will continue to innovate to produce potential anti-bacterial food washes to satisfy consumers' increasing concern over resides on the surface of fruit and vegetables. Hence, P&G had attempt to raise its competitive ability in fruit and vegetables food and dishwasher machines cleaning market instead of bar and liquid soaps human clean market. It seems P&G threats of new entrants and threats of substitute clean products. In fact, P&G considers it soaps or other washing products whether which will cause chemical harmful to human skin or foods or dish washers after consumers have used its washing products. In the absence of that safety relationship of P&G social responsibility, its brand can act as a substitute in managing buyers' exposure to risk. P&G branding simplifies the decision making process by providing a sense of security and consistency of buyers which may be absent outside of a relationship with a washing product supplier.

P&G brand addresses a number of dimensions of purchase risk which have been identified as: physical(Will it's soap or washing products cause consumer skin harm or foods harm or dish washers harm?); psychological (Will P&G soap products or washing products satisfy consumer's needs for safety of mind?); Performance (Do P&G soap products and washing products work in accordance with consumers' satisfactory requirement?); Financial (Will P&G soap and washing products provide adequate performance with consumers' budget?). Due to consumers will compare P&G soap and washing products to its competitors' risk level to choose which brand washing products can give the minimal risk to harm to their health to decide to buy from supermarkets. Hence, P&G brand needs be built objectively measured (bar or liquid soap products or washing products are such as unique shape and smell and reliability) and the subjective values that can be defined only in the minds of its consumers (such as perceived personality of P&G brand is unique compare to other washing products brands). It means that P&G will be recalled that its brand processes functional and emotional attributes. P&G brand has been variously described as having personality that are ' fun', 'reliable ', 'traditional' and ' adventurous' and it needs to let consumers to feel it can give no harm to whose health after who use P&G soap or washing kind of products. In fact, P&G developed a single strong P&G brand strategy to sell different kinds of washing products, such as bar soaps, liquid soaps, dishwasher cleaning fluid and anti-bacterial food washes etc products, It aims to let consumers who choose to buy to use these kinds of washing products, then who must remember P&G brand. One approach to P&G branding is to apply the same brand name to every washing products which produces. The big advantage of this approach is the economic of scale in promotion. Instead of promoting many minor brands through small campaigns, it can concentrate all of its resources on one campaign for P&G one brand. But, the main disadvantage of this approach is that P&G can pose significant risks of confusing the values of it's brand. If P&G positioned its bar soaps, liquid soaps, dish washing fluid and anti-bacterial food washes etc. products range as premium priced, top quality, confusion may arise in consumers' minds if it applied the same brand name to a budget version of its washing products. Does P&G brand still stand for top quality?

This is a particular problem for P&G new washing product, such as anti-bacterial food washes and dish washer cleaning fluid products which are of unproven reliability. Hence, P&G sells in low price strategy in supermarkets to let many families can buy its different washing products to do trial test whether its innovative washing products which are better quality to compare to other brand washing products to satisfy who to choose to buy P&G brand washing products for every families to use long term.

In fact, UK soaps product is a imperfect competitive market. The different soap manufacturing companies produce similar color and shape bar or liquid soap products and they build different brands and they are targeted at specific segments, such as family group and they need promotion to promote their brands and soaps price is premium sustained. Hence, P&G needs a differentiated product may have significant monopoly power in that it is unique, but if it fails to satisfy customers' needs, its uniqueness has no commercial value. However, P&G had innovated it different bar soap products to liquid soap products, even it also launched dishwasher cleaning fluid detergents products, due to dish washer machines reduce housewives to use hands to wash plates to use soap to clean whose hands after eating as well as it launches

potential anti-bacterial food washes to satisfy consumers' increasing concern over resides on the surface of fruit and vegetables. Hence, P&G aims to be any new cleaning products leader to raise its cleaning market share effort.

The soap and other detergents manufacturing industry of Procter & Gamble (P&G) trends and characteristics who its primary intended is target client group(s). I think families (householders) or student individual daily consumption are P&G main target client groups. Soaps are personal care products. Consumers will compare different brands of soaps to decide which brand soaps ingredients can give health to them to wash their bodies and skins. The soap industry includes (P&G) and other soap manufacturing companies primarily engaged in making soap, synthetic organic detergents, inorganic detergents and crude vegetable and animal fats. In general, skin care soap sales include bar soap, body wash and liquid categories which can sell in supermarkets and discounting retailers and drug stores. Traditional , bar soaps, which are considered a mature category, exhibit very low growth, when newer products (shower gels and body washed) substitute products are launched. However, natural soaps still have opportunities for growth if which can be launched to raise care to skins and bodies health to human. The soap and personal products industry is being driven to a large extent by the changing age composition of the population, specifically, baby boomers have established anti-aging preparation as the chief benefit of health products aimed at correcting or improving the physiological condition of the skin. They have led the broad personal care sector of the economy to focus on the potential in aging consumers. Growth is occurring in a variety of age-sensitive product markets from soaps and skin creams to massagers and body fat analysis machines. As baby boomers lives get busier, stress relief soap products will become more important to carry on launching their skin care health quality for human benefits in daily washing. The group composed of 45 ages old to 54 ages old females is responsible for the highest amount of sales of body care and bath products in mass stores, who can influence householder families members spending effort in soaps consumption. P&G soaps are displayed to supermarkets to retail, the supermarkets' shelves are remained unaffected by the changing population in the personal care products sale areas. Even retailers like Brook stone and Sharper Image expanded their interest in branded personal care items. Not only was more retail dedicated to the personal care products, but they were often placed in specific "spa shops" within the store, with displays used extensively to merchandise the personal care category.

Body boomers are not, however, the only group important to the growth of this personal care industry. The number of personal care products designed specifically for children is increasing. Health and beauty aids suppliers are using licensing to tap into the growing spending power of children. The traditional soaps manufacturers must carefully review their marketing and other business strategies in order to adapt to the transformed market. The changes also create better opportunities for new personal care product companies to enter particular market segments. The mass bath and body care category has made recent introductions reflective of several trends that department stores, salons and special boutiques have been offering for years. The world consumers are changing their personal care demand to cause a result of soap product innovation, so P&G also needs to replace older well known soap products with newer ones that contain special formulations. New product activity and the increasing popularity and liquid soap increase competition in this personal care market. A growing perception among consumers that who must deal with problem skin and rising levels of concern about germs are helping drive sales of personal soap. Although, traditional brands such as Dove, Dial and Irish Spring still hold the largest portion of the toilet soap market smaller special soap manufacturers are increasing their market shares. Hence, P&G needs to focus on concentrating who its specialty soaps. In general, consumers want a soap that fits their particular needs and specialty soaps, often made with natural ingredients to protect bath and hand skin health. However, some competitors choose to sell soap substitute products, such as oils, bath blends, perfumes and fragrances in supermarket. Hence, these personal care products can also influence P&G company liquid soap sales in overall soap retail market.

In soap manufacturer industry, the naturals trends is also evident in the ethic segment of skin care. Ethic consumers are seeking multi-functional products full of botanicals and vitamins butter natural ingredients. So, I think P&G needs to launch this kinds of new class of skin care product to raise its skin class of skin care product to raise its skin care health care to increase consumers' confidence. Due to personal care products market competition is increasing, such as one stop shopping stores can offer for a variety of health related items, healthy foods, dietary supplements, prescription and over the counter drugs, skin care products and other natural personal care products. In addition, smaller natural skin care manufacturers are staying competitive by targeting skin-related over the counter drug markets. Moreover, internet retailing of personal care products has grown rapidly. Web site can offer can be nearly limitless. One important advantage held by online sellers over stores with physical locations is the constraint caused by a lack of shelf space. The characteristics of online sellers allow them to stock a much wider variety of the products consumers want, if also provides an opportunity for small or large manufacturers audience of consumers. One of the greatest difficulties faced by a firm wishing to enter a consumer products market is persuading retailers that they will benefit by dedicating scare shelf space to the manufacturer's products to online selling reduces that problem.

A potentially important negative aspect of electronic commerce for personal products is that inability to feel and especially, smell the merchandise. Many personal care products list fragrance as an important characteristics. To the extent consumers are already familiar with a special products, this is not a problem, but such as P&G getting a new liquid soap products might be more difficult. Soap industry needs to launch to improve soap qualify to satisfy consumer need. It must need enough workers to help P&G to manufacture enough different kinds of soap to sell to different countries soap market. I think its workers include these kinds , such as packaging and filling machine operators, first line production supervisors, cleaning, picking equipment operators, hand packers and packagers, hand material movers and soap researchers because it needs these workers to help it to produce different kinds soaps in the manufacturing process in factory, so it needs to give training to raise whose proficient skills to prepare to produce any new kinds of soap efficiently and it needs to consider the labor supply to soap manufacturing market , e.g. who needs to know what the difference between chemicals and all natural ingredients to prepare to produce its soaps ethically. Because if they have errors in the manufacturing process to cause consumers feel to use P&G soaps to have chemical negative health response.

These workers shall influence P&G health soap products image negatively. Hence, P&G needs to consider its workers' working attitude ethically. However, P&G was the largest soap maker and it did not own the most part maintain in house chemical manufacturing capabilities. P&G must therefore purchase new materials from other suppliers, so P&G needs to consider its raw materials suppliers market to measure whether who can give it the largest benefits and the cheapest costs both, Thus, giving the raw material suppliers global marker to choose who remain a greater incentive to provide superior service to P&G. I think P&G needs to spend time to choose who is its raw material suppliers who can provide the best natural health quality and the least chemical ingredients to cause consumers to use to feel uncomfortable response to their skins negative influence. Hence, I think P&G ought innovate its soap products quality to satisfy to avoid to use any cheap chemicals ingredients to produce its old or new kinds of soap products to sell to consumers unethically if it still wants to a sale leader in this personal care product market.

2. How do you think Procter & Gamble has been able to increase its market share at a time when competition from supermarkets' own-label brands has intensified?

Procter & Gamble operates mainly low value consume products, such as household detergents are among the most competitive and building successful brand is key to long term profitability. Differentiating one product from another in the minds of consumers can be extremely difficult, with one packet of detergent looking very much like another and performing similarly. It seems that it can not be unique to sell in supermarket. However, then it innovated new liquid soap products, it seemed to adopt to change in consumer preference, and maintaining consistent standards when exploiting new market opportunities. Adrian, P. 2012) showed that Fairy liquid was rated as Britain's number one cleaning brand by Marketing magazine and in 2010 accounted for 3 percent share of the UK washing up liquid category by value. The brand has been a regular household feature since the name first appeared in 1898 year on a bar of soap. P&G first launched Fairy liquid in the UK market I think Procter & Gamble (P&G) has this marketing strategy to supply its soap products to supermarket retailers. A supermarket is not only supply to likely to encounter a massive range of products, such as food , drink, homecare, personal care, luxury products etc. Consumers can see categories and see how much the offering changes, the range , the packaging , the branding and advertising or promotion of any brand products sale at shelves. Hence, such as P&G manufacturer in 1960 year. At the same time, the market for washing up products was still in its infancy, with most consumers using solid soaps, and only 17 per cent of households using liquid soap. But P&G gained most from a change in consumers' habits. It educated the public of the benefits of using washing up liquid.

The launch of Fairy liquid soap products involved distributing 15 million trial bottles to about 85 per cent of household in the UK. Creating early awareness and trial of the Fairy liquid soap innovative products led to Fairy gaining a market share of 27 per cent by 1969 year. It had a proud positioning as a slightly more expensive product which is better value and worth. So, it created brand values of a soft, caring, homely image by advertisement promotion. It also attempted to adopt in response to changing attitudes, for example, a commercial in 1994 year for the first time used a father instead of a mother at the kitchen sink. During the first twenty years of the brand's life, product innovation had been relatively modest. However, an increasing competitive market, customers have forced P&G to innovate in order to maintain and strength its market share.

Adrian, P.(2012) showed that with emergence of many 'me-too' competitors from supermarkets, Fairy needed to offer additional unique advantages to raise its competition. In 1984 to 1985 years, P&G introduced a lemon variant of Fairy and its total market share increased to 32 per cent. By 1987 year the market share had increased to 34 per cent, with the newly introduced lemon variant accounting for one-third of sales. In 1988 year, a new formulation was launched , offering 15 per cent extra mileage, as well as more effective grease eradication. In 1992 year, the original Fairy Liquid was replaced with Fairy Excel, which claimed to be 50 per cent better at dealing with grease. This helped to increase the market share to 50 per cent . In the following year a concentrated version of Fairy Excel Plus was launched, with the slogan ' The power of four for the price of one'. P&G launched this low bulk, high concentration product to retailers, such as supermarkets, who were tiring of filling their valuable shelf space with more and more variants of basically low value products. Excel Plus offered supermarkets more cost effective and profitable use of their shelf space. Increasing ownership of domestic dish washing machines posed a threat and also an opportunity to Fairy.

The threat came from a relative decline in sales of liquids used for hand washing of dished. The opportunity arose from increased demand for dishwasher cleaning fluid and the Fairy brand was extended to dishwashing detergents. In 2006 year, P&G introduced Fairy Active Bursts for dishwasher. Excel Plus was launched in the UK, Denmark, Finland, Germany, Holland, Ireland and Sweden etc western countries' supermarkets to help it to sell.

Innovation and reliability have been at the heart of Fairy's branding strategy, in a market which has been contested by other manufacturers' brands, and increasingly by supermarkets' own label brands. Preferences for new scents of detergent are continually emerging and provide an opportunity for innovation. Following a series of food safety scares, some observers of the market have pointed to a potential market for anti-bacterial food washes which would satisfy consumers' increasing concern over resides on the surface of fruit and vegetable.

Its innovative liquid soap products, it needs supermarkets where which compete with other soap product manufacturers for the attention and hopefully the purchases to shoppers choice. It's a soap products from bar soap to liquid soap kind of products. P&G brand have been a player in the household and consumer personal care products market for nearly 200 years. They started life making candles at a time when there were still a common source of domestic lightly. But they moved on from those to other related products, soaps and cleaning products. Today, P&G have around 300 brands, including Crest Oral Care brand, Pampers Nappies brand and Baby products, Tide and Arial brand washing powders, Tampax Sanitary products etc. different brand in this personal care market. To keep a range as wide as this refreshed and to develop new and improved produce to feature on the supermarket stages around the world needs a powerful innovation engine. P&G had built a world wide research and development operation which involves some 7500 scientists and a spent of around USA$3 billion per year. It might be not as much as the high technology pharmaceutical industry, but still very impressive for its sector. P&G had some very effective systems and structures to ensure efficient soap products innovation project selection and progression . P&G had an impressive record on new product launches and many of their new categories billion dollars brands, products magic whose annual sales could be high as US$150 to US$200 million. But, in the late 1990 year, there were concerns about this approach to innovation. When if worked there were worries, not least the rapidly rising costs of carrying out research and development cost.

However, I think P&G should not raise its new kinds of soap products sale price, such as liquid soap products. Even it had spent too much research and cost development expenditure. Hence, I think it still needs to keep competition to attract different countries consumers to buy from different countries consumers to buy from different countries supermarkets globally. Hence, low sale price is its major market strategy in supermarkets sale make. For long term, I suggest P&G chooses to outsource its research and development internal business department to one or more than more external technological research and development consultant company/companies to carry on researching any new soap products to avoid spending too much expenditure to raise soap products sale prices to reduce its competition to sell in supermarkets. P&G 's pioneering use of advertising, direct distribution , marketing research , brand management and produce innovation strategies to raise it's growth throughout the 20th century. Diversification, globalization of it's brands, innovations in distribution and supply chain management and P&G 's technological and product innovation strategy continues to drive its success into the 21st century. P&G had pioneered a series of strategic innovations had sustained its competitive advantage in a number of highly competitive market and its primary focus was process innovations in many areas.

Firstly, background on P&G was from its origin to 2008 year briefly reviewed. Next five strategic innovations were each reviewed along with its competitive implications in the areas of direct to consumer advertising, direct product distribution, marketing research, brand management and technological and product innovation. Hence, P&G soap products innovation was divided to two stages of two different periods to aim to satisfy consumers' body and skin health needs of bar soaps choice to use liquid soaps choice in this personal bath and washing care market.

Adrian, P. (2012) showed that in 1915 year, P&G opened a facility in Canada representing its international operations. A chemical division was created during 1917 year and 1918 year which was responsible for research and development of new products. To sell these new products. P&G created a market department in 1924 year. The purpose of this department was to study consumer preference and purchasing inhabits (Data monitor, 2008:7). In 1926 year, a perfumed bar of soap was introduced. By the end of the 1920 year P&G had no longer produced candles, thereby signal a major shift in its core business . Then, 1933 year, the acquisition lead P&G into hair care products. In the early 1940 year, P&G established a drug products division which also developed and sold a variety of toiletry items.Then, P&G introduced new products and entering new markets, it had not stopped innovating on its established products , such as tide liquid soaps was launched in 1984 year. During this time P&G also purchased Blendax a popular tooth paste brand in Europe. As the 1980 year, P&G made a significant move in Asia by entering into a joint venture to produce products in China. In 2007 year, it invested US$35 to US$50 million in its Gillette manufacturing facilities in South Boston, USA. At the same time, it announced a restructuring whereby P&G. Beauty and health division would be managed under the P&G purchased HDS cosmetics laboratory skincare line that focuses on specific skin conditions that require more attention than general cosmetics.

P&G 's history of marketing innovation began in 1980 year with Ivory soap on what had been promoted around the world as the floating soap (Dyer et al., 2004). Ivory represented P&G 's first attempt to brand a product through the use of advertising to connect with customers. Direct to consumer advertising was an innovation P&G pioneered with its customers and as such was a major innovation versus the traditional practice of advertising to wholesalers and practice of advertising to wholesalers and other distributors. During the 1800 year's soap was cut from huge soap slabs at the local grocer. Soap was a classic commodity with each manufacturer's product virtually indistinguishable from others. It is believed that P&G 's technological innovation was making Ivory out of Palm and Coconut oils, both less expensive than olive oil that was the basis of better soaps of the soaps to be mass produced and felt of finer higher quality soap (Dyer et al., 2004).Unlike other soaps of that, Ivory ingredient was lathered, easily and floated in water without melting. The unique blend of the soap meant that P&G could sell the soap in a premium market, such as supermarkets. However, since it used less expensive inputs, this led to higher margins. Those higher margins provided the mass to pay for advertising to raise the profile of the soap (Dyer et. al., 2004), thereby creating the brand and the beginning of a product differentiation strategy to sell in supermarkets.

3. To what extent can the principles and practices of brand management used for fairy liquid be applied to other goods and services, such as televisions and package holidays?

I think the brand management principle used for P&G brand, fairy liquid soap products sale which is more similar to apply to any television brands management products sale. Otherwise, the brand management principle uses for P&G brand, which is not more similar to apply to any package holidays travel services. Firstly, televisions and liquid soaps which have similar characteristics, such as they are products and it can be touched, seeing it existence and they are needed to launch to adopt consumers' taste, e.g. consumers link to accept to use liquid soaps more than bar soaps popularly as well as consumers like to watch colorful and clear image of televisions more than black and white image of televisions. Hence, any soaps and televisions companies which need to launch high technological televisions or more health ingredients of soaps to satisfy consumes' needs seriously if which wanted to build their brands famously and which wanted to retain old consumers and attract more consumers to buy their products in this skin care and television entertainment markets. Otherwise, if some companies did not continue to launch their television or soap products. I believe these companies brands will be not popular, even consumers will forget their brands existence due to other companies continue to launch their televisions or soaps to build strong brands in those skin care and television entertainment both product markets competitively.

Anyway, any one travel agent's package holidays travelling service is not similar to P&G brand fairy liquid soap products characteristics. Due to package holidays travelling services which can't be touched and can't be seen, the package holiday visitors who can only feel the travel agency whether whose travel journey itinerary arrangement, e.g. travelling destination, travelling date and time, travelling living apartments, hotels, restaurants, leisure activities, air tickets prices, airlines choice etc. whether this package holidays travelling is suitable to him/her only or whose family or whose friends with her/him together. The most importance, package holidays travel services are not similar to soap or television products which need to often launch whose skin care and seeing entertainment products to adopt consumers' needs. Although, the travel agencies sometimes need to reorganize new travel journal itinerary , e.g. seeking England, United States fresh and unique travelling places or cheap hotels who travelers choose popularly. But, travelling industry is seasonal period leisure business, it means that public holidays will have many consumers. Hence, basically, the seasonal periods are limited to travel agencies to build whose brand easily. It means that the client numbers are influenced by the seasonal periods, their numbers will not have much changing, even the travel agent often spend much effort and time to seek any new and unique travel journey itinerary holidays package. Although, travel agencies do not need to spend much money to invest to launch its package holidays travel arrangement service. But, they are existence in one competitive travel market. Every travel agent package holidays travel service price is controlled by the seasonal period whether the period is holiday or is not holiday and what the travelers' feeling to the country, e.g. safety extent, shopping places and prices extent, air ticket prices extent, accommodations and restaurants prices extent.

These factors are controlled by the travelling countries. Agencies are difficult to differ their packages holiday travelling services to win other travelling agent competitors to build strong brand management famously. Due to which cannot control external factors to influence their price competition easily, such as airline companies air tickets prices, the destination (country) which hotels, restaurants, leisure services and transportation prices which are controlled by the travelling destination country's businessmen directly. It implies any travel agencies are difficult to build unique strong brands to attract many travelers who choose to find which to help them to arrange packages holiday travelling services to earn more commissions easily. However, if the travel agency had owned only concentrated on arranging packages holiday travelling services experiences and it had many prior packages holiday travelling consumers who feel that it can arrange the most suitable packages holiday travel arrangement services to let them to satisfy all different packages holiday services. I believe who will only choose this travel agent to help them to arrange any packages holiday travel arrangement services again, even who will introduce its packages holiday travel arrangement services to their friends to know the travel agency's brand by mouth speaking individually.

It seems that a new or an old travel packages holiday travel arrangement services agent who ought need more old customers who can speak to whose friends to know how it can give excellent travel packages holiday travel arrangement to them individually, so television or radio or newspapers media travelling advertisement channels do not need promote long time if whose old consumers feel which can provide excellent packages holiday travel arrangement services to make them to enjoy satisfactorily. Hence, it's old consumers' feeling whether who satisfy or who do not satisfy its packages holiday travel arrangement service which will influence the travel agent to build its brand successfully in this packages holiday travel arrangement market. Otherwise, a new or an old television products brand sale company needs more magazines, radios, televisions advertisement to promote which television products for long time due to every family who have different demand to choose to buy the television products, e.g. size, design, manufacturing history and manufacturing country's price. It implies the family can't influence to whose friends to decide to buy or not buy the television brand easily. Due to every family has different demand to choose which kinds of television company brand. The television brand's any different style of television products of the family to choose is not same to or influence to whose friends television brands, so the television brand's buyers speaking will not influence whose friends whether to choose or not choose to buy the television brand easily. Furthermore it will take a closer look at the motivational world of the travel agency staff and how both groups interact. These questions will be analyzed with regard to its significance and applicability in brand management. The results of a neuropsychological systems of package tourists and travel agents with a psychological test.

When investigating the travel market it must be taken into consideration that it is subject to considerable changes due to , for example new dynamic production processes, price comparing systems, the growth of online providers etc. Every travel agent needs to make each brand unique and distinguishable in its perception . The key issues discussed where: Why do package tourists buy? Which scopes and potentials are there ? When positioning style brands? How can potential customers be better addressed and won as a customer? Central question concerning travel agents where: What is there main motivation (commissions, incentives) ? How can travel agents be addressed more effectively? How can travel agents help to increase the sale? Sensing versus intuition concerns perception itself, thinking versus feeling are decision strategies based on perception and judging versus perceiving relate to the handling of these decision . Because individual travel agent needs explain why their choice of packages holiday arrangement is the best suitable to every consumer considerately when the consumer is the first time to contact the travel agent , so the travel consultants need have professional image to make whose visitors to believe whose packages holiday arrangement is the most right to satisfy them to travel in their journeys. Otherwise, one of television brand seller who does not need to build more professional image, due to who is only the television company brand representative, whose duties are needed to explain what the television features and functions to let whose customers to compare to other brand television products when who enquires any one of television brand seller. However, travel agent must need to seek any packages holiday travel informational to let any consumers to choose to let them to compare whether which packages holiday arrangement service is the most suitable to who from the travel agent immediately. Hence, a package holiday travel agent seems to be a travel economist, who needs to compare which packages holiday arrangement is the most right and the most reasonable price to follow travel data gathering to adopt to every customer needs after whose customer spends whose packages holiday arrangement to feel satisfactorily if who want to help whose travel company to build famous brand of providing excellent packages holiday arrangement successfully in this travel market.

Hence, any packages holiday businesses which travel consultants seem to be individual mouth speaking advertising to every visitor when who enquire whose packages holiday arrangement ideas to achieve aim to let every visitor to feel travel consultant can suggest the useful packages holiday arrangement because who must not have confident to arrange their travel plan by himself or herself. It seems that a new or an old travel packages holiday arrangement service agent which needs more old customers who speak to whose friends to recognize its existence to build its brand for long term. So television or radio or newspapers travelling advertisement do not need to spend long term if whose old customers feel which can provide an excellent packages holiday arrangement service to them to enjoy satisfactorily. Hence, its old consumers' feeling whether who satisfy or who do not satisfy its packages holiday arrangement service from the first time, they shall influence whose friends or relatives who decide to attempt to enquire the travel agent successfully. Otherwise, any one of television brand sale persons who do not need to build more professional image, due to the sale persons are only the television company brand sale representative, whose duties only need to explain what the television features and functions to let the customers to compare to compare to other brand television products to decide whether who ought to buy the brand television or ought not to buy the brand television. However, any travel agents must need to seek any packages holiday information about airline air tickets prices, itinerary journey and hotels, transportation, restaurant meals, leisure activities of the travel destination country to let any consumers to choose the different packages holiday arrangement programs to compare whether which packages holiday arrangement program is the most suitable to their travel needs immediately. So, their satisfactory extent to the packages holiday arrangement from the travel agent's consultant who can influence their friends or/and relatives to feel whether the travel agent can help them to arrange packages holiday satisfactory. Otherwise, a new or an old television product brand company needs more advertising from magazines, radios, televisions to promote which television products for long term, due to every family who have different demand to choose to buy the television products, e.g. television size, design, manufacturing history and manufacturing country and prices etc factors which can influence every family choice. It implies the family can't influence to whose friends or/and relatives to decide to buy or not buy the television brand easily. Due to every family members who have different demand to choose which kinds of television company brand. Furthermore, it will take a closer look at the motivational world of the travel agency staff and how both groups interact. These questions will be analyses with regard to its significance and applicability in brand management. The results of a neuropsychological study, which measured the implicit personality systems of package tourists and travel agents with a psychological test. When investigating the travel market , it must be taken into consideration that it is subject to considerable changes, due to , for example, new dynamic production processes , price comparison systems, the growth of online providers etc. Every travel agent needs to make each brand unique and distinguishable in its perception. The key issues discussed where: Why do package tourists buy? Which scopes and potentials are there? When positioning style brands? How can potential customers be better addressed and won as a customer? Central question concerning travel agents where: what is there main motivation (commissions, incentives)? How can travel agents be more effectively? How can travel agents help to increase the sale? Sensing versus intuition concerns perception itself, thinking versus feeling are decision strategies based on perception and judging versus perceiving relate to the handling of these decision. Because individual travel agent needs to explain why whose choice of packages holiday arrangement is the best suitable to every consumer considerably when the customer is the first time to contact the travel agent , so travel agent is needed more professional travel knowledge to arrange the best packages holiday to serve every visitor to enjoy their holidays satisfactory to build their brand. Otherwise, any television brand company sale representatives who only need to introduce what the style of television product which feature to let the visitor to know to decide to buy or not buy it. So, any television product brands which need more different kinds of advertising to help them to promote to build their brands long term.

In conclusion, P&G fairy liquid soap brand management principle, which is more similar to apply to television product brand management principle, which need to launch their different style products to satisfy clients needs. Such as P&G brand company needs to continue to change its product ingredient to let many customers to feel to use safely , e.g. it launches bar soap products to liquid soap products as well as any television product companies to launch how to change television images and colours to be more clear to attract many customers to choose to buy whose television brands products. Otherwise, packages of holiday arrangement tourism service, tourism consultants need to own professional travel knowledge to help whose visitors to arrange any the most reasonable price and the most safe and the most unique journeys to attract any visitors to choose whose packages of holiday services. In fact, travel agents who do not need to spend much money to invest to carry on launching their travel service to raise time to gather travel information to increase whose ideas to achieve to persuade every visitors to choose packages of holiday arrangement successfully. Hence, it seems P&G fairy liquid soap product brand management principle which can not apply to packages of holidays travel arrangement service clearly and it's expensive price and many similar products competitors factors which can influence consumers to choose to buy its products. So, in behavioral economy analysis, consumers are influenced to choose to buy its products by economic variable influence.

CHAPTER IX

Mobile phone company phone call price charge strategy

Critically evaluate methods that mobile phone companies could use to assess buyer's likely response to new features, such as video on demand and whether its sale number is not influenced by economic environment changing influence?

Behavioral economy analysis, it indicates mobile companies need have internet, video function, GPS location search etc. different high technological functions to attract mobile consumers to choose to buy their mobile products. Thus, if the mobile product can have unique high technological functions to satisfy mobile consumers' undiscovered useful needs. Then it charges higher price and it won't decrease mobile customer number.

Mobile phone is a product to satisfy customers' verbal communication needs during who leave home to need to communicate with anyone urgently . Mobile products are only bought for the verbal communication benefit. In other words, a mobile phone product is of value to someone only as long as it is perceived as satisfying some extra need, instead of verbal communication, such as watching video demand from internet when people are sitting on buses, or trains , or drive cars to watch video entertainment from their mobile phones. So, a mobile phone can be a material product, it can also provide an intangible service, such as verbal communication and watching video or sending email from internet by an 3G or 4G telecommunication fast speed internet service provision channel when who leave their home, who can also enjoy to watch video and call anyone and send email such as staying at home. However, mobile phone is a high level of emotional involvement communication product by the buyer due to there are many different and similar style of mobiles to provide to customers to choose to buy, so I think the mobile phone can provide watching video from internet feature is prefer to buyer to choose more than the mobile phone can not provide watching video from internet , even it's price is more than the non video watching mobile due to young people like to watch video instead of going to cinemas to see movies, it is possible who have no time or who feel movie tickets prices are expensive. Mobile phone is low level of accessible product, due to buyers can use home telephone when who stay at home or who can use any restaurant phone if who is walking on the street , it's location is near to restaurants.

Mobile phones are shopping goods, due to consumers generally put a lot more effort into choosing shopping different style of mobiles to buy. Their evaluation include price, credit facilities, guarantees, after sale service, email or video entertainment from internet service. Different brands of mobile products are distributed through fewer retail outlets and therefore there is likely to be a higher margin for the retailer. Customers are usually willing to travel to an outlet to find a brand style of mobile, rather than expecting it to be available on their doorstep. Large amounts of money may be spent on advertising to develop strong brands, such as 3G and 4G telecommunication provision service to watching video or sending email from mobile internet. In fact, mobile product needs to provide intangible service, such as verbal communication , watching video, sending email. Hence, many mobile users ought prefer to buy the brand of mobile company which can provide these kinds of services because who feel these services are whose basic needs, specially the students like to use mobiles to watch video entertainment or working people like to use mobiles to send email to their offices to keep communication when who need to leave offices to work outdoor. However, watching video on mobiles is one new idea to focus of whether who need this service, it can be unclear who the customer is and it can be difficult to conceptualize the exchange that takes place between the provision video watching service of mobile buyer and the mobile seller of the idea. Hence, mobile phone companies need to do market research to evaluate who are the preferable ages segment group and what factors which will cause who do not choose to buy their mobile brands of watching video mobile products. Mobile phone industry is a product innovation industry.

Nowadays, mobile phones have these features, such as cameras, MP3 players and web-browsing. The life cycle of mobile phones as a broad product category is now at the mature stage, some would say saturated. But when individual product formats are examined, a pattern of continual development, launch, growth and eventual decline is evident.

Mobile phone companies vision is to affect people, process and technology by enhancing workflow, improving access to knowledge, increasing the speed of business transactions and providing better modes of video watching feature. Some mobile phone companies are already using mobile applications to deliver video image to increased client matching feeling satisfaction. The mobile phone video watching speed convenient availability and price is factor to influence individual client to choose the mobile phone company's style video mobile or chooses another mobile phone to buy.

Some mobile companies have complex products that need to be maintained at the client's premises. Photocopies are a good example. The quality of field service and support is an obvious factor is establishing customer satisfaction as well as in building the kind of customer loyalty that leads to repeat business. The mobile companies have leveraged the potential of wireless support tools are gaining ground in the marketplace. I think mobile phone is not seen simply as a way to communication function. It ought to spend on carrying on researching and development on internet to deliver email message communication and it also needs to provide on line video watching entertainment service new features when every individual client is using every mobile phone company's different style of mobile phone if the mobile phone companies still wanted their mobile phones can sell to clients in this global mobile phone competitive market. Today, mobile phone is popular communication tool to every family. Due to beyond the rapid consumer adoption and usage of mobile phone is the opportunity mobile phone companies offer for brands to connect more meaningful and personally with consumers. Considering it every individual direct line and immediate connection with audience when who is leaving at home to communicate easily.
Most brands spend less than one percent of their marketing budget on mobile. The argument is that the one percent spend level is too low, given the fact that most consumers devote about 10% of their media attention to their mobile device.

During the 20 century, marketers employed mass-market media channels-Television , radio. The result was that brands created marketing massages that out of necessity had to appeal to a broad spectrum of consumers. It implied that watching video had been every person's habitual behavior everyday. If mobile phone can provide video watching feature to satisfy every client's seeing enjoyment. I think the individual client will choose to buy the mobile phone, which can provide video watching feature more than the mobile phone which can't provide video watching feature, even the individual client feels the owing video watching feature of mobile phone which price is higher than the lacking video watching feature of mobile phone. Because there are many people like to bring their mobile phones to watch video when who are leaving at home.

I shall suggest to do one marketing research of open to close survey method to new features, such as video on demand by whose mobile phone. The survey questions can be conducted , such as whether the client will determine to buy mobile phone with video feature more or who will determine to buy mobile phone without video feature more when the client need to buy one mobile phone to use; whether the client shall compare all different style of mobile phone with video feature which price, size, design and functions before the client determine to buy one mobile phone with video feature; whether what the factor is the most importance to influence the client choose to buy the mobile phone style with video feature, such as function, design, price, color, size, quality more durable use production of year; whether what factors influence the client to buy other companies' mobile phone with video feature, such as cheap price, unique indifferent design, attractive color, smaller size or larger size, production of year, whose friends or family introduction, advertisement promotion, convenient availability more durable use and quality; what kind of mobile phone with video feature, the client won't accept to use, such as screen picture is small size, image lacks clear color, too big size or too small size mobile phone feeling difficult to control . Hence, after any mobile phone had gathered their questionnaire researchers idea, then which can analyze whose data to carry on evaluating to estimate whether video features on mobiles demand on the difficult countries' consumer numbers. For example, every country sample of 100 people whose ages were between 10 ages to 20 ages segmentation group, a sample of 100 people whose ages were between 21 ages to 30 ages segmentation group, a sample of 100 people whose ages were between 31 ages to 40 ages segmentation group, a sample of 100 people whose ages were between 41 ages to 50 ages segmentation group, a sample of 100 people whose ages are between 51 ages to 60 ages segmentation group etc. If the 10 ages to 20 ages segmentation group had 50 people out of 100 people who prefer to buy video feature on mobile. It can estimate the country's this age group whose people numbers whether how many population shall prefer to buy video feature on mobile in the country. Hence, market survey research method can identify to measure every country's different age segmentation of client numbers who prefer to buy video feature on mobile clearly.

2. In terms of a new product development process, how could the development and launch of Tele point services have been improved in order to avoid the problems that were experienced ? What lessons can be learnt for the development of 3G (or 4G services)?

Adrian, P.(2012) showed that Hutchison is not new to taking big risks in the mobile phone market. It was behind the Rabbit network of semi-mobile Tele point phones launches in the UK in the 1980 years. These allowed callers to use a compact handset to make outgoing calls only, when they were within 150 meters of a base station, these being located in public places such as railway stations, shops, petrol stations, etc. As in the case of many new markets that suddenly emerge, operators saw advantages of having an early market share lead. Customers who perceived that one network was more readily available than any other would all other things being equal be more likely to subscribe to that network. Operators saw that a bandwagon effect could be set up to gain entry to the market at a later stage could become a much more expensive market challenger exercise. Such was the speed of development that the Tele point concept was not test marketed. To many, the development was too much product led, with insufficient understanding of buyer behavior and competitive pressures. Each of the four companies forced through their own technologies, with litter inclination or time available to discuss industry standard handsets which could eventually have caused the market to grow at a faster rate and allowed the operations to cut their costs.

The Rabbit network came with the announcement by the UK government of its proposal to issue licenses for a new generation of personal communication networks, these would have the additional benefits of allowing both incoming and outgoing calls, and would not be tied to a limited base station range. By 2006 year, the next generation of mobile phone services were under development, with Japanese trials of 4G faster than 3G telecommunication service. 3G phones were also challenged by the development of alternative wireless access services, notably Wi Fi. Many companies, such as T-Mobile had began offering mobile Wi Fi services, which allow users to log on a local access points and gain access to their email and browse internet. Subscribers to VOIP telephone services could also effectively make the free phone calls from a Wi Fi access point. For many business travelers, using their laptop, Wi Fi access seemed a more attractive and less expensive option than using a 3G phone connection to check for email. It was likely to become even more attractive, with development of longer range Wi Max services that extended beyond the very limited 50 meter or so range of Wi Fi. The pressure of 3G telecommunication services was intensified when the UK government announced in 2006 year that it would license the development of a national Wi Fi network.

It seems that 3G and 4G telecommunication service can be capable of speeds faster then Tele point Rabbit telecommunication in any places conveniently. It causes Tele point Rabbit telecommunication becomes obsolete to mobile to use. From 2003 year, mobile phones industry seemed that the new digital technology would be a third generation of mobile phones (3G). By 2008 year, work was well with the development of the next generation of fourth generation mobile phone (4G) telecommunication service. In terms of a new product development process, the mobile companies need to consider the development and launch of Tele point services have been improved in order to avoid the problems that were experienced. The mobile product mix comprise range of mobiles that a company offers to the mobile market. Tele point service launching whether it is the individual mobile is with its core or secondary and augmented elements to influence consumers to buy mobiles essentially. I think the external factors, such as UK mobile phone companies whether which can sell the augmented mobiles or the secondary level mobiles or the core mobiles which can influence Tele point service demand, such as if the mobile company can only provide the core benefit, but it's style of mobiles which lacks the better characteristics in the secondary level to attract consumers, which shall reduce mobile sale numbers, features are such as mobile design, color, shape, reliability, texture, packaging , even if it lacks the augment level competitive effort, such as after sales service, brand name, credit facilities, speed of delivery and warranty. Thus, even Tele point service launching is useful to mobile buyers, if the consumers feel the mobile products prices are expensive and they are not valuable to attract them to buy mobiles. Tele point service is not the main factor to influence the buyers to choose to buy mobiles in UK mobile market when this mobile phones are launched to sell in the beginning.

The another factor is that Tele Point was new telecommunication service in 1980 in UK mobile telecommunication service market. There is likely to be a lot of promotional effort by Tele Point service to promote to mobile markets to secure sales. It is likely that the network of semi-mobile Tele point phones telecommunication service needs have high costs in the development of its service, costs that in the early stages may not be covered by revenue. Potential customers for a new network of semi mobile Tele point phones telecommunication service may be few and far between and therefore sales in early stages may be quite slow. This stage is known as the introduction stage. However ,Tele point phones telecommunication network service had this limitation. It only allowed callers to use a compact handset to make outgoing calls only, when they were within 150 meters of a base station, these being located in public places ,such as railway stations, shops, petrol stations, etc. If it's service proved popular, more people will show an interest and start purchasing it. However, due to many other mobile network telecommunication competitors who copied Tele point network telecommunication service technology to launch more fast speed and no location limitation and they can make incoming and outgoing calls both functions, even 3G or 4G telecommunication internet service is provided to mobiles. Hence, Tele point telecommunication network can not adopt to consumers demands.

Although, Tele point is the first network telecommunication service to adopt to handset in UK, but it handset network innovation can't identified as a source to mobile users' long term competitive advantages in this mobile phone network competitive market. Due to other telecommunication network companies can improve or revise to Tele point network service to launch more advance telecommunication service to provide mobile users to use more conveniently. Tele communication network fails due to mobile consumers useful demands are raising, its existing telecommunication service may no longer satisfy their needs, telecommunication technological change may make Tele point existing network service obsolete, telecommunication network service competitors can provide more convenient telecommunication network to mobile phone users and the social and economic environment may have changed, creating new mobile users needs in the global mobile telecommunication network service market.

The development of information and communication technology (ICTS) with mobile can bring the benefits of within each of virtually all the world's people social communication, such as Japanese mobile phone focusing on 3G technology. Factors promoting it can be summarized as follows: Deregulations by government/ mobile number portability and collocation; competition among carriers, such as introduction of new change plans; technological development, such as connection speed and contents and applications. Dynamic models are based out only on the assumption, such that carriers don't instantaneously adjust to satisfy their long term demand but also on network externalities. The Japanese mobile market has shown a remarkable growth with more than 106.2 million 3G subscribers and 4.4 million 2G as of Dec. 2009. The 3G diffusion rate accounts for 90% followed by that of Korea and this implies the market is almost saturated. Another remarkable transformation is found in its usage: Data communication exceeded voice services. Japanese 3G(4G) mobile phone originally had much variety of functionality other than voice service, being based on supply and demand side of the services: The founder is 3G technology which enabled new services, such as m-commerce and e-entertainment while the latter is due to existence of consumers who are willing to utilize various services. Although, the global mobile phone market has reached to the saturation stage and the growth rate of subscribers has been slowing down. Moreover, the recent development is found in the fact that data communications exceeds traditional voice communication and being the first phenomenon in the world. However, the effects of price elasticity and product differentiation of various carriers and network externalities increase the demand for mobile phone. Hence the technological innovation , such as electronic payment, high speed access and consumers' attitude toward entertainment and m-commerce are important factors for the success of 4G telecommunication service need is more than 3G telecommunication service need to every mobile phone users popularly. Moreover, new business models including a flat rate charging plan can play an increasing important role. Operators under these circumstances are confronted with competition due to the short product life cycle and the pressure to differentiate. Although, 2 G networks are adequate for voice, there was a growing interest in shifting from 2G to 3G even 4G based on a number of important drivers. First, the higher speed of 3G technologies translates into added convenience, capacity and functionality for the user. Second, there is much excitement over adding internet protocol (IP) capability and hence internet access to the mobile phone. In developing 3G standards, international

telecommunication union worked with regional organizations and industry associates to reduce a large number of initial proposals to a smaller number of global standards.

In accordance with the development of mobile technology services already provided on 2G mobile phone , such as upgraded and consumers needed not feel difficult when using those services including email services (electronic mail, phone mail and video mail), web access and download music, movie and game. Moreover, carriers provide their customers more innovative functions, such as video mail, video-clips, video phone , broadcasting type video program, walk navigation, ringing tone songs, high speed internet connection, digital television broadcasting etc. via 3G mobile phone. In short, 3G services add multimedia facilities to 2 G phone by allowing video, audio and graphic application. Since 2G mobile had technological limitation of networks and handsets data transmitted via 2G was mainly text when due to development of networks and handsets, pictures and flash moving pictures are available and some handsets enables to view HPS for personal computer. Google and Yahoo started mobile search engines. Thus, 3G mobile becomes platform to use mobile contents, such as games and mapping services etc. Data communication , such as viewing web showed remarkable increase in 3G mobile phone, but monthly changes also increase and this became serious problem. In case of the internet in fixed

communications, the flat rate changes are already introduced.

In addition, mobile carriers don't adjust to satisfy clients' long term demands and than dynamic model approaches are available . Especially, network externality or network effect has to be considered in telecommunication. Mobile telephone is the most widely used form by communication in the world today. Mobile communication boost the earnings of many users change the local economy and even significantly, raise the GDP of many countries. The mobile phone has a number of benefits but there is a huge gap in 3G mobile phone why there is the case only two countries . Japan and Korean have more 3G than 2G subscribers. Similarly, why do leading nations like the USA, UK and Germany have 3G penetration rates of less than 30%?

The conclusion, we obtained technological innovation were achieved first, than based on this various service innovation were followed. It should stress that the former includes innovations in handsets as well as those relates to networks and IP technologies. The diffusion on new services depends on how they meet clients preference and needs, but behind services innovations those always technological innovations. On the other hand, some other social backgrounds, such as consumer's attitudes, economies and businesses systems are required. For example, the Japanese and later other service providers solved the first start up problem for mobile internet (mobile internet uses 3G with entertainment content that was supported by a micro-payment system) . In conclusion, Tele Point telecommunication service failure was due to it felt it was the telecommunication service provider to Unite Kingdom people to use mobile, it believed UK people, even any countries' people ought only chose to use its telecommunication service monopoly. So, in this mobiles market, it did not continue to develop and launch its telecommunication technological service. However, due to its telecommunication service had geographic location distance limitation and out calling only limitation to every mobile UK and overseas users in different countries. Hence, many mobile users who would feel inconveniently. However, then other telecommunication service providers copies it's telecommunication technology to launch and research to develop 2G, even, 3G and 4G telecommunication technology, its competitors can provide no geographic location distance limitation and in calling and out calling both to every mobile user who can use conveniently. Finally, Tele Point telecommunication service was not accept to choose to use to its old mobile customers popularly, even the new mobile customers would choose to use any telecommunication service providers, due to which telecommunication service could give more advantages to compare it's telecommunication service.

If Tele Point telecommunication could spend time and technology to continue to launch to improve its telecommunication communication time speed, raised incoming call function and reduced no geographical location distance limitation difficulties (weaknesses). I believe that Tele Point telecommunication ought

attempt to continue to launch to improve its weaknesses of such as above weaknesses to adapt mobile consumers' demand easily, then it ought continue to keep its competitive position in this global telecommunication market till to nowadays.

3. Consider how the launch of 3G services in a less developed country with a less sophisticated telecommunications infrastructure may differ from a launch in a western developed county?

The growth has 3G telecommunication service in less developed country risk for the companies involved, especially where new technological displace the technology which went before them, calling for ever increasing capital investment, and no chance of a return from customers until long after the initial investment has been made in new capacity. Mobile phone companies need to predict the less developed countries, such as Africa country which has how many people who need mobile phone usage whether Africa has high businessmen who can support place, promotion, people and service to assist mobile phone companies to launch 3G or 4G telecommunication service. I think mobile phone companies need to let Africa country people to know mobile phone 3G telecommunication service technology is as the key to a whole new world of mobile telephone in which the mobile phone would be positioned not just as a device for voice communication, but a vital business, leisure, and information tool. So, mobile phones can assist Africa people to communicate in any places conveniently.

A less developed country is a planned economy, the government makes all decision for society. Producers only make what they are instructed to make. The main benefits are that most workers are employed and most people enjoy a similar basic lifestyle. The problems cause to launch 3G mobile telecommunication service include that a planned economy gives little capacity for development, so growth and investment is limited, the infrastructure is usually under-developed as government spends on other areas, such as defense, wages are state controlled, so people have less motivation to perform at higher levels, mobile charges are fixed by government, consumers often can't afford luxury products, such as computers or mobile pones which are taken for granted in developed countries. Otherwise, a western developed country is in market economies (also known as free enterprise), the government's role is limited to providing legislation to protect businesses and consumers and making sure or organization restricts competition. It also provides essential services (like policy defense) and ensures the developed country's money supply is stable . Thus, businesses are motivated by profits to make products that clients will buy. Customers' demand for products and services affects the levels of supply and the pricing, if clients don't less be more efficient or produce on alternative product. For example, During 2003 year, the Hong Kong based Hutchison Whampoa became the first company to launch a 3G service in the UK, with its 3G telecommunication network. The launch was accompanied about the wireless internet and video capabilities. The world was going to be transformed by streaming of video and football matches live to customers' mobile phones and a whole new world of mobile advertising media would open up. However, launching 3G or 4G mobile telecommunication service to developed country , such as United Kingdom or less developed countries, such as Africa , I think the mobile phone companies need to consider what kinds of needs are the country people who prefer to get needs mostly. UK is a developed country, the people will need to get video entertainment, internet extra service from their mobile. Otherwise, Africa is a less developed country, the people live very far. It seems that location technology was value added data services. Even the emergency services stood to benefit from 3G's ability to precisely pinpoint a caller's location.

By 2004 year, 60 per cent of calls to the UK emergency services were made mobile, but in instances callers did not know exactly where they were and ambulances and fire brigades only had very approximate locations. A less developed country is developing economy . It often face great difficulties in improving its economy. For example, in a planned economy, assets like land or property are owned by government. Individuals and businesses are not used to make decisions and operating to make a profit. Developing economy likes a less developed Africa country may also be market economy. But share features, such as the population lives on very low incomes, poor infrastructure , such as transport (roads or railways) or local government, poor communication systems, low levels of basic health and education and a low gross national product (GNP). Over 75% of the country's workforce is in agriculture which can be affected by the climate. Telephone landlines are scarce, expensive and difficult to install . It has less bank branches which are based in cities and tourist areas. Many Africa people are self employed business people, such as small farmers. The impact of mobile telecommunication technology on developing countries. The connectivity provided by mobile phone technology supports economic development. Its impact on a developing country likes Africa country has been extremely positive. Many families live in remote areas of the countryside . Installing landlines over those distances is expensive and difficult families are often separated as the main earners are forced to live in order to earn enough to keep their families. Many are self-employed small farmers or trades people such as plumbers and builders. For small business, better access to mobile technology means that who can advertise to a wider audience and don't have to rely for work on word of mouth. They can be sure that clients can contact them with ease. Due to far remote distance between houses and mobile phone companies, to launch in less developed county, any a mobile company must need a mobile network is quick and easy and secure to install and less expensive than landlines. For example, in a less developed country as Africa country, any mobile phone companies need to provide 3 G telecommunication service to any customers when who go to an accredited shop and in return for cash which has credit registered on their mobile to pay rather difficult than a pay as developed country mobile clients top up their mobile card. So developed countries mobile clients must pay their charge more convenient to compare to developing country mobile clients. Hence, mobile phone companies need to locate mobile card payment stores in developing country, such as Africa country's petrol stations, supermarkets and retail bases stores places. Hence, any mobile phone companies ought need to spend more capital expenditure to launch rapid commoditization of 3G or 4G telecommunication equipment and rising separation of network and service provisioning are pushing the operators to adopt multiple strategies with network infrastructure sharing in the core and radio access networks to improve network costs to a less developed country, such as Africa country more than a developed country, such as Hong Kong country. However, Africa is a potential mobile phone market. Due to limited land line availability, the cell phone is becoming Africa's computer of choice. Never before has a technological innovation been adopted as quickly as the introduction of cell phones in developing countries. Africa county mobile market will be larger to compare to fixed telephone lines, broadband, computer in home telecommunication markets.

By international telecommunication union (2011) source indicated that global mobile usage, 2011 yr. of mobile subscriptions per 100 inhabitants statistic, Africa region had 53, Asia & pacific had 74, America had 103 and Europe had 120 inhabitant numbers. It implies Africa, less developed country had the least inhabitants to compare to any developed countries, so its mobile market will be large (Sullivan, 2007). In conclusion, extensive cell phone networks already are in place throughout the developing countries. These networks constitute and infrastructure providing clear solutions to many problems with building mobile transaction systems. These networks are not exist, but the majority of those in these nations, such as Africa country now uses cell phones for conventional voice communication and text messages to availability of inexpensive handsets and reasonable industry pricing structures. The features of mobile phones transaction systems in developing countries, include interface, network type, date, storage, power source for recharging cell phone, telecommunications provider, financial institution transactions of cash in/out receipt service. So, due to its new technological development can raise its competitive effort, it will bring its advantage to raise its mobile sale price which won't reduce consumer number by behavioral economic method analysis.

CHAPTER X

England NHS public hospital patient price structure of marketing strategy

What do you understand by the concept of a pricing model? Critically discuss their relevance to a public sector service ,such as the NHS? Does its medical charge service price raising will influence patients' choice?

Behavioral economy analysis, UK NHS public hospital needs to consider car park location and parking charge because there are many patient visitors drive their cars to visit their patients. If it can not provide reasonable parking fees and extend parking time, then it will influence their patients choose to go to this hospitals or their patient visiting time. So, hospital's parking service is one important issue. Moreover, it needs have free phone calls service to patient visitors, it does not charge phone call fee to patient visitors when they need to pay phone call to use public phone facilities. Public phone facilities ought to be used by public (non-patient visitors) only. Because it also cause patient visitors feel it is unreasonable to charge them when they feel need to phone call anyone in hospital.

A price model reflects the fact that companies can generate revenue through a variety of combination of the basic price and prices charged for optional additional items. Some price models may be sustainable by giving away a product at very low price initially, but then charge higher prices for essential items that are needed to make the product function. Sometimes, the dominant pricing model in a market is challenged by a new entrant, with the result that consumers' expectations are changed. The price model can occur in perfectly competitive market or non perfectly competitive market. A perfectly competitive market characteristics include there are many producers supplying the market, each with similar cost structures and each producing an identical product. No single supplier on its own influence the market price because it is not monopoly, water and electricity is managed by government to control the public utility company which can not charge high fee to every householder user at the reasonable price ; both buyers and sellers are free to enter or leave the market and there are no barriers to entry or exit and there is a ready of information for buyers and sellers, for example about competing alternatives, e.g. oil products and stock markets where shares are bought and sold are exist in perfectly competitive market. In perfectly competitive markets, firms are price taker and their ability to set prices is limited by the level of demand and supply within the market they serve. If the total demand go up, all other things being equal, the going rate of prices in the market for their product will rise. Likewise, if there is a drop in total supply for whatever reason (e.g. because of bad weather, there will be further pressure for prices in the market to rise. The final price paid in the market will reflect the balance between supply side and demand side factors.

The model of perfect competition presented the forces of competition may be ideal for consumers because the tendency of market forces to minimize prices and/or maximize firms' outputs. But in such markets, suppliers are forced to be price takers rather than price makers. in a perfectly competitive market, firms are unable to use marketing strategies to affect the price at which they sell. At a higher price, buyers will immediately substitute identical products from other suppliers. Lower prices would be unsustainable in an industry where all firms had similar cost structures. Otherwise, an non perfectly competitive market, firms are able to use marketing strategies to affect the price at which they sell. Such as UK medical service market , private hospitals and public hospitals and clinics which can raise their service fee to their patients to follow their patients demand due to their doctors and nurses service performance, medicines quality and price and patient beds supplies factors to influence their service charges to their patients in UK. Hence, NHS needs to provide different and excellent medical service to its patients to make them to feel it's service is better to other private hospitals and clinics if it wanted to apply price model to its car parking or hospital phone system service charge to its patients because it is a public sector medical service organization. It ought not charge extra service fee to its patients in its hospitals. If it charged extra service fee, such as car parking and hospital phone system service which are same or higher or lower than other private hospitals or clinic , which need to ensure which medicine quality, doctors and nurses performance which are better than private hospitals and clinics and its patient beds need have enough supply to any patients when who feel need to sleep in its hospital. Because NHS image is a non profit medical organization to any UK poor patients, who choose NHS medical service are due to its medical service charge is cheaper than private hospitals and clinics and who feel it can provide free car parking and free hospital phone system service.

A market is defined here need not be a physical location where exchange takes place (as happens in retail and wholesale grocery markets). A market in the economist's sense refers to all individuals and firms who wish either to buy or sell a specific product. A market is defined in terms of products or service and geographic description, so the UK soft drinks market refers to all individuals in the UK who seek to buy soft drinks and the suppliers to that market. The UK medical service market structure can describe as the number of consumers, such as patients and medical providers , such as private hospitals and public hospital , such as NHS (National health service) and clinics; the barriers that exist to prevent new private hospitals or clinics or public assistance hospitals from entering the UK medical service market (or prevent UK patients do not prefer to choose NHS medical service); the extent to which the supply medical services is concentrated in the UK small number patients normally and the degree of collusion that occurs between patients and/or private or public hospitals or clinics medical service providers in the UK medical market. Governments often seek to regulate the prices of key products and service, such as electricity and telephones and public hospitals medical services, so it is important to understand how firms can reconcile the sometimes conflicting approaches of market forces and regulation, such as NHS public sector medical service in United Kingdom. Of course, if NHS public sector medical service planned to charge some non major service fees, such as car parking and hospital phone calling service to its patients and hospital visitors and staffs which are same to private hospitals, it needs to consider pricing model should never be seen as an isolated element of hospital's marketing decision making. It needed to consider its service performance of its doctors and nurses, its social responsibility of public medical service image whether it is better or worse than private hospitals that it had created and NHS 's distribution strategy whether it's patient beds supply numbers are enough to patients and whether it's medicine quality and supplies and prices which are reasonable to compare to private hospitals or clinics in this medical service market in United Kingdom.

Private business organization with a broad range if products or services are often price different with their portfolio in quite different ways. They may have developed a price model, which describes the way that it uses pricing of its portfolio to maximize its overall revenue. Hence, one product or service may be charged at a very low price, on the assumption that it can raise higher price if many clients choose to buy its product or consume its service. In some sectors, a number of different pricing models co-exist. For example, in the emerging multi-channel television broadcasting market, some channels are provided free of charge to users, but make revenue from selling advertising space, when others charge to users, either on a monthly/annual basis or a pay to view basis. The idea of a pricing model is familiar to private sector organizations, but do they have a role to play in the public sector? In the UK, pricing models are increasingly being discussed and developed for services which have previously been considered a vital service and available freely to all.

Adrian, P.(2012) showed that the National Health Service (NHS) has a long and proud tradition of providing health service to all, according to an individual's need, paid for out of general taxation, according to individuals' means. Pricing has historically had very little role to play in the NHS. However, from the mid-1990 year, individual NHS trusts began exploiting charges for ancillary services as a means of boosting their revenue. One of the first targets for charging was users of hospitals' car parks. Trusts argued that providing car parks was not central to the mission of NHS trusts, and conveniently, government was encouraging more people to use public transport and leave their cars at home. Critics argued that patients were essentially captive and public transport was not a realistic alternative for most people. However, it showed that at one hospital in London, a patient who attended A&E on the advice of her GP, was charged UK$3.75 for the first two hours' use of the hospital car park and UK$7.5 thereafter. She was ten minutes over the two hour period and therefore had to pay higher charge. She also questioned the fact that charges were reduced to UK$1 per hour after 6:00 PM, when many hospital departments were closed. For private sector service, a lower evening price, when there is not much demand from customers, and plenty of spare capacity, it quite common.

But is it right that a hospital should only charges lower prices at the not busy time when much of the hospital itself is closed? If lower prices are designed to stimulate additional demand, it this a realistic prospect when many hospital departments are only available between 9:00 AM to 5:00 PM? Another source of revenue exploited by many hospital trusts from the use of bedside telephones by patients. Many trusts entered agreements with private telephone service providers which allowed incoming and outgoing patient calls only through the officially appointed system, which used a premium rate number. A proportion of the revenue was retained by the hospital.

Conveniently, hospital trusts pointed to evidence that mobile phones could harm sensitive medical equipment , and therefore used this to eliminate competitive pressure from patients' mobile phones, forcing them to use the hospital's own telephone system. The ethic of hospital telephone pricing was challenged by the House of Commons Health Select Committee, which accused some trusts of using excessively outgoing call, adding to patients' costs, and boosting hospital revenue. It cited a hospital in Essex where people wishing to telephone patients were being charges 49p per minute at peak time and 39p off peak. By comparison , a typical household rate for a long distance phone call was around 7p in the peak and 2p in the off peak. The select committee also expressed doubts about whether a ban on mobile phones in hospitals was actually a result of possible interference with medical equipment and recommend visitors should be able to use mobile phone within certain areas of hospitals. So, it seems that UK private hospitals patients phone calling service fee is below than householder phone calling service fee and it is not every patient must need to use phone when who stays in hospital as well as the visitors should able to use mobile phones and who should not use hospital phones within certain areas of hospital, who will not interference with medial equipment.

Otherwise, by banning mobile phones, had private hospitals been more concerned about creating a monopoly environment for pricing their telephone service, than any possible risk to their equipment? However, I think National health service (NHS) which is one public government assistant hospital, it can not be same to private hospital to charge unreasonable car parking fee or hospital phone service fee to its patients, due to these ancillary services is not hospital main income source and it is one non profit hospital, it needs to provide the fair and non expensive medial charges to its poor patient segment because who are not rich, so who will prefer to choose NHS medical service to compare to choose private hospital services in United Kingdom.

National health service (NHS) is a privatization, fragmentation and market competition of health care provision supposedly to cut costs and improve the efficiency of the health service in England. The NHS was set up in 1948 year to be a free and accessible care, publicly owned and funded sector service in England. NHS needs to consider to redefine its relationship with health service, limiting the quality and quantity of care it can expect to receive, how it access that care, who is delivering if and even how it is paid for.

The result will be poorer, fragmented services with larger differences in quality and access. Services/treatments will cost more and the public will increasingly have to pay for aspects of its care that used to be free at the time of treatment. Traditionally privatization has been through the sale of public assets and services to private owners through the mass sale of shares, e.g. the sale of telecoms, railways, energy or water services. These companies than own the services and are able to make profits from them like any other are able private businesses. In the NHS until now, this model of privatization is taking place through a combination of the reduction of the role of government in regulating health provision, the transfer of services to the private sector through commissioning from any qualified providers, such as independent sector treatment care centers, outsourcing of parts of services to the private sector, the creation of market mechanisms for the distribution of funding within the NHS (e.g. commissioning, payment by results mechanisms, the purchaser-provider split and so called patient choice policies). The use of private finance initiatives that use private money to build new buildings and infrastructure and then the state has to pay, the creation of foundation trusts that are run much more like private businesses and have the ability to raise funding through private patients that pay for services, allowing services to become not for profit organizations, such as social enterprises, cooperatives or mutual and thus leave public ownership, limiting access to certain services previously provided by the NHS. Provided healthcare tends to cost more. It requires a large bureaucracy to operate, with huge transaction costs that come with contracts, billing and litigation. In general, as the proportion of private spending on health care rises, so does the overall cost. The creation of healthcare market can also impact upon the continuity of care people receive. There is always the threat that the private sectors or other providers who take on a service that doesn't secure the expected financial returns may cut losses and withdraw from the provision of that service. NHS is under increasing financial pressure. For example, surgery like hip and knee replacements are more expensive areas of care, the results cause the loss of training opportunities for junior doctors expenditure spending and other health professionals as ever large shares of routine surgery and medical procedures are diverted away from the NHS.

Centers for research and medical innovations are also threatened. This can lead to service being out. NHS hospitals will therefore fail financially and be pushed into greater debt. This could lead to hospital mergers, closure or the private sector coming in to run the service on profit making contracts. NHS will bring poor health care service if it will not increase its service charge price to patients. The poor service will be caused, such as permanent damage may have been inflicted on patients with serious conditions due to the lack of follow up care after treatments. In a second worrying example dangerous delays affected the patients of a privatized out of hours. A competitive market system leads to greater rationing and gradually drives patients to take on more responsibility for funding their own care. It seems this already in the privatization of long term care and dentistry. Patients may soon have to top up the cost of their hospital care in the same way that many already do for community health services. The concern is that the NHS will provide a less comprehensive range of treatments. For the private sector, the aim is to make a profit from every contracts, which is not the same as providing the best service . For example, Southern Cross, where the need to make profit lead to the rapid closure of care homes, leaving old people with no home. Hospital people with learning disabilities and challenging behavior were subject to physical and psychological abuse. Privatization will lead to fragmentation of the health services. This is a process on a commercial footing and redesigning the system along market lives. With different organizations delivering different service in different locations, it is also likely to lead a new health service with some area receiving much better care than others, hardest, leading to greater health inequalities. Fragmentation of services leads to worse clinical outcomes as staff have less opportunity to work in a fully integrated dynamic multi disciplinary team. Patients with complex needs can be particularly considerable.

The impact of privatization on current NHS staff, who are transferred from NHS employment to non NHS organizations would be changed terms and conditions at the time of transfer. These terms and conditions could be changes at some time in the future, staff would no longer be covered by the national negotiating arrangement in the NHS, meaning they would not be entitled to any future pay uplifts or agreed charges to the change terms and conditions of service . If staff moved from this employer to another outsourced community service, who would lose their entitlement to access the NHS pension scheme and would be treated as new staff rather then former NHS staff, the new service provider could argue that the service who will be providing is so different that they will not be requiring staff to transfer. Those staff will than be made redundant. In conclusion, NHS is one public medical service non profit organization. It's pricing model ought be public service price model, such as no price discrimination and non competitor based pricing aim. It may be difficult or undesirable to implement a straightforward price-value relationship with individual of public services for a number of reasons: Such as NHS public sector medical service pricing can be actively used as a means of social policy, subsidized prices are often used to favor particular patient segment groups, such as car parking fee charges to visitors or hospital staffs only as well as hospital phone system service charges to visitors only or prescription medical service charges favor the very ill and unemployed patients and low income patients and students patients.

2. What factors should influence the level of charges at an NHS car park?

Principles for fair hospital car parking, such as NHS is important because its car park service represents the hospital reputation. Charging for car parking is often necessary, but needs to be fair, providing a travel plan for users of all types of transport, controlling parking fairly, with concession for those whose health conditions or work commitments mean they have to park frequently or at anti social hours, showing car park and transport costs and how charges are invested, thinking about the environment and how transport can reduce the NHS 's impact , being open and involve patients and the public. It is important to get car parking and transport policy and it is communication, right to ensure fair access, good patient and staff experience and to protect hospital organization , such as NHS reputation.

Clinical and social changes as car ownership to patients, staff and visitors to hospital sites has increased. For services with rural or urban , as public transport infrastructure is less convenient and reliable . When for specialist treatment, some patients need to travel greater distance and modern hospitals have often been located on the edge of population centers.

Car parking is also a factor in patient's experience of using healthcare. When much progress has been achieves to improve the patient environment inside the hospital, including cleanliness and new buildings, patients frequently report dissatisfaction with transport and parking arrangement. Visitors concerns both cost of car parking and also the availability of space for people with an essential need, illustrating the competing demands that managers need to balance. Patient experience is an important objective for hospitals; poor experiences can undermine confidence in clinical quality and stress can be worsened by poor transport and parking policies. Car parking can have a major impact on the local and national reputation of the NHS hospital . As patient choice increases, reputation and loyalty will be key drivers for provider's commercial sustainability.

It seems car parking is one important factor to influence patients who choose hospital more than location/ transport/ easy to get to/ reputation of consultants factors. Ensuring that patients can access hospital when they need to is an important part of healthcare delivery. Many patients who need to travel to hospital by car, either because of mobility or illness, a lock of alternatives or through choice. However, providing a car park is not the only component of a travel plan. Access to healthcare should be considered in terms of service planning, decisions on location of services, building design, access routes and the other transport modes. One of the factor of the current changes to the way that NHS hospital services are delivered is that healthcare should be localized where possible. In many cases, people who used to have to travel to hospital are being treated in community health centers. The NHS hospital can also ensure services are accessible. Most notably, ease of access has recently been improved by reducing waiting times and by enabling patients to choose and book their appointment at a time and location that is convenient to them. Another of factor is whether NHS hospital had or had not ran a bus service from a nearby park and ride car park that runs every 15 minutes. The service has proved popular and is now run by the UK country council. The hospital is been to extend the shuttle service to the other three park and ride car parks which serve the city.

The other factor influences NHS hospital charge includes the control parking fairly with concessions for those whose health conditions or work commitments mean they have to park frequently or at anti-social ours. In order to ensure that those patients who really need to access hospital by car are able to NHS often need to ensure that car parking space is available on site. Space is usually constrained, NHS hospital is in city or town center with high land costs and planning constraints. Charging some patients, visitors and staff to park can manage demand for space when ensuring that those who really need to park are able to access services. Where charging is required to manage demand, the overriding principle should be to ensure that where possible those patients who have the greatest need to park are prioritized. Where managing demand is a reason for charging for car parking, there may be scope for varying rates for different times of the day and the week, for example, increasing charges for non essential users in peak hours but applying a minimal charge at night when there is less reason to ration space. As well as prioritizing car access for those with greatest needs restrictions on car parking may also be required to deter non hospital traffic, particularly where NHS hospital is located in controlled parking zones, near shopping centers or other facilities that might need to illegitimate required use of NHS hospital grounds. In these cases , NHS hospital may be required to be charge the same as local car parks to avoid abuse by non visitors. However, alternative arrangement could also be explored, including day permits for people with appointment. NHS car parking fair policies should need to be fair application. This is often a cause of concern for patients and visitors. Concessionary schemes and season tickets should be well publicized and available, since a patient may not known in advance low frequently who will need to attend a clinic in the next month. Penalty charges, or towing away should only be applied extreme circumstances with a presumption of good faith that no patient or visitor chooses to stay in hospital longer than necessary and may how on arrival how long who will have to wait for treatment.

Running a car park can be expensive. These are maintenance, security, insurance and running costs and the NHS hospital has to pay for the space the car park uses. Costs are particularly high where land prices are high or there is increased risk of crime. At the same time, patients and the public rightly don't expect healthcare to suffer to pay for parking. The transport costs of non car owners are not subsidized by the NHS budgets to provide subsidized free car parks . To make car parking fee would be to penalize those using public transport. Therefore, fair charging is often the most sensible answer to adopt these two demands. Climate charge and pollution and congestion factor also have health impacts. Reducing car dependency is also a public health objective in order to reduce traffic accidents and increase physical activity. These NHS organizations have

a number of environmental and health reasons to seek to encourage people to use other modes of transport. Parking charge together with the expansion of alternative bus an cycling options to encourage a modal shift from cars to alternative transport. Patients , visitors and staff need to be made aware of these aims. NHS hospital can achieve a travel plan to develop to its car parking with the aim of during a period of busy time reducing single occupancy car journeys by 15% over three years, ensuring tat patients and visitors do not have to

search for a space for more than ten minutes at peak times, encouraging the number of direct bus routes to the site to increase reducing staff parking spaces per employee by 10% as staff numbers grow. Car parking charges were introduced as part of the plan with certain categories of staff on exempted from charges (night and weekend staff, disabled staff, volunteers, car sharers and tenants of residential accommodation. From an environmental perspective, NHS travel plan supposed to reduce numbers of cars arriving at the site and the numbers of bus car raise. It aims to improve bus services to cause air pollution at the busy car parking period and cycle parking spaces and improved cycle facilities have encouraged staff to commute by bike. Additionally, a park and ride scheme aims to reduce car traffic of the NHS hospital in the busy time.

Moreover, it is absolutely wrong to charge cancer patients regardless of income, for unavoidable parking costs. From a staff point of view, NHS hospital car parking is an indirect tax on healthcare. However, most unions also support the aim of reducing car usage, as long as policies are fair. Because NHS hospital needs to develop transport policies for patients requiring regular cancer treatment. This approach has potentially negative publicity into a positive image to public. These ought be free parking for the duration of a cancer patient treatment or as often as is needed.

3. If you are studying at a university or college, critically reflect on the pricing strategy that it has adopted for ancillary services.

The development of a costing and pricing strategy will provide an university staff with greater access to price information, thereby providing a more accessible platform from which to base negotiations with commercial organizations. As prices will be informed by cost, the university will be seeking to apply pricing strategies that maximize university as opposed to maximizing income. In fact, any universities is education industry which is different to common businesses which provide service or product to raise price when client numbers are increasing easily. Due to if an university which planed to increase school fee to charge students, which needed have unique courses to attract students to choose to study and its lecturers educational experiences and education methods needed to make student to raise learning interest and feel the courses are useful to choose to study the university subjects, so who shall compare the university subjects to other universities subjects, then to evaluate their school fees and lectures educational experiences and qualifications to decide whether who ought to choose the university or another university to study.

So, I believe that the university can not raise its school fee easily if it has no more confident its subjects and lecturers which can make students to study to feel more satisfactory till to graduate. Otherwise, it will reduce student admission numbers if it still increase school fees, due to it has not researched what the subject contents are students who like to learn. Hence, any universities can't increase its school fee easily.

However, university ancillary services have primary paths to reduce internal cost to raise competitive advantages, such as services differentiation, low internal cost or internal span structural advantage. I shall recommend these price strategy to

adopt to reflect some university ancillary service (non major) service. The pursuit of a service differentiation strategy to an university advantages. The university needs truly understanding its unique core service (value) and then focusing resources on its ancillary services. An implicit part of having a focused

price strategy is not only defining what the university is going to invest in, but is also clearly articulating what the university is no going to do. For example, if the university investigated its students did not like to eat some foods taste, which ought to change some foods taste which could satisfy its students eating needs in its university canteens.

Even the university could charge cheaper student parking fee to compare outside public car parks when they park their cars in university parks from the morning to afternoon studying busy time. It could only permit students to park their cars in its students private car parks.

Hence, university staffs and visitors could not permit to drive whose cars to park in university private student car parks, so university staffs could park whose cars in university staffs car parks as well as visitors could park whose cars in university visitors car parks. However, who also needed to pay cheaper parking fee to compare outside public car parks to buy car park tickets to park their cars in university staffs and visitors both car parks in any limited time. Even, the university book shop could sell lower second hand books and new books prices to compare other private book shops to attract students to choose to buy studying books from university bookshops. However, if the university tried to pursue too many areas of service differentiation, which was likely to invest too broadly and thus reduced the return on investment for previous capital possibly because it needed time to research whether which aspects of it needed to change to adopted students tastes to satisfy their needs, then it needed time to change its services and it also needed time to evaluate whether it's changed services which can satisfy its students demand to make decision to raise its service prices. Hence, it ought concentrate on changing one aspect of ancillary service to ensure it's changing was right to adopt students' taste to attempt to raise service price. Then, it could attempt to evaluate whether what ancillary services which needed to change to achieve price raising possibility. University recognizes that focusing on the core is hard to do, given the history and culture of university. But the worst case scenario for an university is to be relatively expensive and completely undifferentiated.

Whether will who pay high school fee per year to go to an university that is completely undistinguished on any ancillary service?

An university looks to areas where which can make cuts and achieves efficiencies, an university should start farthest from the core of teaching and research ancillary services. Cutting from the outside in and building from the inside out. Growth in programs and research, increasing faculty and student demands and increasingly compliance requirements have all contributed to the growth of administrative costs. The reasons are often very legitimate. But as new programs are added, old programs often are closed down in some university ancillary services, e.g. unimportant administration internal service . The resulting breadth of campus activities creates too much complex it for staffs to manage with any efficiencies of scale in university. Units don't trust one another or the center to provide ancillary services. Data center management is a good example of fragmentation on campus. At the university, the central information technology group managed fewer than half of the servers on campus in its data center. For the servers located in the colleges, fewer than half were managed by college information technology groups, the rest were considered hidden at the department or faculty level. Despite the internet data and security risk of having too many unmanaged serves on campus in the university's central information technology department. In similar cases, outsourcing data centers would be a good solution. Third party data centers could provide more solutions, higher levels of securing, greater flexibility in capacity and lower cost than internal solution. Redundancy, an university is an many other campuses, it was managed at the department level, there were no product standards and each department negotiated its own vendor contracts. A sample of purchase order showed that the same item was being bought for as much as e.g. 36% more in some departments than in others. By centralizing end, standardizing more if its procurement to expect to save more expenditure.

An university hierarchy, most campuses have too many middle managers. Before it reorganized , an university has average spans of control (the number of employment). Campuses engage to save cost. An university campuses engage in too many activities that require to broad a skill set to effectively deliver in house. Take information technology application management for example, not only does it need to support classrooms and research needs across a diverse set of disciplines (history, music, law, engineering, biomedical science etc. different subjects), it also has to cover functions (finance, human resource, research, administration, student registrar, libraries and student services etc. functions). It weren't enough, information technology also has to serve industries beyond the core academics, including bookstores, retail food, debt cards, total museums, publishing houses. A single IT group would have a hard time managing all it that well, given the expertise required, leading to either poor service delivery, sub scale and costly delivery.

Outsourcing more of non core activities would reduce campus complexity and cost. Third party provides have greater scale capability and skill because the outsourced service is their core business, enabling them to deliver the same or better service at a lower cost. In order to reduce administrative costs without diminishing service and perhaps even enhancing it's campuses will need to subscale operations by creating shared service or outsourcing improve processes by eliminating low value work and automating much. Better manage university assets to whether it is real estate, physical assets or intellectual property, a number of activities where partnership with third party providers would allow for financial relief and improved performance. Hence, an university can also invest its intellectual property to build its build to raise its market value for long term to raise its sale price for long term.

In conclusion, an university can attempt to use these two kinds of price strategies to adopt to reflect to its ancillary services. Such as the first is competitors price strategy, the university can set its students and visitors and staffs car parking fee by examining what its competitors such as, it's close public car parks are charging their car parking fee services whether they are similar in terms of the university car parking service characteristics fee to satisfy its parking car users' needs as well as the university can set its canteens meals price by examining what its competitors, such as it's close private outside restaurants meals price whether they are similar or different taste and low meal price to attract students or staffs or visitors to choose to eat their meals . The another is demand based pricing strategy, the students are prepared to pay represents the upper limit book numbers to the university's every year studying books. Such as the university book shops can decide every years different subject second hand or new teaching books price to follow the students demand. For example, if the subject second hand or new teaching books supply numbers is less than the student demand numbers, the university can raise the subject books sale price. Otherwise, if the subject second hand or new teaching books supply numbers is more than the student demand numbers, the university needs to reduce the subject books sale price, even it needs to reduce their prices to be lower than outside other private book shops marketing price to sell in the year. Hence, it seems that any universities can adapt price strategy to reflect to their services or products prices. So, if it can have reasonable car park charge service and free phone call service to patients' families or friends visitors, then its high medical price charge will not influence patients' economic choice behaviors to its hospital.

CHAPTER XI

Tesco supermarket value chain rapid transport strategy

Identify the elements of the value chain involved in the supply of fresh fruit and vegetables to Tesco stores by non-economic influence factors.

Behavioral economy analysis, Tesco supermarket needs to arrange itself fruit warehouses to close to farmers because fresh fruit transportation time is one important factor to influence fruit customers to choose to buy its fruit. If its warehouse is very close to farmers. Then the farmers can delivery many fruits to its warehouse in short journey and short time, then it can deliver its different kind of fruits to different fruit stores to keep its fruit fresh to let its fruit customers to eat at the same day or next day.

Hence, transportation location factor is very important to influence its fruit customer number.

The place(P) of the traditional marketing mix decides about channel intermediaries or middlemen to use an outdated, yet user friendly, term and the management of physical distribution. Placing products involves managing the process supporting the flow of goods or services from producers to consumers.

The process has sometimes been described as developing the best routes to market for a firm's products. Products must be made available in the right quantity, in the right location, and at the times when customers wish to purchase them. Marketing channels can perform an important role in the later stages of a value chain, in particular outbound logistic (e.g. order processing, storage and transportation); marketing and sales (e.g. market research, personal selling, sales promotion) and after sales service. However, it depends on which kinds of business to need outbound logistic, such as Tesco supermarket only needs ordering fresh fruit and vegetables from local farmers, then these foods need to be stored in refrigerate in warehouse and transport these foods to different supermarkets by vans. So, Tesco value chain only needs outbound logistic activity, but it does not need marketing and sales and after sale service to sell its fresh fruit and vegetables to its clients from its supermarkets (stores). In fact, Tesco stores is such UK farmer's intermediaries which can add value by breaking bulk. This might involve purchasing in large quantities of fruits and vegetables from UK local farmers and then selling smaller, more manageable, to keep volumes of fresh food stock in warehouses, then its vans will deliver these fresh fruits and vegetables to different stores daily.

Discrepancies of fruit foods quantity are reduced by Tesco (intermediary) who provides every store clients with individual preferable fresh foods items that suit their needs daily. Tesco stores can offer superior knowledge of a target market compared with farmers, for example by ensuring which kinds of vegetables or fruits foods numbers are stocked in every store to match the economic and lifestyle needs of Tesco store shoppers who live in the area. Probably the most important gaps between Tesco store shoppers and UK local farmers in channel management are indicated at those of location and time. A location gap occurs owing to the geographic separation of farmers and the store shoppers of their fresh fruit and vegetables foods. UK farmers generally want to grow their fruits and vegetable food in one central location (farming), but farmers' food buyers typically want to buy their growing foods locally. A time gap arises when the UK local farmers' fresh foods buyers want to buy whose fresh growing foods at a time when a UK local farmer may considerate it inconvenient to make the available. UK local farmers may like to grow fresh fruits and vegetable foods at night from 8:00 PM to 12:00PM, then who will collect these fresh foods from 5:00 AM to 7:00 in the morning, but their buyers may want to buy in the evenings or at weekends afternoon. Tesco stores (intermediary) need to facilitate vans to transport these fresh fruits and vegetables foods from farmers' farming to its one central warehouse to deliver to different stores to sell the budget numbers of different kinds of foods to every local store consumers more exactly (Adrian, P. 2012).

Tesco stores is one of the world's largest retailers, it has social responsibility to protect fresh fruit and vegetable to sell to clients. It had attempted to predict customer behavior about hope much fresh fruit and vegetable and what kinds of fresh fruit and vegetable whose consumers will buy from data statistic in warehouse. It aims to reduce excess fruit and vegetable stocks in warehouse to cause perishable. In the winter might have seen choice reduced to basic items such as potatoes, cabbage, apples, supplemented by canned fruit and vegetables. Look in a Tesco supermarket today, and clients may find difficult to tell the season of the year or the distance from the countryside, simple based on the fruit and vegetables with are on display. In UK supermarket sector is intensely competitive, and has seen continuous innovation in the way it seeks to satisfy customers' needs. As consumers have become wealthier, the supermarkets realized that buyers would no longer be content with the staple foods such as cabbage and potatoes in the depths of winter-significant numbers of them now wanted excitement on a plate, and all year round. Furthermore, if they were planning a menu, they wanted to be sure that when they went to their local supermarket.

By and large, supermarkets have been key drivers of the value for the groceries that they sell. They have been close to their customers and identified their changing needs. They have built confidence with their customers, who can trust freshness and provenance of food they sell and the reliability of supply. It is therefore the supermarkets who have gone seeking sources of supply, rather than growers aggressively seeking to sell the produce that they have available. Before, the development of very large supermarket chains, retailers were more

fragmented. They did not have the power or resources to innovate with new product lines which they could then commission a grower to produce. Today, supermarket such as Tesco invest heavily in their food technology laboratories, and can then go to suppliers and place large orders with exacting standards with regard to price, quality, and delivery. Above all else, supermarkets have put themselves at the center of a slick distribution system which connects an international networks of growers through transport networks of trucks, ships and planes to put fresh produce in their network of stores, every day, all year around. The efficiency of the logistics, and the bargaining power of the supermarkets has often led to the price being charged at a British supermarket being lower than the price changed in supermarkets thousands of miles away where fruit and vegetables were grown. Tomatoes grown in Bulgaria and sold in Britain can be cheaper in Britain in local Bulgarian shops. The bizarre situation has occurred where the supermarkets import apples from France to be sold in Kent, the traditional home of British apple growing, plums from Poland to be sold in the grown product in Lincolnshire. Supermarkets argue that sourcing from overseas is not just an issue of cost saving more importantly, the supermarkets seek a continuity of supplies from large growers who can guarantee to deliver a specified quantity at a specified quantity at a specified time and place.

The supermarkets capable of achieving this. British supermarkets are among the most efficient in the world, and their desire to ensure that customers can always get what they want may explain the mass transport of food. Local farmers' market may could environmentally friendly, but they rarely guarantee a continuity of supplies. As part of their drive for efficiency, supermarkets have a tendency to move food , such potatoes could being transported several hundred miles between distribution centers before they end up on a supermarket shelf just a few miles from where potatoes were grown. The environmental campaigning group Sustain has estimated that the average children travels 2,000 between the farm where it was grown and the supermarket shelf and furthermore the distance products travel from farm to end customer increased by an estimated 25 per cent between 1980 year and 2007 year (Priesnitz 2007).

Global warming had become an important issue with many clients and there was growing concern that supermarkets' practice of transporting fresh produce long distances around the world was irresponsibly adding to greenhouse gas emissions. Hence, distance travelled was one of value chain factor Terso supermarket needs to consider their fruit and vegetables food to keep fresh in refrigerate to transport to retailers to sell in UK. The most contentious food miles are clocked up by fresh fruit and vegetables flow in by plane from overseas. Although, air freighted produce accounted for less than 1 per cent of total UK food miles, it was the fastest growing way of moving foods around. One response By Tesco was to introduce a greatest proportion of local produce. To achieve this, it placed buyers and marketing teams in the regions in order to get a clear picture of local markets and to develop relationships with suppliers. By 2007 year, Tesco claimed to have 7,000 regional lines from throughout the UK, which were promoted as local produce, supporting local growers and reducing greenhouse gas emissions. Throughout its history, Tesco has demonstrated its ability to listen to what customers want, and this has been true in respect of its distribution system. The weaknesses of commodity systems are particularly for major customers, such as Mc Donalds, commodity systems do not lead to reliability in supply, quality, quantity or price nor high rates of innovation on which they can differentiate their offer from their competitors. The opportunity and challenge of fresh food product differentiation, so Tesco stores need to innovation to give rise to a number of strategic options to keep vegetables and fruits to be fresh in the short time to sell full numbers. If a firm, such as Tesco is the lowest cost producer than commodity market strategy can be an attractive strategic option. As Tesco stores fresh food sale that it's larger competitors shall find difficult to copy. Otherwise, Smaller size stores can sometimes be a competitive advantage.

Tesco stores (fresh food retailer) need to co-operate with suppliers and fresh food growers to align the whole chain to the changing needs of consumers. The food chain strategy aims to deliver superior value to specific groups of customers.

Tesco stores work closely with its fresh food suppliers to develop specific products for each range. Both the supplier and growers understand the Tesco marketing strategy and their role in the innovation process. Tesco is actively seeking new

chain ideas and is prepared to pay for such efforts. From a primary producer and supplier perspective the range of brands enables Tesco to work with suppliers to market the total crop .

2. Critically discuss the factors influencing Tesco's sourcing of fresh fruit and vegetables.

At a time when the media enjoyed the big supermarkets, such as Tesco, being seen to source fresh fruit and vegetables food locally and being good to the environment helped to restore. One observe from Friends of the Earth noted the local produce sold at a branch of Tesco in Excess had in fact travelled served hundred miles as it was moved from the grower to a regional processing center, then to a regional distribution center, and finally back to the supermarket where it was sold. There has also been debate about where sourcing fruit and vegetables locally actually reduces greenhouse gas emissions. There is an argument that Tesco supermarket would be better for environment to grow them in countries where fresh fruit and vegetables need less heating and fertilizers than if they were grown in British. The greenhouse gas emissions resulting from growing them locally in Britain may be more than the emissions associated with transporting them from warmer countries.

The first factor influences Tesco's sourcing of fresh fruit and vegetables is the main stages of horticultural value chain are as follows: The first stage is inputs elements needed for production, such as seed, fertilizers, agrochemicals fungicides and pesticides, farm equipment and irrigation equipment, production for export includes the production of fruit and vegetables and all processes related to the growth and harvesting of the produce, such as planting, weeding, spraying and picking, packaging and cold storage means grading, washing, trimming, chopping, mixing, packing and label are all processes that may occur in this packing stage of the value chain . Once the produce is ready for transport, it is chilled produce is ready for transport, it is chilled and placed in cold storage units ready for export, processes fruit and vegetables include dried, frozen, preserved, juices and pulps. May of these processed add value to the new foods by increasing the shelf life of the fruit and vegetables and the final stage is distribution and marketing means the produce is distributed to different channels, including supermarkets and small scale retailers and wholesalers and food services.

The second factor indicates several basic conditions must be for a country to enter the fresh fruit and vegetables value chain. These include climate allowing for year found supply, adequate road and transport infrastructure, such as ports and airports, essential for moving fragile foods to market efficiently, establishment of sanitary and to prevent disease spreading. The value chain needs to upgrading into the packing segment and processing segment. Upgrading into parking is dependent on understanding the market needs investment in capital goods and availability of supporting activities within the country, such as United Kingdom. Maintaining open lines of communication regarding demand preferences in fresh foods, quality, packing and fostering buyer involvement is critical in all stages of the value chain. For example, organize trips to key markets and they observe interactions at the point of fresh food purchase, a wide variety of equipment to attain very high standards of hygiene within the pack house operations as well as on site laboratories for fresh fruit and vegetables research and staff health tests, horticultural sector has been greatly inhibited in its upgrading along the value chain by the lack of fresh food quality packing materials. Much of produce destined for the Europe is shipped to neigh countries where it is repackaged, resulting in a significant of value.

However, upgrading into the processing segment of the value chain has been difficult to achieve for low income developing countries since the processing of fruit and vegetables is cost prohibitive at low levels of crop production. Therefore, countries must gain a level of expertise during the production stage to increase output to a level that will enable the country to upgrade to the fruit and vegetable processing stage. For example, given the importance of ability to read pesticide labels and understand barcodes amongst others, standards have led to additional training initiatives to improve adult literacy. Skills training must be carried our in all job categories of value chain to maximize growth and upgrading opportunities. Investments in training are required for all job categories, from farm workers to managers, such as farming activities and the workforce within the agriculture sector, packing and storage positions and the processing stage in which workers are classified under the industrial workforce. Hence, fresh fruit and vegetables packing and processing services, such as washing, chopping, mixing as well as bagging, branding and applying bar codes are often carried out at the fresh foods source rather than at the end market destination. These processes which were previously based in the developed country, such as UK have created considerable new employment opportunities in developing countries.

The third factor influences Tesco's sourcing of fresh fruit and vegetables, which indicates today, the fruit and vegetables sector operators as a buyer driven value chain and large supermarket chains are the leading actors both in key export markets with controlling market and shares across the Europe and United States as well as increasing in emerging markets. These buyers including Sainsbry's Marks and Spencer and Walmart seek enhanced cost competitiveness, consistency and product differentiation, such as convenient, ready to eat fresh foods from their global supply chains. It causes considerable value chain method how fruit and vegetables are produced, harvested, transported, processed and stored to achieve how fresh fruit and vegetables characteristics of quality, size, pesticide use and the social and environment conditions of cultivation and post-harvest handling will influence buyer behavior decision. This ensures that the perishable food reaches its destination in good condition cold storage units are used throughout the chain to keep the produce fresh and both air and sea freighting supported by the cold chain are key elements to ensure timely delivery. Export is divided between production for fresh and vegetables and fruit consumption and production for processed fruit and vegetables that are not accepted for sale as fresh produce are as well as inputs for the processing stage, but in order cases, such as orange juice or preserved peaches a specific variety and grade quality is required and production occurs separately. The next segment is packaging and cold storage unacceptable low grade produce will be redirected to processing plants or the domestic market.

Washing, trimming, chopping, mixing, packaging and labelling are other processes that may occur in this stage of the value chain. Once the produce is ready for transport it is chilled and placed in cold storage units ready for export. Packaging usually requires economies of scale due to the high costs of cold storage and other capital investment necessary at this stage .Processed fruit and vegetables include dried, frozen and preserved produce as well as juices. Processing plants purchase fruit and vegetables inputs from the producers. These firms may export their products under their own brands as well as under the buyer's brand. The last stage of the value chain before consumption is distribution and marketing. In this final stage, the produce is distributed to different channels including supermarkets, small scale retailers, wholesales and food services. Air freighting for horticultural foods and more cold storage segment of value chain in order to increase their access to key markets and avoid competition form new countries entering cold storage technologies allow suppliers to adapt to geographic constraints, such as size and distance to market.

3. Assess the level of power that Tesco exercises in the supply chain for fruit and vegetables.

The themes identified were the perceptions of freshness, having good relationships with growers and suppliers , good quality of fresh fruits and vegetables, competitive and pleasant environment for shoppers. Globalization of the fresh fruits and vegetables, retailer system has impacted on the distribution and marketing of fresh modern supply chain outlets now dominate the fresh food retail market. The increasing population and rising personal income is resulting in significant shifts in fresh food demand. Supermarkets are perceived to be the place where more wealthy consumers choose to shop. Consumers purchase almost everything there including fresh fruit and vegetable, meat, children and fish and other household supplier like dry food, bread, detergents, stationary and toys in supermarkets, such as Tesco stores, not choose to buy from fruit and vegetable markets or food retailers. The traditional markets and grocery stores comprise wet markets, fresh markets, farmer's markets are popular among consumers when purchasing fresh food are the oldest food distribution channel. The traditional market has been defined as a market with little central control or organization that lacks refrigeration and doesn't process fresh foods into brands foods for sale where each vendor specialized in one fresh food line (meat, fish, fruit or vegetable) or in a sub line (fruit and vegetable).

A fresh market and/or wet market generally occupies one or two floors of a building that is located adjacent to a housing area where there is a high population density and high traffic flow. The ground floor is normally rented to retailers who sell fresh food or ready to eat items. The upper live level is occupied by retailers who sell ready to items or non food products/ These stores are family owned retailers that sell a limited variety of foods ,such as fish, fruit and vegetable, bread and milk, stationary , toys and household supplies. However, consumers may limit their purchase from these stores due to the high prices and limited product lines. Another distribution power level to Tesco supply its fruits and vegetable to deliver to its clients in the short time. Tesco faces its customers occurred with respect to its home delivery service. With the launch of its Tesco online service, it effectively extended the supply chain right through to customers' own homes, adding value to its product offer by avoiding the need for customers to even visit a supermarket.

Was it good for the environment to have fleets of delivery vans around town and countryside? Simple evaluations were difficult to make supermarket buyers again, Tesco was keen to be seen as a good citizen in this final leg of its chain, for example by launching electric delivery vehicles which Tesco decided to reduce global warmth when its vans do not need to deliver fresh foods and vegetables to different supermarkets from its warehouse in the long distance. Tesco stores is a retailer to UK local farmers that buys their fresh fruits and vegetable for the purpose of reselling them to end consumers in its different local stores daily. The Tesco stores are large, self service stores carrying a very wide range of different kinds fresh fruits and vegetable foods to sell in its different local value chains from UK local farmers supply daily. For example, Tesco stores are often the first with new store shoppers initiatives such as loyalty cards and low fresh food prices are based on large scale efficiency to sell in Tesco smaller independent stores to match. Hence, the factors can influence Tesco stores channel selection power include that the expectations of store shoppers who expect to buy local stores or who prepared to travel to a retailer that the farmers' fresh fruit and vegetables keep to save more than one day or more days to buy. This might mean taking into consideration factors such as a geographical preference to buy locally, or a tendency to feel more comfortable visiting a particular type of store; Tesco fresh foods attributes can be important, fresh produce that is highly perishable requires fairly short channels. Bypassing channels, a UK local farmer may seek to cut out intermediaries , such as Tesco stores by dealing directly with the public and Tesco may feel difficult to open up any new local stores for the farmers.

Over saturation, a farmer may be accused of using too many fresh fruits and vegetable food distributors within a given geographical area, making it difficult for any individual distributor to achieve a satisfactory level of fresh foods sale , such as Terco stores. Too many links, in the supply fresh foods chain, Tesco stores may be required to buy excessive fresh fruits and vegetable foods from any farmers daily, who may be perceived as a fresh food farming competitor, rather than a cooperative channel member. New channels, these can have a similar effect to bypassing an intermediary, for example, many UK local farmers have opened up internet sales channels, thereby taking fresh food sales away from established intermediaries, such as Terso stores. Cost cutting, in order to increase volume fresh fruit and vegetables food sales, a UK local farmer may seek to distribute through higher volume, low cost intermediaries, which may make it more difficult for a smaller, full service intermediary , such as Terso stores sell the farmers' any fresh foods and UK local farmers can give incentives and rewards to other intermediaries to help them to sell in UK any stores to raise Terso's competition in UK foods supply market. So, consumers will be influenced by non economic factors

CHAPTER XII

A national chain of restaurant mobile advertising strategy

Critically assess the likely opportunities and problems
of mobile advertising for a national chain of restaurants by non economic influence factors.

Behavioral economy analysis, the national chain of restaurant needs have mobile advertising method to help it to advertise : such as different country food customers can find its any one of restaurant locations from their mobile easily when they do not know that the country has this restaurant existed when they arrive the country. Mobile is one popular communication tool to any travelers, so they will prefer to find any information from mobile more than television or newspapers when the customers are travelers, due to they feel it is convenient to let them to find any information when they feel unknown and need to know, then they will turn on their mobile to find these information in anywhere, e.g. streets, shopping centers etc. outdoor location.

A global crisis in the advertising industry largely linked to the impact of the internet is transforming the business models of media industries, the content they create and distribute, and the audiences who consume that contents. Such as consumers can use whose mobiles to find where the chain of restaurants are located and meal and drink prices and meal and drink types and

restaurant opening and closing time etc. information for the national chain of restaurants from internet advertising when who leave at home conveniently. The opportunity to mobile advertising for a national chain of restaurants, it can expand its national chain of restaurants brand to different countries visitors and instead of its self country visitors to let them to know whether where its chain of restaurants can provide what kinds of food or drink to serve to them to eat before they prepare to go to any one of the national chain of restaurants immediately. Hence, when visitors travel to its country, it will be more easy to let them to remember where any one of the national chain restaurants are located in the nation when who enter the national chain restaurants website or enter yahoo website to type" national chain restaurants" word, then who can seek any one of the national chain restaurants from whose mobiles easily.

In fact, if a national chain of restaurants chose to use television advertising, due to the national chain of restaurants which locate at itself country locally. It is only concentrate on promoting it's country's domestic eating consumers target to know it's existence when its country's domestic eating consumers are

watching television at homes. Usually, working people need to work and students need to go to school to study from morning 9:00AM to 6:00 PM at night. Hence, the national chain of restaurants can only advertise at night time. Furthermore, the overseas travelers watch the nation's television when who are staying in the nation's hotels at night time. Hence, the national chain of restaurants can only use television to advertise to attract the largest numbers of local and foreign visitors to watch its advertisement at night time possibly. Due to mobile

advertising exists, television advertising is more difficult to attract the durability of audience segmentation models to build upon demographic and it also lacks new opportunities to implement psychographic and behavioral models for understanding audiences. Such as, many young people who accept to use mobile to communicate, so it implies every family usually has a mobile to use and mobile advertising will also have much opportunity to help any businesses to promote whose services or products to let many families to know whose advertising. In fact, mobile users can use mobile to watch movies or news, so who ought to link internet to watch during who are sitting on any transportations or walking, so when the nation's people who feel hungry, who can use their mobiles to link to internet to seek any restaurants to decide which restaurants are the most close to their locations to choose. As a national chain of restaurants, it is more effective to advertise it's different chain of restaurants' locations to let any it's different locations of national mobile users to seek its any one of chain restaurant conveniently when who are walking on the street if who feel hungry who can turn on mobile to find map to seek the national chain of restaurants immediately. In fact, the global households who the average viewing audience composition, the number of global households using the television set and the various times it is in use, the average audience (home viewing during an average minute of a

program) and the total audiences (homes viewing the program in excess of minutes) which are decreasing. Otherwise, the mobile phone users view mobile advertising numbers are increasing.

Broadcast channels as well as whatever is available on their various devices, including computer, mobile devices, gaming devices, time-shifting devices or internet enables devices. As such, it is providing more and more difficult to track the audience and known who they are and the best way to target them. Additionally, the rise of social media adds another dimension to audience research. Social media provides new ways of segmenting audiences that currently can not be done on television. Hence, a national chain of restaurants can get better ways of segmenting its viewers from mobile advertising over a variety of platforms. So mobile networks can be better package to the nation chain of restaurants advertising programming and the national chain of restaurants advertiser can make a more effective to attract foreign visitors or domestic visitors to make them to enter its website to view its advertising from their mobiles. For example, car owners, such as those who own a BMW or Audi famous brands cars, which have very homogeneous demographic characteristics, but each car brand has a specific type of owner with a unique personality.

A similar look as television audiences could allow advertising of those car brands (who attend the upfront presentations every year) to match their car buyers to specific television shows. Demographics have not caught up with these changes and presume that viewers are still watching in only the conventional way. For instance, there is not yet a way for the networks to get credit for online viewers and it is as more viewers more to online platforms, like a network in landing site.

Instead, a psychographic profile of the audience, one based on psychological segmentations , such as behaviors, attitudes, interests, values, opinions feelings which is a valid and valuable way of narrowing down the audience into segments for an advertiser. So, psychographic data can measure, such as peoples' activities how who spend whose time, their interests what they place importance on in their immediate surroundings, their opinions how their view of themselves and the world around them and some basic characteristics, such as their stage life cycle and income and education and residence location. The result of the research then provides a detailed profile that allows the marketer to be better visualize the target audience. Psychographics start with people and reveal how the people feel client specific subjects, which can lead to be more effective marketing.

When psychographic segmentations are used, the consumers are divided into group based on lifestyle and personality, often with all of this in mind, the research questions proposed here as follows: What psychographic measurements are being used right now to determine the television audience or mobile advertising ?

How are the various branches of the industry , such as restaurant industry adaptive to the new television landscape ,such as mobile advertising and what actions are they taking?

What are some challenges and resistances to psychographic measures between television advertising and mobile advertising?

What incentives or lack are there to change between television and mobile advertising?

What would be helpful for advertisers , such as a national chain of restaurants or networks , such as internet advertising to know or do in order to more towards wider use of psychographics?

A reason behind dividing audiences based on engagement can be illustrated with the Pod mobile phone, such as the national chain of restaurants organization has shown that audiences' attachment to specific the restaurants' brand corresponds directly to how much the audience will pay attention to the national restaurant brand's advertisements from mobile and how likely who are the actually to choose to go to the national chain of restaurants to eat lunch or dinner or breakfast more than its other restaurants.

The problem is how the national chain of restaurants to advertise it's foods taste, price and service and locations uniquely to win its other restaurant competitors from mobile specific program, providing the network to be best convenient that it's restaurant brand to advertise on that specific program. Another key problem is trend segments viewers based on domestic and foreign consumers' behavior are more specifically their viewing behavior mixed with their restaurants choosing eating behavior in whose countries, watching the national chain of restaurants television advertising from whose mobile , what who are watching to know its existence and on how to let them to know what their actual eating taste to the national chain of restaurants can provide. Hence, I suggest the national chain of restaurants can attempt to use surveys to carry on researching the different countries foreign visitors and domestic visitors whether what whose tastes are preferable to choose what kinds of foods and drinks who hope to eat in this national chain of restaurants from mobile advertising website. The problem is who may choose not to fill its surveys from its mobile website advertising. If they use computer to fill its surveys at home, it will have more opportunities to gather data from survey due to who can sit down to fill surveys in quiet environment. Hence, I suggest it ought use computer internet to do market research about what whose tastes are preferable to eat in its restaurants. When it estimates whether the foreign visitors and domestic visitors numbers, how many people choose to eat different kinds of foods and drinks to its identifications. After it can achieve mobile advertising to promote its restaurant brand more confidently in this mobile marketing advertising strategy.

2. Discuss methods that could be used to assess the effectiveness of mobile advertising.

Measuring social media marketing , such as mobile advertisement, effectiveness and identifying the target market. The use of social media sites as part of company's marketing strategy has increased significantly. Regardless its popularity, there is still very limited information to answer some of the key issues concerning the effectiveness of social media marketing , ways to measure its return on investment and its target market. The social media was started around ten years ago. It began with linked in, which was launched in 2003 year, followed by both My space and face book in 2004 year. You tube in 2005 year and Twitter in 2006 in year. The popularity of social media sites has also spread to companies as part of their strategies. Executives are concerned with their budget justification for a social media plan in computer or media online advertising, when there is lack of supporting materials to confirm the effectiveness of the social media platform , i.e. conversion rate, the relation between buyer-seller relationship and increase in sales and the rate of return investment that they can earn from this plan. Others also believe that their companies' performance are not affected by their lack of involvement in the social media sites.

Clearly, the fact that social media marketing is still relatively new among business practitioners has raised some major concerns , such as its effectiveness, the main purpose of including social media mobile advertising in a company's media platforms, it's relation to the existing platforms and the target audience of this strategy. The methods to assess effectiveness of mobile advertisement include that marketing research method is about target client segment of respondents' social media activities and buying decisions relationship survey. Survey questions can include whether how long time and how often who turn on mobile phone to use internet, such as a week is less than 20 hours average or a week is between 20 hours and 30 hours average or a week is between 30 hours and 50 hours or a week is more than 50 hours, why who like to use mobile to use internet and not use home computer to use internet, e.g. reducing to use home electricity, interesting, convenience, no computer at home, what who will seek to see from mobile advertisement, e.g. advertisement , news ,email , message, movie, whether who decide to buy products or consume services choice is from which kinds of channel advertisement influence mostly, such as television, radios, newspapers, magazines, computer internet, mobile internet. It aims to gather target client segment of respondents' social media activities and buying decision relationship to estimate whether there are how many numbers of target client will decide to buy the company's product or use it's service from mobile advertisement channel.

Hence, the survey result can indicate these five respondent groups, such as highly affected, somewhat affected, neutral somewhat not affected and not affected at all groups. Mobile phone advertisement is needed to any organizations to use internet to operate. Hence, to access the effectiveness of mobile advertising which may begin by using measures that were very easy to capture and understand, such as the number of website hits or percentage of users who clicked on an advertisement. These measures were very useful fro examining trends in traffic patterns, but the impact of this traffic on sale and other marketing objective was sales and other marketing objectives were little understand. Standardized approaches for capturing and summarizing websites behavior were eventually developed to help make sense of web traffic and patterns. Metrics, such as number of unique visitors and the amount of time who spent viewing web pages provided marketers with new insights into who was assessing the site and how who were using it. But even with a high level of detail about how customers were interacting with the company via the web, marketing manager often lacked the information how user

behavior data translates into increased profits and business value. For example, organizations using websites primarily for after sales support have used exactly the same kinds of metrics as these selling directly from the site. This is not due to a lack of available data. Many organizations using web analytics gather and store vast amounts of information and develop large, complex databases to house it. But much of that information is never used. Because organizations who first began to market over the internet often lacked a clearly formulated strategy. In addition, the rapidly changing internet environment made it difficult for marketers to formulate clear expectation about the impact of activities. Both the amount of returns and amount of investments are difficult to measure. I suggest organizations may estimate the value of a visit to a particular web page by estimating the number of visitors who will become customers and then multiplying that number by the average value of all clients to estimate returns. What the 'clicks and hits' and 'measurement driven' approached have in common organization's strategic objectives and provide quantified models that plan and track internet marketing investments from intermediate outcomes to financial results. Hence, it can indicate how marketing expenditures in mobile internet advertising method to lead to increase shareholder value aim.

I think investment in internet marketing , organizations will need follow these stages. In the beginning is inputs stage: Organization and business unit strategy includes structures, systems, resources as well as marketing strategy includes structures, systems as well as information strategy includes structures, systems and market strategy transfers to websites, search marketing , advertisement and public relations, mobile marketing and marketing research. Next, it is outputs stage: It includes intermediate outputs, such as awareness and perceptions, attitudes and intentions, value provisions, channel optimization and market information as well as it includes final outputs, such as marketing assets: customer value, brand equity, knowledge as well as financial flows: increased revenue, cash flows, reduced revenue, lower cost, lower working capital, lower fixed capital and reduced risk. Finally, it is outcomes stage includes shareholder value, return on investment and corporate profitability. For example, Donald restaurant uses its website to promote lower calorie food and fruit options as well as its global campaign tied to the Olympics, nutrition (Business week 8-7-06). Each organization should carefully identify the outputs it seeks to achieve. How can process produce these outputs? Organization can attempt to enhance of website functional or initiation of an email campaign. The final question to organizations which will ask : How outputs contribute to the long term financial performance of the organization from mobile advertising ? Is critical for organizations seeking to enhance return on investment from mobile advertising? In addition, whether mobile advertising can give these benefits to any companies, such as market capitalization and shareholder value can be enhanced by increases in marketing assets (customer value, brand equity and knowledge base) that produce future corporate financial flows from mobile internet advertising method.

Hence, marketing assets include customer value, such as using dynamic pricing to manage demand, supporting sales through online information sites, shipping directly to reduce need for inventory possession, shifting in store sales to online sales, eliminating clients with prior post sales problems from promotion lists; brand equity, such as additional revenue through brand premiums, using customer relationship to speed adoption of next generation products target marketing to loyal clients during predicted slow periods, reducing customer turnover and support costs, shifting responsibility and risk for inventory management to major suppliers, pool inventories with suppliers and clients to reduce warehouse space across the supply chain, using trust in brand to reduce unwarranted lawsuits, knowledge base, such as developing mass customization capability, reducing time to market through online concept trials, time promotions to smooth demand, eliminating product features that are not valuable to clients. Watching production timing to demand, direct in store sales to products that generate high contribution margin per square foot of fixed space and anticipating and respond to stakeholder concerns. Finally, customer value and brand equity and knowledge base shall transfer to financial flows aim, such as increased revenue, accelerated cash flow, reduced revenue volatility, lower cost, lower working capital requirement, lower fixed capital requirement and reduced risk. However, Metrics can be used to access effectiveness of mobile advertising, both financial and non financial metrics are needed to effectively measure performance. Some non financial items , such as market research activities are difficult to measure and companies often avoid measuring those items.

However, if the item plays a critical role in delivering organizational value. Measuring it, preferably in quantifiable terms, such as monetary changes or percentages. Even when such measures are difficult to obtain or depend a rough estimates, they provide a basis for examining trends over time and can provide useful information to managers. For example, two metrics for the output awareness are: The number of emails opened recipients and the number of clients that clicked on a promotional mobile advertising. Those two metrics can provide different perspectives on the meaning of awareness, thus the choice of metrics helps clarify the objectives, just as clear objectives can help in identifying specific and to be relevant must be specific and to be relevant they must be customized to meet the unique dynamics of the organization . It aims to achieve the best to capture and reflect the organization's unique sets of activities and results some may be relevant to all organizations and many can be readily adopted to be useful for decision making.

3. Discuss the relationship between mobile advertising
and other elements of the promotion in campaign
planning.

Mobile advertisement defines as the use of the mobile medium, it is as a communications and entertainment channel between a brand and an end user. In basic terms, it is the process of planning and execution conception, pricing, promotion and distribution of products and services through the mobile channel. Advertising is a form of communication intended to convince an audience (viewers, readers or listeners) to purchase or take some action upon products, information or services etc. The relationship between independent variables elements and mobile advertising which are environmental response and emotional response with behavioral aspect of consumer buying behavior with mobile advertising. It is time that people purchase those brands with which who are emotionally attached elements. Almost every one grows up in the world which is flooded with the mass media, e.g. television, films, videos, magazines, movies advertising and internet channel is either mobile advertising or computer advertising.

Advertising is a subset of promotion mix which is one of the 4'p in the marketing mix, i.e. product, price, place and promotion. As a promotional strategy, advertising serve as a major tool in creating product awareness in the mind of a potential consumer to take eventual purchase decision. Advertising, sales promotion and public relations are mass communication tools available to marketers. Telecommunication technology, such as mobile advertising enables business and industry to grow at a faster pace when contributing to the economic development and at the same time telecommunication infrastructure can be reliable. Cellular phone industry has been one of the profitable businesses in Asian. The country's growing population and huge demand potential have always been an attraction for many high-technological multinational companies. Societies used symbols and pictorial signs to attract their produce users. There elements were used for promotion of products.

A company can't make dream to be a well known brand until which invests in their promotional activities for which consumer market have been dominating through advertisements. As the primary mission of advertiser is to reach prospective customers and influence their awareness, attitudes and buying behavior.
The major aim of advertising is to impact on buying behavior, however this impact about brand is changes or strengthened frequently in peoples' memories. Memories about the brand consist of their associations that are related to brand name in consumer mind. These brand cognition influence consideration, evaluation and finally purchases. The promotion in campaign planning to mobile advertising focuses on young people because who choose advertising information and characters as whose role models, who may not only identify with them but also intend to copy them in terms of how who dress and what who are going to buy. As the market is surplus with several products or services, so many companies make similar functional claim, so it has became extremely difficult for companies to differentiate their products or services based on functional attributes alone. Differentiations based on functional attributed, which are shown in advertisement, are never long lasting as the competitors could copy the same.

Mobile advertising may differentiate companies' products or services promotion channel to attract client's attention, e.g. the company can use movable product images on internet video to show on mobile. However, mobile advertising time ought depend on the business nature, e.g. facial health products target segment is female, so it's mobile advertising time ought choose form 9:00 AM to 6:00 PM working time between Monday to Sunday, due to housewives or working women shall go back home to cook, who shall not turn on mobile phones at home. Hence, if the company had differentiated which brand and it had chose what time is the more popular to accept to let mobile users to turn on their mobile from mobile advertising. The company mobile advertising will have more promotion effort. For example, if the company sold toys, it's target segment would be 3 ages to 10 ages old. It's mobile advertising ought let every family to find its company website easily. If the family didn't know it's brand, but is was difficult to let the family to find what its toys sale from whose mobile phone because there are many toy companies were using internet advertising to promote which toys. So, it might let every family types " toy" word on yahoo, Google websites, then this toy company name would appear on their websites, the family only clicked its name on their mobile phone, it could show it' toys images, prices, which country manufacturing and which year manufacturing different kind of toys, sale payment and delivery method, e.g. visa card payment, air or land or shipping transportation flight delivery, toys manufacturing ingredients indication from website advertising and it's toys advertising time ought to choose family working time, such as between 9:00 and 6:00 PM , due to who shall bring their mobile to work usually. Hence, the toy company needs to consider family will choose what time to use mobile phone. It ought not choose night time to advertise its toy products from mobile due to family would not turn on whose mobile at home at night time usually.

Economic theory has sought to establish relationships between selling prices, sales achieved and consumer's income, similarly before the company chooses to spend mobile advertising expenditure, it ought frequently compared it with sales actual income each month.

Social media marketing, such as mobile advertising effectiveness is highly influenced by three aspects: content quality, involvement and integration with the other media platforms methods to assess whether effectiveness of mobile advertising.

On the first aspect, content quality isn't quantity. It shows that managers should not totally reply on the monitoring software to measure and analyze their social media campaign. For example, the twitter website analysis show that some brands/companies, e.g. Microsoft used their Twitter account to connect and to

communicate with customers . Their Tweets were about communicating and connecting with their follows, through some personal conversations in subjects. That were relevant to their customers . As a results, Microsoft clients were able to

beat their main competitors in financial performances and Twitter activities. So, Microsoft can use twitter website to assess whether how many numbers of people use internet service to enter phone, then who decide to buy its software products . If Microsoft found the result of the number of buyers who decide to buy its software from mobile phone Twitter website advertisement channel which is more than mobile phone Yahoo or Google websites advertisement channel after who turn on mobile to see advertising.

On the another aspect, building trust and long term relationship to mobile advertising to indicate to how to persuade to increase many shippers to decide to buy any products or seek service, e.g. travel tickets booking service after who use mobile to seek advertising habitually. Today, media marketing is about building relationship and trust through effective two way communications , e.g. talk about something that customers are interested in and creating products or service that will help to solve customers' problems from mobile advertising. Some of today's social media marketing campaigns are still driven by the old fashioned marketing and focus on short-term effect sales, which is also known as incentive induced behavior. To assess trust and genuine buyer/seller relationships achieved through consistent and engaging conversation will increase the messages (SMM) level of influence. Trust is the key factor to get the followers to actually to something , i.e. change in buying decisions influence

their peers and turn it into revenue for the companies. It is crucial to build a strong relationship with customers and enhance brand loyalty. Hence, it implies mobile phone companies need to build trust relationship to let them to pay extract internet charges to aim to read email, news, watch movie habitually. Then, it will increase chance to let potential buyers to prefer to seek advertisement to choose to buy and products or consume service from mobile websites habitually. Hence, assessment of mobile internet habitual users who use mobile internet time per week from survey is one effective method. Also, firms should start their involvement by inviting their customers or prospects to join their social media community. For example, firms can post the icons of the social media main websites or giving some special deals to customers who become their fans or followers . In the online community, firms should start writing more effective posts.

An effective post should reflect honesty and conciseness, it is as key elements of an effective post. It should also be informative to satisfy clients' need for information and experts; opinions. Effective contents should be able to actions from the audience (conversion) so that by the end of this process. Followers will place on order, subscribe newsletter or participate on online surveys. In the offline community, managers should share expertise with their speaker in the local community, which will help to attract more followers or fans and to strength connection with the community. A debate has been going on whether or not consumers are willing to receive mobile advertising. America consumers seem to willing to accept mobile advertising to subsidize the cost of other mobile services , such as email and news services.

A study conducted by HRI Research on behalf of Nokia brand found that the core mobile phone subscriber market (16 to 45 year old) is not only receptive to experiencing mobile advertising, but also actively welcoming mobile advertising in the form of electronic coupons promotion. The relationship between mobile advertising and the four key elements contributing to mobile advertising's acceptance of the promotion in campaign planning. There were mobile advertising should allow users to decide whether or not to receive messages, users could bypass sales messages easily, users should be filter the message received and users want to get mutual benefits of something back. The SMA advertising campaigns of mobile advertising industry plays and consumers have been made afraid of the spam phenomenon deriving from negative email spamming experiences. The personal nature of the website phone markets spamming especially invasive compared to spam received via other channels and devices. Mobile advertising has the potential to be one of the most powerful one to one digital advertising mediums of utilized in the right manner. SMS trials across the would have show the power of mobile advertising in building direct one to one relationship. The online companies like AT&T, AOC wireless, Microsoft and Nokia to mention few companies that are focused on the potential of mobile marketing via mobile handsets. Factors contributing to the success of mobile advertising include that ability, setting up research. measurement, tracking systems, availability of specialist expertise in agency, service provide and establishing consistent rate mobile cards. Other factors impact of drivers on the development of mobile advertising include that personalized medium, users able to opt in , call to action , i.e. immediate response possible , location specific, interactive profiling, appeals to younger customers , one to many communication.

In conclusion, the relatively between mobile advertising and other elements of the promotion in campaign planning include as below: The first element is by utilizing mobile advertising, companies can run marketing campaigns targeted to tens of thousands of people with a fragment of the costs compared to other direct marketing mediums, such as direct mail or telephone and this in just few seconds of line. The advertising industry uses two types of cost calculation cost per thousand impressions (CPM) and cost per rating point (CPP). CPM is used for both print and electronic media when CPP is more popular for electronic media. For instance, if an advertising campaign costs US$5,000 and has an audience of 300,000 consumers, the CPM will be approximately to the initial CPM measure in media selection , such as quality of the audience, audience attention probability and believability of media selection when the CPM for direct mail is between UA$500 to US$700. For email the CPM ranges from US$5 to US$7. However when email marketing is losing its efficiency, mobile advertising offers new ways to promote products and services. A significant factor contributing to consumers' willingness to accept mobile advertisement is the capability of mobile handsets to service certain type of messages , such as multimedia messages. Evidently, most consumers in the future will carry on smart phone with them. The smart phones allow advertisers to reach consumers in different locations with personalize messages at a given time. Another element is the industry of SG or 4G network service is faster connection speed is a obvious enables users to receive digital photographs, moving wide images, high quality sound for their mobile handsets. From advertisers; perspective this opens various opportunities to plan and implement more advance m-advertising campaigns and integrate those with existing marketing channels. However, to develop and provide applications, for example, interfaces to the carrier's wireless network need to be provided in multiple areas: location, presence, billing, personalization, provisioning, packet network, transport and messaging systems.

Next element is location awareness cab be seen as the driving force of many wireless applications and suits also well types of mobile advertising. When mobile phones are almost always carried with and intelligent location awareness technical solution are available. The final element is personalization means building customer loyalty by building a meaningful one to one relatively by understanding the needs to each individual and helping to satisfy a goal that efficiently and knowledgeably addresses each.

Personalization is about mapping and satisfying of client's goal in specific contest with a business's goal in its respective context. Personalization means understanding different kinds of individual preferences , needs, mindsets and lifestyles and cultural as well as geographical differences. Mobile are already equipment with a profiting options, e.g. silent, meeting, outdoors. For example, the utilization of time and location awareness as personalization variables has the benefit that mobile advertising is a marketing medium has features that other marketing channels lack. Hence, email advertising needs to keep every mobile users' personal information to be confidential, solicited message, relevance to users need and the right frequency. So, non-economic mobile advertisement will attract consumer's attention to find its restaurant location to eat.

Reference

Adrian, P. (2012). Introduction to marketing theory & practice,

3 rd edition, London: Oxford press.

Couper, M.P. J. Blair and T. Triplet (1999). A Comparison Of Mail And E-mail For a Survey Of Employees In USA Statistical Agencies. Journal Of Official Statistics, 15, 39-56.

Data monitor (2008). The proctor and gamble company. Retrieved Nov. 15 2009 from http://www.datamonitor.com/

Dyer, D., F. Dalzell & R. Olegario (2004). Rising tide. Lessons learned from 165 years of brand building at Procter and Gamble. Boston, MA: Havard Business School Press.

Priesnitz, W. (2007) Counting Our Food Miles. Natural Life, 1 July.

Sullivan, Nicholas P(2007). You can hear me now: How Micro loans and cell phones are connecting the world, San Francisco, CA: John Wilsey & Sans, 2007.

CHAPTER XIII

Organizational time management how influences consumer behavior

To research consumer behavior, it has different theory to explain why and how the consumer is influenced to make the choice by different factors. For example, utility theory,it explains that consumers make choices based on the expected outcomes of their decisions. They are viewed as rational decision makers and they only consider self interest.

Utility theory views consumer is as a " rational economic man". However, the factors influence consumer behaviors may include these activities, such as need recognition, information search, evaluation of alternatives, the building of purchase intention , the act of purchasing choice, consumption and finally disposal. Hence, it seems that all the consumer's activities in whose purchase processes. They will influence their choice. For example, when the property purchase consumer , he plans to research different kinds of properties information concern price, location, housing areas, room numbers, building facilities and environment facilities. He will find some sample target properties information to make comparison in order to decide to buy which of property is the most suitable to satisfy his living need.

However, it is not only one activity for the property purchase buyer in his decision making process. It also include evaluation of alternatives activity when he ensures the accurate property information number in order to evaluate whether which one of all these property choices is the most suitable one. Hence, it explains that property information research and evaluation of alternatives both activities are needed to spend much time for this property buyer. If he does not plan to find one property to live in short time, it is possible that he can spend one month, even more than one month or more than three months time to do the only property information gathering activity.

Hence, it seems that time factor is not the main factor to influence the property buyer to do property purchase decision immediately. Otherwise, if the property buyer plans to find one new property to live within one month. Then, time factor is possible one important factor to influence this property purchase choice decision. For example, if he felt that he needs more time to spend to gather information concerns the large house area size and the properties have more than three bathrooms and/or bedrooms properties information. Then, he will be possible not to find any this kinds of all property information. So, it means that all these properties won't be his choice. It is because long time property information gathering activity factor influence.

I assume that the property buyer is a economic man and he does not spend much time to do the property information gathering activity. So, this kind of property needs him to spend long time to gather properties information in order to make this kind of properties comparison. Moreover, because he expects to live one new property within one month. So, he only chooses the properties, they have less than three bedrooms and/or bathrooms to gather sample properties information in order to make property purchase decision within one month. Hence, the time variable factor can only influence the property purchaser when he/she needs to make decision to buy one new property to live in the short time. If some kinds of properties choices number has a lot and the property buyer feels to let that he/ she must need to spend long time to find the suitable properties number to make evaluation alternatives comparison behavior.

Then, the time variable limiting pressure factor will be possible the main factor to influence the property buyer's choice in order to make the most suitable kind of property purchase decision. Hence, it is one case example of how time limiting pressure factor can influence consumer purchase choice decision, such as property purchases market case. The reason explains why the property buyer needs to spend time to do property information gathering. I assume that general property buyer behave rationally in the economic sense. They won't only believe property agent individual property photos advertisement , it concerns where the property location is and facility etc. information on property photos in order to evaluate whether the property price is reasonable to pay. Generally, property buyers need to attempt to gather property information and visit the different actual property locations to make choice. So, general property consumers would have to be aware of all the available different kinds of properties consumption options from themselves properties information gathering and the properties agents' verbal properties introduction both be capable of correctly rating each property alternative and the available to select the optimum course of the final property purchase action.

Hence, in the property purchase and sold market, limiting time pressure factor will be important influential factor to decide whether the kinds of properties will be option to some property buyers when they feel need to find one suitable property to buy in short time. Otherwise, in some food consumption market , time limiting pressure factor will not be the main factor to influence consumer option. Such utility theory indicates consumers are as one rational economic man, whom do not expect to spend much time to do any options evaluation decision making.

However, in coffee market, buying a coffee comes almost automatically and does not need much information search. Hence, time limiting pressure factor won't one main factor to influence coffee consumer to choose to buy the kind of coffee to drink. However, there are other factors to influence coffee consumers' kind of coffee drinking option from cultural, social, personal or psychological factors. So, coffee taste producer can follow these factors to estimate how coffee consumers might behave in the future when making any kinds of coffee making purchasing decisions.

Firstly, social factor can affect coffee consumer behavior significantly. Every coffee consumer has someone around influencing his/her coffee buying decisions. The important social factors include reference groups, family, role and status , e.g. when the coffee buyer has high income job and his friends have good educational level and high income. Then, he will compare his reference group, such as his friends' coffee buying behavior choosing which kinds of coffee taste to drink in habits or lifestyles. If he chooses the kind of coffee taste to drink, its price is cheaper to compare his friends' drinking coffee tastes. Then, he may be influenced to follow his friends to drink the same kinds of coffee taste in order to keep their same social status and role between him and his friends.

Secondly, the coffee consumers will be influenced how to choose which kinds tastes of coffee to drink by personal factors, such as his age, life cycle state, occupation, economic situation , lifestyle and personality and self-concept. Age related factors are such as taste in food, e.g. the kinds of coffee taste. Although, coffee price is cheap, but if the coffee consumer's income is more and he/she can often spend to buy different kinds of taste coffees to drink. Then, his/her income level will have much purchasing power to influence his/her purchasing behavior. Hence the coffee consumer's frequency of consumption of different kinds of coffee taste drinking choice behavior will represent whether his/her income level is high or low in possible. For example, the consumer needs to go to automatic coffee shop to buy at least three cups or more different kinds of high class good taste coffee brands to drink per week. Although, these high class coffee brands' prices are higher than the low class of coffee brands. But the coffee consumer still only buys any one of these kinds of high class brands' coffee taste to drink. Hence, it seems that this coffee consumers ought have high income to let him to buy at least three cups of high class brand of coffee taste to drink from automatic coffee ship per week.

So, income factor can influence the coffee consumer to choose either coffer purchase from supermarket or coffee drinking at automatic coffee shop. If the coffee consumer only chooses to buy coffee from supermarket, due to the bottles of different kinds of brand coffee can provide more different tastes of coffees choices from shelves to let him to buy to drink at home. So, it seems that the coffee consumer's income level is low in general. Otherwise, if the coffee consumer only chooses to go to automatic coffee shop to buy the high class brands of coffee tastes to drink at least three times or more per week. It may mean that the coffee consumer has high income level to support him/her to often go to automatic coffee shop to buy different kinds of high class coffee tastes to drink frequently every week. Some high or low income level factor can influence every coffee consumer individual drinking coffee behavioral options.

Moreover, when the coffee consumer is younger coffee consumer will be possible to buy much coffee to drink. Because younger age people can accept to drink coffee habitually more than older age people. Also, it is possible that younger people feel often drinking coffee behavior will help them to bring more health feeling and /or raising nervous to learn , due to they need often to go to schools to study. Otherwise, older age people feel often drinking coffee behaviors won't help them to bring more health and they do not need to raise nervous to learn.

Finally, even, cultural difference factor will influence coffee consumers number for any countries. For example, western countries' people like to drink any kinds of coffee tastes traditionally. Asia countries' people like to drink any different kinds of teas tastes traditionally. So, different kinds of teas tastes will be Asia people's traditional drinking substitute to replace different kinds of coffee tastes more easily. Hence, culture difference will be one factor to influence Asia coffee buyers number. So, it seems that time limiting pressure factor won't influence coffee consumers' coffee taste choices to different kinds of high class or low class brands, visiting coffee shops or visiting supermarkets choices, frequent or not frequent coffee drinking behaviors.

How and why time limiting pressure
influences consumer choice
Can consumer buying decisions be influenced by time limiting pressure. For these three situations, they will influence consumer hoe makes different buying decision, e.g. in the little time available, but the consumer needs to do more effort needed to choose to buy which kind of product among variety kinds of product choice or in a moderate amount of time available, or a considerable amount of time available. In this first situation, the consumer can not real attempt to find any weaknesses or unique characteristics of the products, because it has no enough time to allow whom to choose. So, his/her product evaluation won't be the most accurate to satisfy his/her needs because little time can only allow him/her to find some weaknesses of the products. Otherwise, in the final situation, because the consumer has a considerable amount of time to allow him/her to attempt to find the weaknesses and/or strengths characteristics of the products choice. So, he/she ought do the more reasonable or accurate evaluation of these products to choose the most effective economic beneficial product to buy. Thus, it seems that time limiting pressure factor can influence the consumer to make more rational or more reasonable economic beneficial consumption decision making to buy the product or consume the service.

Thus, a consumer buying decision will require these situations to do buying decisions, they may include either little time and conscious effort or a moderate amount of time and effort or a considerable amount time and effort. The products may include cheap products/services , e.g. fruit, DVD, university courses, computers, facial services, surgeries, sport shoes, reference books, soft drinks, magazines as well as expensive products/services, e.g. cars, houses, luxury goods, e.g. jeweler, female hand bags, holiday travelling entertainment. So, any expensive or cheap products or services, the consumer will need to spend either little or moderate or considerable amount time to do gathering information about the different kinds of products or services in order to find which brand of product or service can bring more economic benefit when he/she chooses to use the product or consume the service. He/she will compare his/her preference sample brands limiting number of products or services choices to decide to buy the brand of product or consume the brand service easily. However in the consumer's consuming decision making process, he/she will need to spend either little or moderate or a considerable amount of time to do the evaluation and choice consumption behavior. It means that time limiting pressure factor will influence the consumer how to make consumption choice consequently.

What are the impacts of reduced branding on consumer choice and time limiting pressure to influence consumer behavior? When one consumer needs to choose products to buy one in a time limiting pressure consumption environment, when branding on packaging is reduced, e.g. the brand of product has 10 different style of packages to let consumer choice, but it reduces to only 5 different style of packages to let consumer choice. How does it influence the consumer decision making when the consumer has little time to allow to choose these 5 different style of packages ? For example, when the consumer expects to spend only 10 minutes to choose any one style of package to buy this brand product. Currently, this brand of product has reduced different style of packages number from 10 to 5. Do you feel that the consumer will feel easy to do decision making to choose to buy the most attractive style of package product from this brand's 5 different style of packages choices? Is 10 minutes consumption choice time enough to let the consumer to make final purchase decision from these brand's 5 different style of packages choice? Will the time limiting pressure be reduced , due to this brand's 10 style packages are reduced to 5 style packages to let the consumer to choose within the 10 minutes expected limiting consumption choice time.

It is one interesting psychological consumption behavior to research whether the brand's reducing different style of packages number factor will influence the consumer to do the decision making in the short time in the time limiting pressure environment. For toothpaste, shapmoo products example, if the brand of these products' style packages choice is reduced to 5 style packages from 10 style packages choice. When one consumer finds the brand of toothpaste or shampoo has only 5 style packages on the shelves in supermarket. If the consumer has moderate or considerate amount time to let him/her to choose these both kinds product any one style of packages to buy. The 5 style packages to these both of products will be impossible to satisfy the consumer's choice need because he/she has much time to stay in supermarket to choose. Otherwise, if the consumer has little time to allow to stay in the supermarket , e.g. only 10 minutes. Then, he/she expects to spend only 10 minutes consumption choice time to do buying decision making within 10 minutes. These both kinds of the brand's products, its style of packages choice number is reduced to 5, it is possible to satisfy the consumer's choice need to buy this brand of product either toothpaste or shampoo and both of thee brand of products to be chose to buy in the supermarket. So , the reducing style of package number to let consumer choice will be seem to let the consumer to do buying decision making in the limiting time pressure consumption environment.

In fact , package is such a visual to influence consumer decision making in the short time or personal limiting time choice process. If the product has more attractive package design, the it can bring more attention effort to influence the consumer to choose to buy the product in the short time information transfers to influence the consumer decision making to choose to buy more easily , when he/she is active in communication process. So, package, communicating with consumer in the selling place , has become an essential factor to influence the choice of consumer.

Scientific researches have proved that package decisions can attract consumer attention, transfer the desirable information about the product, position , the product in consumer conscious, differentiate and identify of among similar kinds of products. In that way elements of package influence consumer decision making process and can determine the choice of consumer and the package itself can become more competitive advantage.

However it is not absolute that the brand of product has more package choices, it must have more customers to choose to buy its product. For example, there are two brands of shampoo in the supermarket shelf. One brand shampoo has 5 different style of packages and 5 different fruit productive elements to cause similar fresh fruit smells to attract consumers to buy. Another brand shampoo has 3 different style of packages and 3 different fresh fruit smells to attract consumers to buy in the same shelf location also. When one supermarket customer has little time to expect to stay in the supermarket, e.g. he expects only to stay the supermarket maximum to 15 minutes. he expects to buy one bottle shampoo and meats and fruits and vegetable within 15 minutes. Hence, he expects only to spend about 5 minutes to choose one brand of shampoo product as well as he demands to spend maximum 10 minutes to buy other foods within 15 minutes. When he stays in the sham shelf location, he finds only two brands of shampoo products are displayed on the same shelf location. One brand of shampoo has 5 different style packages to let him to choose, but he feels that these 5 different style packages are not very attractive. Otherwise, the another brand of shampoo has only 3 different style packages to let him to choose, but he feels that the 3 different style packages are very attractive. Due to he feels time causes pressure to choose these two brands of shampoo immediately. So, he does not want to spend more time more than 5 minutes to choose on brand of shampoo to buy. He will be influenced by the brand of different styles of packages more attraction to influence his buying decision making obviously. So, whether the shampoo brand's package is attractive or not, it will influence the consumer's buying decision making to choose either to buy the brand's shampoo product in preference.

So, the more packages choice to the brand's product which may not mean that it has high opportunity to influence consumers' attention. Otherwise, the attractive package element if more important to compare right number of packages choices. Consumer package can influence these elements, e.g. colour, size, imageries, graphics, materials, smell, brand name, producer/country, information, special offers. Of the brand of products can have much attractive elements. Then, it can attract consumers to choose to buy the brand's attractive package products in short time decision making process, such as perception of needs, search for information , evaluation of alternatives, decision making, behavior after purchase. Such as supermarket case, I assume that any supermarket consumers do not expect to spend much time to choose which brand of product is the most suitable or earning more economic benefit to buy when they need to stay the shelf to need spend much time to select which brand of product to buy in the supermarket. Because in general, supermarket consumers ought plan to buy more than one kind of product or food, even more usually. So, limiting time pressure factor will influence their decision making. Similarly, as my explanation indicates why although, the product had attractive package elements and its has many packages number choices, but it does not mean that it can win the similar product which has not more attractive packages, even it has more packages choices number to let supermarket consumers to choose. So, an attractive package element factor will have more influential and potential to cause supermarket consumers to choose to buy it in the supermarket limiting time pressure consumption environment.

How the time consumption pressure
factor influences irrational consumption
decision making

When one consumer has a large number of options, he/she will feel time pressure to cause whose accurate and reasonable evaluation. Then, the personal time limiting pressure factor will bring these questions: How does the time limiting pressure influence the consumer evaluation? Will the consumer personal limiting time pressure bring advantages and / or disadvantages in whom consumption decision making? How to help the consumer to solve short time decision problem when he/she encounters extreme time pressure and choice overload?

I shall assume every consumer is general one economic man. He/she feels time is important, he /she does not want to spend much time to choose one brand of product to buy among a number of brands of products choices. I also assume that any consumers decision making satisfaction, which is based on search until they found a sufficiently good item, or run not of time. So, it seems that which the consumer needs to buy one kind of product, but the product has a lot number of different brands to let the consumer to choose. The consumer ought need to spend much time to make choice decision making. However, consumer is one economic man, he/she ought not to search all different brands to decide whether which brand of product can bring the much economic value or utility value to choose to buy. So, in general, consumers will only choose sample brands of products to decide to buy the satisfied brand of product. For example, when the consumer needs to buy one television. The television has 20 brands of similar televisions to let he to choose. He will not spend much time to search these similar 20 televisions information. He will only gather sample 10 to 15 or less different brands of televisions to compare what their strengths and weaknesses, unique characteristics. Then, he will make decision to choose to buy the best television from these sample televisions. Hence, in general, consumers will feel time pressure when they feel need to spend much time to choose a lot different brands of similar products. Because they feel time is not enough to let they can do other important matters when they need to spend much time to do search information behavior when they need to buy any products usually. Hence, it is general consumers psychology that they will feel real choice under time pressure and choice overload, when they have too much a lot of similar brands of products to let them have opportunity to choose to make decision making to buy only one brand of product.

However, when a brand of product is familiar and given its simplicity and familiarity to general consumers' acknowledgement. It will have perference advantage to attract or influence consumers' attention or consideration. So, when the market has similar different brands of products are available to let consumers to choose. The largest choice set is not large enough to create overload to influence the brand's sale when consumers need to spend much time to choose these different brands similar products to buy. Because when the brand's any products are familiar and given its simplicity and familiarity to general consumers' knowledge. Then, it can build utility confidence to influence general consumers , it will be preference sample brand of product to do buying making option. Hence, the brand's familiarity factor will influence general consumers' preference buying decision making option. So, any product manufacturers need to concern how to build its brand familiarity to let many consumers to acknowledge in order to raise its competitive effort. Raising brand's familiarity may be a good method to solve consumer individual choice under time pressure overload , because when the brand of product is preference sample brand to any consumers. It's sale opportunity will also be raised. So, it brings the question: How can the brand of products can cause general consumers' preference choice. For food example, food brands were more likely to choose the implicitly preferred brand over the explicitly preferred one when choices were made under time pressure.

Imagining one customer enters a supermarket 10 minutes before closing time. He failed to write up a shopping list. So, when the staff is preparing to close store at the night, the consumer hurry not to for set too many of the ingredients for dinner . What brands of products , he opts for, as he can choose from a variety of similar foods, but time is short and the staff is looking at the consumer impatient? It is possible that the consumer will probably quickly decide in favor of the foods he likes best, pay, and leave the evening.

Hence, supermarket consumer's first time feeling to the brand of food will influence whom choice. One target category and one attribute category share same response key: Pleasant vs unpleasant feeing, if the supermarket consumer has pleasant feeling when he sees the food photos and touch the package of the brand of food to feel pleasant in the short supermarket closing time. Then, his pleasant feeling will be chooses to buy the brand of food to eat. Thus, the consumer individual pleasant or unpleasant feeling factor will influence whom consumption choice, such as this supermarket closing time pressure consumption.

In fact, many factors may influence whether consumer behavior is under more or less control. Hunger may influence control in the domain of eating behavior . So, such as the supermarket will close soon,it has store closing time pressure to influence the consumer needs hurry to make choice decision to buy food. If the consumer feels more hungry, he will not spend much time to find the right food to buy. He will be influenced by the different brand's food packages whether which brand of food package can bring a more pleasant to let him to feel, when he touch and sees the brand of food package. He won't spend time to search whether the different kinds of brands of foods have how much different health elements because the supermarket will close store soon. So, he only depends his individual pleasant feeling to make final food purchase decision. If he feels all of the kinds of brands foods are unpleasant food packages when he sees and touch them first time as well as he does not feel much hungry. Then, it is possible that he won't choose to any one food to eat. He will choose to go to restaurant to get dinner to replace buying food to cook to eat dinner at home at the night.

The another case is that time pressure concerns how on choice of information source impacts purchase decisions. When the consumer who buys one product , he needs to use the same number of information sources to search the product's information regardless of time pressure. Because he has more available time, he devotes more time , but only to selected the right sources to search information about the product. He will mostly use marketing dominant sources, e.g. magazine. he feels magazine can give more accurate information concerns to the product's good or bad quality real more reasonable and fair evaluation to let the consumer to acknowledge. so, when the consumer has much time to choose to buy which brand of product is the most best choice. He will buy magazine to find information. He believes magazine has more fair evaluation to different brands of product. It won't mislead consumers to make wrong decision making. Hence, in general, when consumers have much time to find information source to search which brand of product is more value to buy. They will attempt to buy consumer magazine to acknowledge whether the different brands of product , which have unique characteristics, strengths or weaknesses in order to compare them to make more accurate evaluation to choose to buy which brand of the kind product. When they have no time pressure to influence their choice process time to be shortened or reduced. Otherwise, these consumers will depend on newspapers, television, radio advertiments information sources when they feel time pressure controls their consumption choice decision making process time to be shortened or reduced. Hence, time pressure will be possible to influence consumer individual information source channel choice.

Time pressure consumption decision
making process characteristics

How we can predict or know the consumer time pressure in whom decision making process? Will it bring advantages or disadvantages to influence the businessmen benefits? I shall indicate some different consumption situations or environments to explain what will be impacted to sale number is increased or decreased to businesses when the consumer feel time pressure to avoid whom behavioral consumption to the product or the service.

Firstly, I shall explain that what effects of product popularity and time pressure on online shopping behaviors are . Electronic ecommerce is popular to any countries, in special, US, UK, China large areas countries, because when one customer feels need to spend one hour even more time to catch any transportation tool to arrive the shop to buy the kind of product. Then, due to far distance reason, he/she will choose to apply internet to buy the kind of product . If the seller has website to let the consumers to choose online shopping. However, it seems that online shopping behavior can reduce the consumer individual time pressure, when he/she feels need to catch any kinds of transportation tool to arrive the shop to buy the product. Moreover, when the consumer can turn on home computer to enter its website to choose the styles of the kind of products, which one is the most suitable to choose. He/she can spend time to search the different styles kinds of product information to compare and evaluate which brand of product will b whose purchase choice easily at home.

Hence, in psychological view, he/she can feel that spending time to search information from internet behavior which is more valuable and it can bring more economic benefit to make final purchase decision more than the behavior of spending long time to catch any transportation tools to visit the shop. Moreover, it is possible to bring failure risk that he/she wastes time to catch any transportation tools to visit the shop if he/she can not find any one of suitable product(s) to choose to buy. Hence, it seems the online shopping can influence the consumer reduced time pressure and wastes time to do any shopping decision.

This is online shopping's attractive strengths to the consumers when they need to spend long time to catch any kinds of transportation tools to visit the shop or when the consumer feels hurry to do other important matters, he/she can not allow himself/herself to spend long time to do his/her visiting the shop behavior. Moreover, another online shopping's advantage is that product popularity can be perceived by examining the information pre sended on websites. For example, research on online reviews confirms the review quantity presented with products become positively influences to consumers' purchase intention and it can persuade the online visitor can make decision to buy the product when he/she has enter the seller's online website to find the most suitable product to choose to buy more easily. Hence, it seems that it is more easy to persuade the online visitor to make final purchase decision more than visiting the shop , when the online visitor can attempt to do the click mouse behavior to enter the seller's online shop, such as website. Then, he/she will be influenced to view the seller's different kinds of colorful and attractive product pictures from the seller's website.

Consequently, it has much opportunity to persuade the consumer to do the final purchase decision. if the seller's website is attractive to persuade him/her to visit its website to find any new products more than five times, even tem times or every weak several times , even day one time frequently visiting behavior from internet channel. Hence, due to internet is convenient tool to let consumers to find any product information from the seller's website at home or public library , computer, or mobile phone. Consumers must find any product information any time in any places easily. So, online shopping can reduce any consumers' time pressure to visit any shops to expect to achieve final consumption decision aim in possible.

Thus, it seems that online shopping method can influence consumers to feel time saving and time pressure reducing consumption both advantages more than visiting shops' shopping method when the consumer is living far away from the shop. When the consumer feels that he/she is experiencing situational time pressure, then, he/she will respond well to seek another time saving situational consumption environment. So , it explains when one consumer feels he/she has no much time to catch long time transportation tool to visit the shop on the day. When he/she has computer at home, he/she will attempt to type the shop name to research whether it has online shopping platform service from internet. Because he/she does not want to spend one hour, even more time to catch transportation tool to arrive the shop, when he/she can't walk to the shop in short time. Even, he/she may feel online shopping behavior won't influence his/her eating , sleeping, or recreational time to be reduced at home or any places , when he/she can behave the online shopping behavior at home or any where conveniently.

Consequently, promoting online shopping is as a time-saver is likely to be effective for these experiencing situational time pressure. Those with situational pressure would almost certainly welcome anything that would reduce their activity level and the demands on their time. In fact, there is really no adult learning method for store shopping because it is something everyone learns to do from early childhood. But for many adult consumers, they feel have interest to learn how to use internet and web to shopping. Some adult will feel interest and it is value to learn how to use internet channel to anticipate the complexity of shopping online. For example, Super Walmart cheap food store that carries many thousands of products and brands to let online shoppers won't feel confused when viewing its online merchant's home page with only a few menu items and links from its website. So, Super Walmart website can let online shoppers to feel difficult that they can save much time to enter any merchants' home page . They only need to view the Super Walmart's website ,then they can find any preference cheap grocercies to compare and evaluate which one(s) is (are) value to buy. So, Super Walmart's website can let global cheap grocery online shoppers feel it can help them to save time to find any merchant's products from internet conveniently. Consequently, online shopping will be one popular time saving consumption channel to reduce time pressure to some consumers nowadays.

Secondly, I shall explain that what determines purchase decisions for airline tickets when the traveller fees time stress. When a travelling planner has no enough time to prepare whose travelling journey, whether the time stress will influence he/she feels decision difficulties and frustration, when it will cause he/she needs to gather significant amounts of information to lead to make to choose which airline ticket is the most right choice? How and number of airline options and time pressure influence the airline ticket buyer's purchase decision?

However, there are both kinds of time pressures to influence the airline ticket buyer's airline choice decision, they focus on either real decision deadlines (physical time), such as the journey beginning day is any day of this week or tomorrow or subjective feeling of pressure with time (sense of urgency or psychological time), such as the traveller expects that he/she fears all airlines' all seats are full booked in this month. Moreover, he/she can plan to catch air plane to travel next month. So, he/she will attempt to gather any airlines' tickets prices, flight day and time and destination arrival and weather information in this month to avoid that it is too late to delay his/her next month travelling plan.

Hence, it seems that the effect of number of airlines choices and air tickets purchase deadlines (physical time limit) will influence how the traveller or air ticket buyer's purchase decision using secondary data to search of airline ticket. for example, if the traveller felt time is no enough to let him/her to go to travel agent to enquire any airlines' air tickets prices and seats and date and time air plan departure available time to concern the traveller's destination choice. Then, he/she will be probable to choose to buy electronic-ticket (e-ticket) from internet. If he/she has computer to link internet to gather any airlines' flying date and time and seat available information at home easily. Hence, it seems that one time pressure traveller will be probable to choose e-ticket purchase at home in preference. If the airline can provide online e-ticket purchase option to the time pressure traveller. Due to the pressure time traveller feels closer to departure, the negative impact of number of airline options is not as strong when he/she can view the airline's website to find the flight date, time and seat available information to purchase e-ticket to pre book the date and time to departure the traveller's country and to arrive his/her travelling destination information from the airline's website channel at home or anywhere any time conveniently. Hence, travel agency can bring a positive relationship between airline number of options and pre-booking airline that immediate possibility. When the time pressure traveller hopes the airline can build the good interactive relationship between number of options and decision time limit (number of days till planned travel effort on e-ticket purchase probabilities. So, if the airline website can let the traveller to predict when date and time is accurate available to arrive whom frequently destination choice country as well as the e-ticket's real price , it is not e-ticket predictive price and the real seats number available, it is not the estimated seats number available on the departure time and date to the travelling or arrival country destination. Then, all of these online information to the airline, which will raise the e-ticket pre-booking purchase chance to let the e-ticket buyer to make whose final e-ticket purchase choice decision to win its e-ticket competitors easily.

Consequently, a real time e-ticket information can attract any time pressure e-ticket buyers to choose to buy its e-ticket (electronic airline ticket) more than visiting travel agent's paper airline ticket option when the travel feels hurry to buy airline ticket to travel in short time.

Reducing time pressure consumption
methods

How can sellers persuade consumers to choose to buy their products or consume their services in time pressure environment easily? It is a valuable research topic to concern how to know how consumer individual decision making to spend his/her available resources (time, money and efforts, or consumption relate aspects) as well as how any why he/she chooses the preference brand to buy its any kind of products or consume its services, when he/she chooses to buy the brand of products or consume its services? Hence, marketers need to obtain an in depth knowledge of consumer buying behavior.

In any buying process, time factor will have about 10 % to 40 % to influence consumer decision. When the consumer feels hurry to consume, e.g. planning to go to travel, when he/she needs to choose to buy which airline's air ticket and what day and time is the right air ticket pre booking purchase decision right time choice; or enrolling which school to be chose course to study decision, e.g. how long time is needed to be choose which school is the most suitable to provide the most suitable courses studying choice change; purchase warm clothes to wear in winter, when is the suitable time to choose to buy the cheaper warm cloths to prepare to wear in winter, e.g. Jan to Mar., April to June, July to Aug. month; when is the most suitable time to buy another new house to live, when the property consumer(buyer) has lived present house for long time, e.g. three years or more. All of these issues will include time factor to influence the consumer feels when he/she ought choose to buy the kind of product or consume the kind of service. However, the other factors will also include to influence his/her decision, e.g. family, friend relationship factor, advertising factor, social status factor, cultural difference factor, personal psychological need level or satisfactory level factor, young or old age factor, income level factor, economic environment factor, material enjoyable need factor etc. factors.

However, time pressure factor will be the consumer individual intrinsic (internal) psychological feeling factor, and it is the consumer individual intrinsic feeling to judge whether when he/she ought spend some money to buy the kind of new product or the kind of consume service (what time is the most reasonable or the most suitable time) to make purchase choice decision. However, when the consumer feels hurry to make purchase decision. So, he/she will not hope to spend more time to gather more information to compare and evaluate which one is the right brand of product to choose to buy or the right service to consume among different brands of products or services. Otherwise, if the consumer has more time or he/she can make the decision to buy any brand of product. Then, he/she ought spend more time to gather more information to compare and evaluate which one is the most suitable product choice to buy or which one is the right service choice to consume. So, time pressure factor will have some influence to any consumers to make decision about what time is the suitable time to buy the kind of product or consume the service. For example, heater product is usually when winter weather time, the heater products need number ought increase in winter weather time or season. But, it is possible that the heater products need number won't increase in winter season / weather possible, when one country , there are many householders or families , they have one heater number at least at home. Then, it is possible that these householders or families won't have consumption desires to buy one more heater product to use in winter at home, because they have had one heater to use at home in winter. So , when the country has have many customers number, they are using the kind of heater products at homes. Most people own at least one heater number factor will have possible to influence enough time available to cause they do not feel hurry to buy any heaters to use at homes, so, their do not feel time pressure to buy any heaters in short time. Because they do not plan to buy the kind of product to use at home in short time when they have one heater product at least to use at homes in present.

Hence, it brings this question: How to attract or persuade the customers, they are using the kind of product to let they feel time pressure to make decision to buy another new or same brand of product to replace to use? The product's better quality , long durable time useful, brand loyalty and past good purchase experience factors will influence him/her to feel time pressure to need to buy another new product in short time. So, when the consumer feel time pressure to make decision to purchase, he/she will choose when is the most right time to gather information, search, select, use and dispose of another new product to replace the old product in the short time.

Hence, the brand of product needs have good product motives, may be raised to the consumer's impluse, desires, considerations which make the buyer purchase the brand's new product to replace the present using product in order to achieve whose satisfactory needs to emotional product motives and rational product motives both. Moreover, persuading or encouraging the consumer feels he/she has real need to buy the kind of new product or replace the present old product (s), the brand of product marketer needs let the consumer feels these any one of nature of motive to raise his/her purchase decision desire in time pressure environment. The natures of motive may include: When the consumer feels desire for saving money, he/she will choose to buy it when the brand of product falls down, when he/she feels fear to be sickness, retirement, he/she will choose to buy insurance policy, when he/she feels pride, or high social status knowledge, he/she will buy premium product , e.g. gold, expensive watch, car , when he/

she feels fashion need, he/she will move house to live from rural to urban, or rural people imitate urban to learn to do their fashion living behavior, when he/she feels possession need, he/she will feel need to buy antiques for its future unique worth satisfactory feeling in possible, when he/she feels health need, he/she will choose to buy health foods, join membership in health clubs, when he/she needs to enjoy comfortable feeling, he/she will feel need to buy micro-oven, washing machine to use at home, when he/she feels love and affection need, he/she will buy gift items to give to whose friends or families for presents in their birthday or lover day etc. special days to let they to feel happy. So, when the marketer can touch the consumer individual different nature of motives to satisfy his/her personal purchase feeling need and it can know how to influence them to feel that they have these any one of purchase motive needs in short time. Then, they will be persuaded to raise time pressure to make purchase decision to buy any kind of products in short time.

However, instead of attractive good product quality method can attempt consumers to make time pressure consumption behavior. The another method is brand loyalty building method, which can be attempted to encourage or persuade consumers to feel consumption desire need to make decision to buy the brand of any products in time pressure consumption environment. For example, when the consumers feel the brand is loyalty and it can build good image to his/her feeling , and this time pressure factor can influence this brand of any products which has high discount price to attract the consumer individual attention , e.g. familiar brand high class cars, the good confident house agent's high class houses, and the expensive and infrequently buying items, come under this category. When their prices are fallen down to sell cheaper , e.g. twenty per cent discount or more than twenty percent discount sale price than the other similar competitive brands' any products' normal prices. Then, it is possible to let these expensive items' consumers have high involvement and high feeling need in time pressure consumption environment. Because they assume that this discount sale price will be short time sale price, e.g. after three months or next month etc. short time discount sale price in short time period. Then, these expensive items' prices will be raised to the normal sale price, even higher price. so, they have time pressure feeling to feel that it is right time to make consumption decision in order to avoid to lose these low price purchase benefit in this non-predictive cheap discount price purchase items. so, if the expensive item marketer can build long time good brand loyalty relationship to consumers. Then, it will have much influential effort to persuade consumers feel consumption desires need by its any extensive items in the non-predictive short term discount period, due to they do not want to loss this large discount purchase price chance. So, short time discounted sale price, it is another method to persuade consumers to choose to buy the brand's any products in short time pressure consumption environment.

The another persuading time pressure consumption method is that it can let consumers to think more habitual buying the kind of products. products like stationery, groceries, food etc. fall under this category. For example, when the consumer fees the brand of any products ,he/she has habitual purchase experience, of he/she feels that the brand's any products won't sell in market temporary, even he/she can not buy it to use again. Then, it is possible to influence him/her to feel immediate purchase need to buy a lot of product or food number to keep to use or eat later in the time pressure environment, e.g. the food consumer buys the brand of any breads to eat in supermarkets habitually, but in this moth, he/she watchs TV advertisement to be acknowledge this brand of any breads won't be bought from any supermarkets as soon as possible. Hence, it is possible to influence him/her to plan to make choice to buy a lot of number of this brand of any breads in order to keep the enough of this brand of breads number to eat later. So, this brand of any breads sale loss in supermarkets that will cause the habitual food consumers of this brand of breads, whom make consumption choice to buy a lot number of this brands any breads in short time suddenly. Because they are eating this brand of any kinds of breads habitually. They feel much eating need to lot number of this brand of any breads in short period, because it can satisfy their habitual taste needs of this brand's any kinds of breads. So, brand loyalty and habitual consumption to the kind of product or food , which will result simply from the habit and it can influence the consumers feel consumption need to buy the brand's any kinds of products or foods when they feel that they may not buy it again or they can not earn discount advantage after the short time. So, any one of these sale strategies will have possible to raise the consumer individual consumption desire to the brand of products in the short time pressure consumption environment. Also it needs to spend much time to gather information in order to make purchase decision, because the brand had built confidence to consumers when they feel this brand's any products or foods are better to compare the similar brands' any products or foods habitually. So, time pressure consumption environment will persuade them to feel consumption desire to buy this brand's any products or foods in short time. When, they feel that they can not buy any more for this brand's any kinds of products or foods or discounting price in this final short purchase time.

In conclusion, these factors can influence consumer behaviors to be changed to feel time pressure need to do purchase decision making behavior from enough time gathering information available feeling behavior. They have these same views, e.g. habits and routines are very influential, particularly for behaviors repeated daily in a semi-automatic fashion. The consumer's past purchase experience to the brand's products, positive or negative emotion to the brand's products, and the brand's familiar, recognition are strong influence , the information available , it is the consumer's mind and the relative important information given to let the consumer knows form different advertisement medias matters for decision making, great between pieces of information and can be influenced by personal psychological timing limited pressure, the consumer's comparison to differences in price or other characteristics, many pursue value (or in bargain), and compare to alternatives or past knowledge, consumer personal greater value on the immediate future and heavily discount future costs or savings to the brand of product, feeling simple and easy decision making process to the product , it can lead the consumer to avoid to spend long time to make purchasing decision and the consumer will easy to choose to buy the product when he/she feels have a loss value if he/she does not decide to buy the product in the short time. SO, it seems that when the marketer can motivate the consumer's consumption desire to feel saving money, promote health, avoid waste time and less nervous workload to gather information for comparison and evaluation alternatives aim. It is seen favorably by the consumer personal time pressure purchase decision making and sense of justice influence factors.

However, sociologists have categorised the motives for consumption behaviors in the short time by the fundamental consumption decision making needs or wants which they satisfy, e.g. having a clear understanding what benefits, characteristics, economic value to the brand's any products , feeling consumption decision making process is a leisure activity. These drivers for consumption behavior will either bring positive or negative to influence the consumer personal emotion, either owning enough time available or time pressure environmental impacts can be seen to influence whether the consumer feels he/she needs how long time to be spent to make comparison and evaluate alternatives in order to make final purchase choice in whom decision making process. Hence, the consumer himself/herself time pressure consumption decision making feeling, it can bring positive purchase choice influence, when the marketer can build brand loyalty to let many consumers to feel in the market. Otherwise, if the marketer can not build brand loyalty to let many consumers to feel, but consumers feel time pressure to compare and evaluate its any products to other similar brands of products in the competitive market. Then, its products may be not the preference choices the many customers among the different brands of products choices. So, building long time brand loyalty relationship to satisfy consumers' needs, it will bring positive preference purchase choice to raise the sale effort to the brand of any products when consumers need to make purchase choice in time pressure consumption environment, e.g. seasonal discount sale period, products or foods shortage supply period, without any forever sale possibility in market. Hence , it seems that brand loyalty building factor will influence any brands of products /foods /service sale or provison number to be raised or reduced in possible. Also, it can explain why and how it has close cause and effect relationship between time pressure consumption environment and the brand loyalty building to the brand of products/foods/services to any marketers nowadays.

What are the in-store and out-store

factors influence supermarket

fast moving consumer decision

It is one interesting question: How can the brand of product seller influence the supermarket/store fast-moving consumers' more visual attention when the supermarket/store visitor is hurry to make decision to choose to buy which brand of product in time pressure environment? Supermarket/store fast-moving consumers do not usually spend much time to say in any supermarket shelf locations to choose numerous similar alternative brands of products. However, I assume the fast-moving supermarket/store consumer's decision is dependent on the interaction between the supermarket different shelf location sale environment and the mind of the consumer. So, the eye tracking explores this rapid processing that lacks conscious access or control to any supermarket or store consumers.

It brings this question: How product packing and placement (as in-store factors) and recognition, preferences, and choice task (as out-of-store factors) which will influence the supermarket / store consumer individual decision making process through visual attention. In split-second decision making, the ability to recognize and comprehend a brand of supermarket/store product can significantly impact preferences. Hence, how the supermarket/store consumer's eye truly sees what whom mind is prepared to influence how much consumption desire to choose to buy the brand's product in short time decision making process when he/she stays in the shelf location, it has less than ten or more than ten different kinds of brands products or foods to let the visitor to choose in the supermarket or store.

Brand owners and product developers will feel responsibilities to overcome promotion or advertising or communication challenge in order to let consumers to know their products are launched on the market. However, it is not until the product reaches the supermarket shelf that has good quality to the effort is judged whether it has how much sale number every day in the supermarket. The judges are the consumers themselves how to make decision quickly through the personal time pressure environment with minor package information processing in the supermarket.

What does it take to be consider an option to influence the consumers' minds on visual attention in point-of-purchase decision making ? The supermarket's in-store activities and the consumer personal out-of-store activities will influence how his / her visual attention to the brand of products in the supermarket / store any shelf locations when he/she is walking to pass any shelf locations. So, it seems that any supermarkets or stores brands of products sale number , it has relation to every supermarket or store visitors' visual attention throughout the point to point (shelf to shelf) decision making process in the supermarkets / stores. So, how much does the supermarket's visitors' time spending to obtain attention to the brand of produc? it will have possible to influence the brand of any products' sale number in the supermarket/store. Hence, in this limited timeframe, the consumer enters a decision making process that is in itself influenced by in-store and out-of-store both factors.

I shall explain what is supermarket / store space quality factor, e.g. top level versus floor level to different shelf variable height, weigh , or shelf space location factor as well as the product price elasticity and price-quality relationship to the brand of products both factors to influence every consumer decision making in supermarket/ store. The in-store factor is more influential factor to compare out-of-store factor to influence consumers' decision in supermarket. For example, where the shampoo brand products are locating to be put on the shelf , it can influence the point to point behavior of shampoo product habitual buyers. If the buyer habitually chooses the shampoo brand products in the shelf location. Also, if all of the shampoo brand products are moved to another shelf locations to display its different kinds of shampoo products to cause the habitual buyer needs to spend much extra time to find where the another new shelf location is displaying the brand's shampoo products.

In this situation, information processing has a heightened decision making role as the buyer needs to spend much time to find where the brand's displayed shampoo products' shelf location to make non-habitual decision making between options. For habitual decisions, the consumer's visual attention is reduced to measuring visual search. However, when the brands of any shampoo products are moved to another new shelf location to display its different kinds of shampoo products. So, the act of another shelf new location search , it will influence the habitual shampoo buyer's visual attention to consider the brand of any shampoo products which are usually used to wash to his/her hair habitually. When he / she can find the other new brands of shampoo products are displayed on the old shelf displayed location of the brand of shampoo products. Hence, the traditional shelf displayed location to the brand of products, when the brand of products are moved to another new displayed shelf locations. This in-store factors that will influence traditional consumers through visual attention concerns to this brand of products more or less.

So, supermarket traditional shelf displayed variable location to the brand of products factor, which will have influence to the traditional consumers' visual attention to do either buying the brand's products or buying another brand's products to replace it, when the traditional consumer feels difficult that he/she needs to spend extra longer time to find whether where is the traditional useful product's displayed shelf location. Then, it will be possible to influence the traditional consumer's traditional purchase decision to the brand's product, and he/she will choose to buy another brand of product to replace when it can be displayed to the shelf location to attract the consumer's visual attention more.

It is one important in-store shelf displayed factor to influence the traditional fast-moving consumer individual purchase decision making behavioral change in any supermarkets or stores when they feel hurry to do personal time pressure consumption decision to make purchase final decision in the point to point counter purchase (the brand's of products are moved from the traditional shelf location visual attention moves to the strange shelf location visual attention) in supermarket time pressure consumption environment.

Hence, in supermarket time pressure consumption environment, in -store and out-of-sore both factors can influence fast-moving consumer individual purchase decision making. The in-store factors can influence product packaging, product placement components as well as the out-store factors can influence choice task, preference and brand recognition components. So, it is common to influence supermarket consumers choose do personal time pressure purchase consumption decision of visual attention purchase behaviors. The different brands' products are displayed to different shelf locations in order to cause shelf displaying products' different decision making effect.

However, instead of shelf displaying location factor, package will also influence consumers' decision making, due to the influence of minute differences in packaging design on visual attention. When, the supermarket consumer feels the brands are not familiar or unfamiliar. Then, he/she will spend more time to evaluate and verify the unfamiliar brands' products whether which one is value to buy in her/his decision making process. He/she will feel visual attention need in order to evaluate in set of brand alternatives to make conscious demand mind cognitive effort by involving working memory. So, if the product's package is attractive, even the consumer is unfamiliar the brand's any product choices which are displayed on the shelf location in the supermarket. The brand's attractive package factor can influence the consumer to raise whom visual attention. Then, the attractive package factor can increase much visual attention chance to many consumers when they are walking to pass through the unfamiliar brand's any products' shelf displaying location considerably. So, it explains when attractive package factor may solve the visual attention problem to fast-moving consumers when they are visiting one strange supermarket to find anywhere unfamiliar brand's products' shelf displaying locations. Because they are the non-traditional consumers to the unfamiliar brand's products, they won't be influenced to choose either buying or not buying the unfamiliar brand's products. When the unfamiliar brand's products are moved to another new shelf displayed location. So, if the unfamiliar brand has attractive package to let the non-traditional consumers feel visual attention when they are passing through the strange shelf displayed location. Then, it can raise purchase chance to the non-traditional consumers target number when they are staying in the strange supermarket.

In conclusion, the brand of products' shelf displaying location and package factors may bring much influence to any traditional or non-traditional consumer behaviors in supermarket or store time pressure consumption environment.

What consumption is most
influenced in preference choice
by time pressure

What kinds of services or products are most influenced to consumer behavioral change by time pressure? Can time pressure factor influence more preference to other factors, such as age, culture, income level, habitual shopping, family or friend relationship etc. factors to influence consumer behavioral choice to these kinds of services or products in consumption market? I shall indicate some kinds of services or products consumption models to explain how time pressure can influence consumers to choose to consume its services or buy its products.

Firstly, for theme park entertainment industry example, has it time pressure to cause any theme park visitors, e.g. Walt Disney entertainment theme park to influence them to feel time pressure to enjoy their emotions to play any entertainment machine facilities and it brings negative emotion to choose the entertainment theme park entertainment consumption activities.

For Walt Disney entertainment theme park example, every visitor needs to pay a fixed ticket fee to enter Disney theme park. So, however, he/she chooses to play how many number of entertainment activities facilities, e.g. only one entertainment playing facility, or more than one entertainment playing facilities. The Disney visitor needs to pay the same ticket fee to enter Disney. So, it will cause the visitors feel unfair , they do not choose to play any entertainment facilities or play only less number of entertainment facilities. Because they need to pay the same ticket price to same to the visitors, who choose to play many entertainment facilities number in Disney. So, it brings this question: Does the Disney visitor feel time pressure when he/she chooses to play many number of entertainment facilities , but he/she will not enjoy to carry on other activities in Disney, e.g. shopping, visiting cinema to watch movies, walking around the whole Disney anywhere to view scene activities. Because US Disney entertainment theme park is very large . It has not only entertainment facilities to attract visitors to play. It has many places are value to visitors to visit or enjoy the other free charge entertainment activities , such as visiting Disney gardens, visiting ocean park, visiting Disney cinema to watch free movies, view scene or seeing free charge ocean animal performance shows , going to Disney shopping centers to shopping, visiting Disney library to read books, visiting Disney ocean park to view different kinds of beautiful fishes non-entertainment machine facility playing activities. All of these activities are value to any Disney visitors to choose to play or visit, instead of entertainment machine facilities activities. So, if one visitor hopes only to spend one day in US Walt Disney entertainment theme park. He/she will feel hurry to choose to play any machine entertainment facilities, or he/she won't choose any machine entertainment facilities to play in Disney because he/she also hopes to play other non-machine entertainment facilities activities, e.g. visiting garden, visiting ocean park, visiting library, visiting cinema to watch free movies, visiting garden to play free charge boats water entertainment activities, watching ocean animal show performance etc. different kinds of entertainment activities, even walking around anywhere fun and excite places in Disney theme park. Hence, the Disney visitor will feel time pressure to choose either playing any kinds of entertainment machine facilities or visiting different places in the whole one day in Disney.

Hence, time pressure factor may influence any one of Disney visitors how to choose any entertainment activities to spend time in Disney. It will bring this question: Because the Disney ticket price is fixed fee, can the Disney visitor will feel unfair to cause negative emotion, if the Disney visitor feels time pressure to choose to play any kinds of machine entertainment activities or doing other non-machine entertainment activities in the Disney visitor's limited timeframe, during he/she stays in Disney? So, it seems that time pressure psychological factor will may influence some Disney visitors to feel unhappy, negative emotion, when they feel their entertainment activities choices are wrong or doing wring entertainment decision making in his/her limited timeframe. Consequently, time pressure factor will influence some feeling time pressure Disney visitors won't choose to enter Disney again. Hence, time pressure factor can have much influence to theme park visitors' behavioral change, instead of whether the entertainment theme park's machine entertainment facilities are attractive or enjoyable playing or how many entertainment facilities are supplied to let visitors to play in the entertainment theme park. So, entertainment theme park service provide need to consider whether their ticket prices are reasonable to let visitors feel, if they do not want to reduce theme park visitors number seriously.

The another example is restaurant food service industry. Can time pressure influence food consumers to choose the restaurant to eat? Instead of food taste, price, seats available providing, restaurant location, public transportation facilities available etc. factors, which can influence the food consumer individual choice to the restaurant.

Is time pressure another one main factor to influence food consumers choice to the restaurant? In what situation, food consumers will feel time pressure to influence whose preference restaurant choice? I assume that the restaurant 's price is reasonable, public transportation facility is convenient to catch to go to the restaurant, food taste is acceptable to the food consumer. Although all above these factors are accepted to the food consumer . But when the food consumer feels hurry to hope to find one restaurant to eat and he/she hopes to spend less time to sit down to eat in the restaurant , e.g. less than one hour. Then, the food consumer will compare all the restaurants are near to whose working place or school , if he/she is one student or one working person. Because he/she needs to eat lunch to go to school or go to office to work. So, the restaurant's food taste, price is not the main factor to influence him/her to choose to eat. Otherwise, whether the restaurant needs him/her to spend how long queue time to wait, or/and the restaurant needs how long cooking time to let him/her to eat, the restaurant needs him/her to walk how long time to arrive the restaurant. All of these factors concern " efficient cooking time, queue waiting time service performance" issues to the restaurant, which are the main evaluation requirements to influence the feeling time pressure food consumer to make decision whether he/she either still ought follow the better food taste, cheap food price factors to be preference decision or he/she ought follow short time queue time waiting or without queue time waiting, fast cooking waiting time factors to be preference restaurant consumption decision.

Hence, it seems that a feeling time pressure food consumer, he/she ought choose the restaurant to eat in preference when it does not need him/her to wait long queue time and wait long cooking time. Otherwise, when the food consumer does not feel hurry to eat, he/she ought choose the restaurant, it can provide good taste food, cheap price in preference to eat.

Hence, time pressure personal feeling will influence students or working people food consumers' preference restaurant choice when the restaurant can provide short time queue waiting or without queue waiting and fast cooking time service preference to satisfy their needs.

However , in some situation, time pressure can influence consumers to choose the service, even its price is expensive than other services. For example, public transportation tool choices service. When one passenger has need to find one kind public transportation tool to catch from the place to another destination, but the destination is far away from his/her location. He/she hopes to catch the kind of public transportation tool to arrive the destination about one hour. Although, his/her location has cheap public transportation tools to choose, e.g. bus, train, tram, ferry, underground train. But, he/she feels that all of these public transportation tools need to spend longer time to compare taxi to arrive the destination. Although, these public transportation tools can be possible to arrive the destination with one house and they must charge cheaper fee to compare taxi. But, however the passenger hopes to arrive the destination in the shortest time. The most important influential factor is that the passenger feels personal time pressure to need to arrive the destination fast and taxi public transportation tool is believed the fast transportation tool to arrive any destination to compare other general public transportation tools , when it has no traffic jam external environment factor influence. So, time pressure factor will influence passenger to choose taxi transportation tool in preference. Also, it seems that when the place often has many time pressure passengers are living. Then, the place's taxi business will be possible better than other locations. Hence, it implies that time pressure factor will bring need or demand number to be increased to some services.

Time pressure also influences how consumers choose to buy the kind of product, when he/she feels that the kind of product will be old fashion or it is not popular to use in society. For example, computer product, the traditional desktop large heavy weight computers will be possible to be replaced to use at home or office or any building places. Due to the laptop small light weight computers , it can be brought to anywhere by the users easily, even it can be brought to catch public transportation tool to use, it can be brought to restaurant, library, shopping center etc. different public places to use conveniently. Due to some working people feel hurry to use computer to do their tasks, e.g. typing one document in short time. If they are not working in office and they have no computer on hand. They will worry about that they can not finish their tasks to give their bosses in limited time on the working day.

Hence, laptop computer will be one good chocie of task tool for busy working people when they need to often to use computer to finish urgent tasks in any time. Hence, it seems that the feeling time pressure working people will choose laptop computer in preference more than desktop traditional computer working tool. Due to the feeling time pressure workers, they feel that they can not finish their daily tasks in office. So, they will feel to need to use laptop computer task tool to help them to do office tasks . When they are catching transportation tool to go home or office time or lunch time , or holiday time. So, laptop computer product is more popular to time pressure working people target consumers.

Laptop computer products can also increase the feeling time pressure student consumers' needs. Because when one students feel home time is not enough to use computer to do their homeworkers at homes. When some students finish all lessons in schools and they need to catch public transportation tools to go home, in this catching public transportation time, they will be possible to hope to use one laptop computer to do their homework. So, one student who often feels time pressure to do whose homework, he will feel need to buy one laptop to carry it to anywhere, e.g. library, garden, school etc. different places. Then, he/she can do whom housework at any places in any time conveniently. Hence, it seems that their laptop computer products will be time pressure consumers' preference task tool.

In conclusion, the different factors influence consumer behaviors. Time pressure factor may be one main factor to influence consumers to choose to buy the kind of product or consume the kind of service in preference. So, when th consumer feels time pressure to influence him/her to do preference choice to consume the kind of service of buy the kind of product. It is possible to occur to influence he/she does irrational economic choice decision. Hence, time pressure factor can being positive or negative both consumption emotion to some kinds of services or products . Hence, the increasing or decreasing number of consumers to some kinds of products or services, it has absolute relationship between of them. So, any product sellers or service providers can not neglect the importance of how time pressure factor influences consumer behavior in our nowadays society.

Time pressure impacts consumer behavioral effect

I shall indicate cases to explain that how time pressure environment factor impacts consumer behavior as well as what effects will be brought by time pressure consumer behavioral cause. Instead of above discussions concern how customer personal time pressure psychological factor influence, whether hoe time pressure environment factor will also influence consumer behavior. What are the difference between time pressure environment factor and time pressure consumer personal psychological factor? I shall explain as below:

Firstly, the impact of life satisfaction is caused by time pressure on consumers responses. Can effective advertising can impact of life satisfaction when the consumer feels need to buy the kind of product in any time pressure environment? Can effective advertising bring direct impact on sales when the consumer feels need to buy the kind of product in time pressure environment? Effective advertising may being advantages, includes customers feel easy to accept of price increases, favorable publicity, and reshaping market segmentation.

However, when the customer feels need life satisfaction in time pressure lif environment. The time pressure life environment ought impact on the consumer responses on advertising. Hence, when the consumer needs to live in the time pressure life environment. The over-commercialization of advertising ought impact the consumer chooses to buy the brand of product, when the seller has attractive advertising to bring purchase incentives to influence consumption desire to the time pressure environment influential consumer. For example, when the summer season will change to winter season, the ice cream consumers begins to feel weather will change to cold weather. Because many people feel more cold in the beginning. This is seasonable time pressure environment feeling, it may influence many ice-cream likers feel ice-cream may be possible shortage in hot weather or summer season, due to many ice-creams will be bought in summer weather to cause supermarkets in possible. So, if the brand ice-cream can make attractive advertisement to persuade ice-in cream number will be reduced in the coming winter season beginning. So, it may influence many ice-cream likers choose to buy this brand's ice-cream in preference in summer. Because they feel fear none of any this brand's ice-creams can be sold in supermarkets in summer. Because they feel this brand's ice-cream , it's problem to let they can buy any different kinds of ice-cream taste to eat from any supermarkets in summer season. Hence, it explains why effective or attractive advertising may increase sale number, when consumers feel the brand's product number will be shortage or reduced from the seasonal time pressure external environment factor influence.

Secondly, I shall discuss what is the relationship between the effects of product popularity and time pressure on consumer responses? When a brand is popular to let many customers to familiarize in society. Does it increase time pressure to influence consumers choose in preference? Time pressure remaining to product popularity concerns how much sale number is raised to persuade consumers to choose to buy a preference for ecommerce online shopping. It seems to be one time pressure online sale environment. The effects of the ecommerce online shopping environment has relationship between pressure and product popularity on perceived risk and purchase intention.

In ecommerce online sale environment time pressure is operation at the time remaining for consumers to sign up the online seller' website and property popularity is operation to the number of products already sold at the moment when consumers visit the web page. Hence, when on online consumer has intention to buy any products from internet. He/she will attempt to type the product name, then he/she will find some webpages which can provide the different brands of product photos, their prices information to let the consumer to compare whether which brand of product price is more reasonable, better quality , good product image from the web pages' advertisement information to let him/her to evaluate. Hence, any product web page will influence how every online customer feeling is good or bad to the web page's any brands of products. If the consumer feel the web page has many high product popularity indicators, it may bring a high consumption desire to let the online customer to evaluate the web page all products in order to compare which brand of product is the best to choose to buy in time webpage view pressure consumption environment. Otherwise, if the consumer feels the web page has high product popularity indicator , it may bring a less consumption desire to let the online consumer to evaluate any of the webpage products to choose to buy. So, online webpage advertising information will be one time pressure online ecommerce consumption environment.

I assume that online shopping consumers won't like to stay to view on any webpage long time. It is possible that they choose to click more web pages to hope to find more different familiar and unfamiliar both brands of products information in order to make more accurate comparison and evaluation from more different kinds of brands of products in order to make the most accurate online shopping decision. Hence, any brands of products online webpage information will be one time pressure limited sale environment to consumers feel that they need to make the most accurate online purchase decision in short time. Moreover, it seems that if the brand of products which can be showed on the popular product webpage, the it will have much sale chance to let online purchasers familiarize in order to increase sale opportunity more easily.

Finally, I shall explain what is the meaning of external time pressure consumption environment is the long time queue waiting consumption environment. I shall explain how to achieve one simplistic queueing system to solve long time queue waiting problem to bring consumers' negative emotion influence to choose to consume the service or buy the product in preference.

For entertainment service example, e.g. queueing at the cinema counter to buy one ticket to watch the movie , or queueing at the music hall to buy one ticket to listen the music performance show activities. The audiences' ticket purchase aims to sit down in the cinema or music hall to enjoy to listen and see pretty music performance or watch the attractive movie comfortable within one to two hours entertainment time. If the movie or music performance show is attractive, the cinema or music hall will have many audiences accept to spend long time to queue to buy the ticket. However, if the cinema or music hall needs audience consumers to queue long time to buy the ticket, e.g. one house , even more than one house queueing time to wait to buy the ticket to watch the movie or listen the music performance show. Then, the long time queue waiting problem will be possible to cause a lot audiences number to be reduced, because they feel that they need to spend much time pressure to queue to by the ticket to listen the music performance show or watch the movie.

However, of these unacceptable too long queue time audiences can have another/ other cinema(s), music hall(s) to buy the same price , even more low price of movie ticket or music performance show ticket in short time. Then, they must leave the present cinema queue and go to the another cinema or music hall to buy ticket to watch the same movie or listen the same music performance show. So, long time queue is one external time pressure environment to influence consumer's preference choice to the service provider, when they feel it has another service provider does not need them or these audiences need to spend same long time queue time to wait to buy the ticket in order to enjoy the service, e.g. listening music performance show, watching movie.

Hence, in a high time pressure queue situation where decision makers, e.g. audiences have less time than needed (or perceived needed). It is very likely that they feel the queue waiting time stress of copying with themselves queue waiting time maximum limitation. So, if the movie ticket purchase audience feels that he/she will need to spend more than half hour to queue and half hour is himself/herself the maximum acceptable queue time level. So, his/her queue long time pressuree negative emotion feeling will influence him/her to leave the cinema to choose another cinema. He/she feels that ir does not need him/her to queue more than half hour in order to buy the ticket to watch the same movie in the another cinema, he/she can feel more comfortable to watch the movie. So, long time queue will influence some audiences choose another service provider to replace it in possible short time, when they feel waiting in a queue is irritating, frustrating and hence costly.

What is a simplistic queueing system and how it can solve above queue problem. For a grocery store queueing counter case example, for one Apply brand computer shop example, the day's most busy queue time , there are about between fifty and hundred Apply brand potential computer buyers numbers every hour in the day. They need to queue to enquire the salespeople concern to any useful opinions to let them to know in order to make purchase decisions. But, the Apple brand computer shop lacks enough salespeople to answer their enquiries concern any computer purchase challenges. Every computer enquiry potential purchaser needs to spend at least half hour , even more time to queue to wait the salesperson to answer his/her enquiry in the counter queueing line. Hence, the feeling long time queue enquiry waiting consumers will feel time pressure to queue. Then, they will choose to leave the Apple brand computer shop's counter queue line. Consequently, the Apple brand computer will lose many potential computer buyers on the busy day.

The most simple solution is that it can increase the salespeople number in the most busy enquiry time every day. Hence, when every computer potential enquiry customer can contact every salesperson to listen whom opinion concerns his/her any computer enquiry issues in order to let he/she feels that they every one can provide excellent sale service computer issues enquiry explanation performance to satisfy his/her enquiry need to let himself/herself to feel in the short enquiry time. Due to they do not need to spend long queue time to wait every salesperson's feedback or opinion to solve their enquiries in the computer shop. Because they do not feel pressure to spend long time to queue to wait the computer shops every salesperson's opinion. So, they will raise satisfactory feeling to the Apple computer shop's every salesperson individual sale enquiry service performance.

Consequently, the day's computer sale number will be possible to raise after the salespeople can spend much time to solve their enquiries effectively and efficiently.

● The reasons cause consumers feel
time pressure

What factors can cause consumers feel time pressure to but the product in the personal time limited dominated consumption environment? It is one interesting question: Why does the consumer feel time pressure to make short time purchase decision making? I shall indicate some cases to explain this possibility as below:

First, I shall indicate household purchaser time pressure consumption behavior. Consumer house buyer behavior, some house buyer will feel personal time pressure to choose the different houses to make house purchase decision in short time. For example, if the house developer has a 30% discount house price to sell only in the short three months. So, after this three months, all house purchaser will need to pay the original house price. If the house developer's houses prices are between US dollar one million to two million every house. For one million house price after 30% discount , the house buyer only needs to pay seventy million. For two million house price after 30 % discount, the house buyer only needs to pay one hundred and fouty million. So, expensive product's financing factor will influence the buyer's consumption time pressure, such as the house discount price case, due to the house developer's houses prices are very expensive. However, if any house buyers can make decision to buy its houses in three months. Then, they can pay les 30% of the houses prices. Such as the original price one million house, the house buyer can pay less thirty million amount or the original price two million houses prices. The house buyer can pay less sixty million amount. So, the large discount financing amount may be attractive purchase method to influence many house buyers feel time pressure to decide whether they ought choose to buy the property developer's houses in these three months. It is one short term cheap house financing price to let many house buyers feel time pressure to make house purchase decision from this house developer in these three months . Hence, short term high discount price to expensive product financing factor will influence consumers feel it is right time to make pressure consumption decision.

Hence, such as this three months house discount price case, when the property buyer gain this property developer's knowledge of three months house discount price message. This sudden three months house discount price message will be one attractive knowledge of factor to impact the potential property buyers' house purchase desires to be raised in three months time pressure house purchase consumption environment. So, it is one feeling sudden time pressure consumption desire good example for this three months large discount attractive houses price to influence house buyers to make house purchase decision from the house developer in these three months. Consequently, house developer will have possible to raise the large house sale number , if this 30 % house discount price can let many property buyers feel it is one worth purchase price in these three months. So, they will consider that they can not pay less 30% discount price to buy this house developer's any houses after three months. So they need to make house purchase decision in these three months short term time pressure house consumption market for this property developer.

So, this time pressure financing advantage will only bring benefit to this property developer, this time pressure financing advantage won't bring benefit to other property developers, because all property buyers feel need to make property purchase decision in these three months suddenly, due to this property developer can provide a special 30 discount price to any property final decision making to choose to buy its houses in these three months temporary short time. It seems that three months short time can cause final house purchase choice time pressure to any potential property buyers. They expect to gain high discount price to buy any expensive houses. So, these expensive house potential buyers will feel need to make final expensive house purchase decision to choose to buy this property developer's expensive houses in these final three months period. So, time pressure can occur in any short period, when the seller can provide any special sale promotion to persuade consumers to feel need to make sudden time pressure that purchase decision is they hope to earn special sale promotion consumption in the short limited sale period for the seller.

Hence, consumer personal time pressure feeling, it can be predictive to any time occurrence psychological consumption, feeling, such as the property developer's sudden high per cent discount price to expensive house less burden factor to influence the expensive house buyers feel that whether they ought do choice house purchase decision in these short term three months , because the house developer's non predictive and sudden attractive expensive houses reducing prices strategy. So, this property developer's short term three months high house discount price time pressure consumption strategy may persuade or attract , even encourage many potential expensive house buyers choose to spend lesser amount to buy this property developer's discount houses, either is paid by house mortgage bank loan lending payment method or installment payment method or on-time all payment method. So, the different house payment choice buyers will be influenced to make immediate property purchase decision in these three months time pressure period from this property developer's expensive discounted house number influence.

However, in this house market time pressure consumption environment, the property developer's expensive house supply number may also have influential effort to excite the expensive house buyers' house purchase consumption desires, for example, if the other expensive house property developers' between US one million and US two million of every property price's these houses in the country's property marker total supply number is one thousand property unit number. The potential property buyers , they plan to buy these amounts of expensive houses , the property buyers estimate three thousand buyers number at least. Hence, it seems that these expensive house buyers' demand id more than three times to expensive property supply number.

Moreover, the other property developer's expensive property developers ' expensive house prices have no any discount in this three months periods, and some property developers' expensive house prices tend to increase 1 to 10 per cent in these three months period. Hence if the property developer can supply at least three thousand property units number between US one million and US two million sale price and all of these expensive houses are reduced 30 per cent discount to sell in these three months .

Consequently, it is possible to persuade all estimated three thousand expensive house potential buyers choose to buy this property developer's houses in these three months in possible. So, it explain that why this property developer's expensive discounted house supply number will influence these property buyers' preference choice. If this property developer has only one thousand expensive houses to be supplied by discounted 30% sale price. Then, it will cause shortage of expensive houses to satisfy these three thousand expensive house buyer estimated number in the country in three month discount sale promotion period.

Consequently, this property developer will lose two thousand these prices of expensive house potential buyers number in all these three months discounted sale period . I assume that all these three thousand expensive house property buyers will be influenced to make choice to buy its all discounted expensive houses in these three month time pressure discounted sale period. So, it needs to do data gather concerns how many of thee expensive house potential house buyers number in its country in order to avoid discounted expensive houses supply number to cause shortage supply challenges and bring these expensive house potential buyers lose number in these three months period.

In conclusion, it explains why that supply number will influence this property developer's sale number in these three months sale period. Consequently, time pressure sale strategy and supply number has close relationship to influence the seller's sale number in the time pressure sale period.

Secondly, I shall discuss how does environment time pressure factor influences consumer behavior? Does time pressure influence consumer donating behavior? I assume that external environment time pressure factor can influence consumer changes whom original purchase decision making. What circumstance's time can influence consumer individual to feel time pressure to consume. For example, when the consumer expects have one hour to choose whether which brand of product to buy among the different kinds of products. The circumstance is changed suddenly. It influences the consumers feel that they has only 10 minutes to make the final purchase decision.

Why does the consumer feel enough brand of product? What external circumstance factors influence he/she feels only 10 minutes time to make the final purchase decision suddenly? For travel fair time limited external environment influential pressure travelling consumption case example, the international travel fair can indicate that time limited pressure has positive significant influence on traveler perceived value and purchase intention in short time. In addition, perceived value is served as a mediating factor between the relationship of time limited pressure and feeling travelling entertainment purchase intention to the travel fair visitors. It has a beneficial reference for planning a travelling show or fair marketing strategy.

One attractive travelling fair/show can promote the country's different attractive travelling destinations to let the travelling show's visitors to know. It can particularly influence the visitors' long time travelling planning , it can be shorten be short time travelling planning, e.g. after one year's travelling planning can be influenced to make immediate focused on choosing the country's travelling decision if he/she feels the country has more attractive travelling destinations, he/she prefers to go to travel in short time, e.g. within 6 months . So, when the travelling exhibition fair/show can provide the country's beautiful scene photos to let the visitors to view. Then, it will bring effective time pressure feeling to let some travelling visitors feel travelling needs immediately in the travelling exhibition show/fair . This travelling exhibition show/fair can bring the time limited pressure benefit. It is as an external environment factor that can influence the travelling visitors' travelling desires to be raised , when they can view many beneficial scene photos of the country' different undiscovered travelling destination . Then, it can increase their travelling desires to the country in possible.

I shall explain why travelling exhibition show/fair can play an important role in travelling consumer perceived quality and travelling country destination choice decision making to influence travelling visitors feel time limited pressure. However, perceived value has been show to be a value has been shown to be a value of perceived quality and perceived sacrifice to cause travelling visitors feel more interesting to choose to travel the country when they can view the attractive beautiful scene photos in the travelling exhibition show/fair.

A successful travelling exhibition show/fair can bring time limited process increases , the travelling visitors pay more attention to key travelling destination features and positive travelling information from the scene photos and travelling destinations introduction. So , the country's attractive travelling destinations scene photos and clear travelling introduction to different destinations information will be important message to let the different countries' travelling visitors to know when they spend a limited time to enter the travelling exhibition show/fair to view the different scene photos . If the travelling visitor feel very satisfied to the country's travelling exhibition show/fair. Then, this travelling exhibition excite whom travelling interest to choose to go to the country to travel in short time, when the travelling visitors are influenced to feel the country has many beautiful destinations where they feel have travelling interest in the limited time pressure travelling exhibition show/fair environment. If the travelling exhibition show/fair needs they to pay enter fee and it has only two hours or less time to permit to stay in the travelling exhibition show/fair.

Hence, if the time pressure limited travelling exhibition show/fair can let the travelling visitors feel attractive and enjoyable view feeling when they look every the country's any scene beautiful photos and indication how to the different travelling destinations and explains why the country's travelling places are value travelling destinations to let the exhibition visitors to know, when they do not know or discover these any one of value travelling places in the country before. Then, this limited time staying travelling exhibition show/fair will bring positive time pressure to influence some travelling visitors feel interesting to visit the country's unknown or discovery travelling destinations in short time. So, all attractive travelling exhibition shows/fairs are one external environment time limited positive pressure factor to excite some travelling visitors' travelling desires in short time in possible.

Instead of travelling exhibition show/fair can bring external environment positive limited time positive pressure to excite travelling visitors' travelling consumption desires, the another external environment positive limited time positive pressure case is that mobile coupons of limited mobile phone sale number or discount mobile phone call payment plan in short time case. How and why mobile coupons can excite any mobile consumption and/ or mobile phone call user choice to the mobile phone sale company or mobile phone call service provider.

An effective mobile plane useful limited time beneficial purchase strategy can encourage some mobile phone consumers to choose to use the brand mobile useful phone call service plan immediate if the mobile phone call service plan is attractive to the mobile phone call consumer . For example, dynamic discounts strategies are used by marketers to send scarce message which lead to higher consumers' mobile phone purchase intention. An utility increasing discount strategy provides mobile phone call users with an increasing discount over time (e.g. 30% discount for in-store consumption for 30 minutes, after which the discount increases to 40 % , an utility discount strategy provides the same discounts for mobile phone call users over a specific promotional period (e.g. 40% discount from 9AM to 5 PM) phone call using time. An utility decreasing discount strategy offers mobile phone call users with a decreasing discount over time (e.g. 40% discount for in -store consumption for 10 minutes, after which the discount decreases to 30%).

However, these three different discount strategies for bargaining have different impacts on outcomes. However, they have same influences to lead mobile phone call users feel time pressure to do choose whether this mobile phone call using plan is suitable. If the mobile phone call user feels this mobile phone call using plan is suitable to use, then this mobile coupon promotion strategy can influence mobile phone user feels limited time pressure to persuade him/ her to choose to use its mobile phone call service under different time limitation, quantity limitation and discount strategies on the mobile phone user's mobile phone call plan using intention.

Furthermore, I hypothesize that the brand of mobile phone quantity, limited scarcity message that gives a perception that the brand of any kinds of mobile phones are limited for purchase, it will have a positive impact on mobile phone consumers' perceived value of mobile products, leading to a greater tend to make mobile phone purchase decision immediately. Hence, mobile coupon is one type of price-incentive promotion. In various price incentives, discount strategy is a mode of price negotiation between the mobile product consumer and the merchant, such as the mobile phone seller , mobile phone call user and mobile phone call service provider.

However, mobile coupons offer discount under a time constraint to induce perceived scarcity. Scarce commodities are more attractive than those with plenty inventory due to the in special and uniqueness of the former perceived by the consumer. However, scarcity has both forms. They include quantity scarce can let consumers feel need to buy the product in short time. Otherwise, due to stock shortage or low inventory to influence they can not brought the kind of product. Time scarcity means products are for sale only for a designated

    May time dominate consumption

final purchase decision making

    Whether can time limited pressure dominate consumer individual to make more rational purchase decision? Can the consumer make more rational decision , when he/she has enough time to make final purchase decision? I shall explain why and how the consumer can make more rational decision when he/she has enough time as well as I shall explain that without time pressure environment. It may dominate consumers to make more rational or more accurate decision making.

I assume that it is the final time limited pressure day to nee the consumer to spend more nervous do time final purchase decision among the different kinds of similar products choices, e.g. air conditions . If the consumer decides that the day is the final purchase decision to choose to buy one air condition among these different brands of similar air conditions in the super store. So, if on the that day, he/she can not make any final decision to choose which brand of air condition to buy on that final consumption day in the super store when the super store visitor sees the final air condition consumption day advertisement in this year in this super store . Then, he/she won't buy any air condition again if he/she can not buy on that day in this super store.

The another time dominates immediate purchase behavior is that I assume that one common air condition can not be bought in short time later if all air condition consumers can not make decision to buy any air condition in this super store. So, his/her personal time limited pressure can dominate whose final or condition purchase decision in this super store on that day. If the store has many different brands of air conditions to lead him/her to spend long time to compare which is th best worth to buy in this super store. Then, it will let him/her to feel difficult to make the air condition final purchase decision in the store on that day. Otherwise, if the super store has less different brands of air conditions to need him/her to spend less time to compare which is the best worth to buy in the store. Then, he/she may make the final air condition purchase decision making more easily on that day.

So, the final air condition purchase day of the super store, the super store's air condition final day's time can dominate the air condition buyer to make air condition purchase decision immediately. Due to he/she feels that all of these day brands air conditions can not bought from this super store after that day. So, he/she needs to make the air condition purchase decision making in this super store on that final air condition purchase day in this year. Because it is the final air condition purchase day in this super store of all sir conditions products. If he/she can not make the choice to buy any one brand of air condition in this store. Then, it is possible that he/she will lose this store's final cheap price air condition purchase benefits. However, if this super store has too many brands of air conditions need him/her to choose. It will cause him/her to spend more time to choose. Consequently, it will cause he/she feels difficult to compare which brand of air condition is the best and he / she does not choose to buy any one in this super store.

Hence, this super store ought have less number different brands of air conditions to let every air condition consumer to choose in order to let they can make final air condition purchase decision on this air condition cheap price purchase final day. So, less different number brands of air conditions will dominate the consumers to spend less time to make purchase decision immediately and easily on that final sale day in this super store. Hence, it seems that the super store's final air conditions sold day time will dominate many air condition visitors to make purchase decision when they visit this super store in summer season on that day in this super store. Because all this super store's air condition consumers do not expect that they can not buy the best quality of air condition in this super store final sold day , due to air condition stocks number shorten challenge is not supplied enough on that final cheap purchase day in this super store. Consequently, that time pressure will increase to influence them to make the final air condition purchase decision in the final sold day' s short time, before this super store closing time on that day. Their time pressure feeling comes from the super store 's air condition number shortage supply in possibility. It will dominate them to make the final air condition purchase decision in this super store in short time.

The another time dominates immediate purchase behavior case is that I assume that one common picture painter(actor), he finds one architect to help him to build one house. The architect only needs to follow his house picture to build one house. The common picture painter tells him that he will give him building expenditure and building profit after he helps him to build the house profit after he helps him to build the house successfully. After six months, the architect made one decision, he did not demand the famous picture painter paid him for the building service fee. But, he needed him give the house picture to him to replace the building service fee. Because the picture painter feels that he didn't need to pay the building service fee to him to buy the architect's building service in these six months building time. Hence, he accepted his offer to give his common house picture to the architect for his reward.

I assume that this six months time dominate the architect to make the final building service fee decision either acceptance the common picture painter customer's building service fee or acceptance his common house picture replaces the building service fee. However, the architect believes that this common house picture can have higher selling price to compare his building service fee income. Consequently, I assume that his evaluation is right, this house picture selling price is more than three times to compare his past six months' building service income. So, it proved that his choice is right, because he could earn more than three times of his building service income after he decided to accept the common picture painter's this house picture to attempt to sell it in the picture auction market. It seems that this six months long house building time can dominate these both buyer and seller's purchase and selling behaviors, such as this picture painter and this architect. When the architect has this six months enough time to let the picture painter to change his building service offer decision from building service fee payment to his common house picture offer exchange. This architect can achieve his intention to let him to accept his free house picture sold product exchange offer more easily. Otherwise, if the architect can not need six months to build this house, he only needs three months or less time to build this house, then it is possible that the picture painter won't accept his this house picture offer to replace his building service fee easily. If he considers that whether his this house picture's selling price has possible to sell higher price to compare this building service fee for this house picture. He will choose to sell this house picture himself. Hence, due to the picture painter can not sell this house picture in this past six months. So, in this six months period, the house painter can not sell this house picture in picture auction market. This six months period can dominate his low market worth selling feeling to this house picture as well as it can influence him to make this house picture exchange decision to replace his house service fee.

The picture painter will ask himself, ought the house picture painter need to wait how long time to sell this picture in auction market, because he does not know whether the architect needs how long time to build this house? So, this house building time can dominate the picture painter's acceptance of the architect's this free house picture product exchange offer, which is easier acceptance or difficult acceptance . In this six month' house building period between the architect service provider and the picture painter house buyer. Hence, the house building time can dominate the house building provider and the picture painter's house building buyer both house picture free exchange purchase change behavioral choice between of them influentially.

The another time dominates consumption behavior case is that time rich or time poor factor, e.g. one fast food famous restaurant , its success is not only due to its fast food good taste factor, its restaurant location whether is close to the time poor people's offices, it is one main factor. Because this fast food famous restaurant only choose to build its restaurants to close to offices in any large cities in different countries. Hence, the franchisees need to pay expensive franchise loyalty income to buy its franchise in order to it can supply fast foods to the franchisees to sell, but they also need to pay expensive rent to this fast food franchiser, due to their fast food restaurant locations has been chose to locate in the main cities in different countries from the fast food famous restaurant's location decision. Hence, whether long or short time fast restaurant rent period to the franchisees , which can dominate the fast food restaurants' royalty and rent income. For example, if one fast food franchisee only sign one year contract to buy the fast food franchisor's loyalty to help it to sell its fast foods only one year, because it does not ensure how many fast food consumers will choose to buy these fast foods to eat, due to its price is decided by the fast food franchisor. If the cities have other fast food restaurants to let them to choose, they may find other fast food restaurants to replace it to eat fast foods very easily. If this fast good restaurant is not the most famous and it operates only short time. So, it can not earn more fast food franchisees' confidence to accept to pay long time rent to operate its fast food restaurants in cities and pay long time royalty fee to it. Otherwise, if the fast food restaurant had operated its restaurant for a long time period to raise its fast food loyalty's to let many different countries' fast food eaters to familiarize or acknowledge its fast food brand in popular. So, long fast food operation time can confirm that it has many fast food eaters, they prefer to choose to eat its fast foods. It can increase the franchisees' confidence to choose to rent its fast food restaurants and pay royalty to it in preference. Hence, the fast food franchisor's restaurant operation time whether it is long or short time, this franchisor's fast food restaurant operating time pressure factor will dominate the fast food franchisees' choices to decide to pay how long rent sand franchise royalty income to rent its restaurant to do the franchisee's fast food business in the cities locations in different countries. So, it seems that the fast food franchisor's business operation time can dominate the franchisees' choice.

In special , in fast food industry, time rich and time poor consumers behavior will dominate their fast food choices. Time rich people feel they have enough or too much time when time poor people feel time is a major constraint in their daily life. The growth of the fast food business, and the increase eating of fast food are indicators of this trend. At the same time, shorter working hours increased wealth and less pressure on domestic routine have opened up new segments of leisure consumption. But, " free time" in certain areas has not for many people, lead to an increases feeling of time richness.

So, it explains that why many fast food consumers who feel not enough time to work daily. They are time poor working people usually. So, instead of fast food taste factor influences consumer number. The people who feel time rich or poor, e.g. employment rich or poor lunch time to the employee, it will dominate the employee chooses to go to fast food restaurant in preference. So, the fast food restaurant can supply rich time to let them to eat lunch in short time, if the employee has less time to eat lunch or more tasks need him to do on that day afternoon. Hence, feeling time rich or poor to the people factor, which will dominate some consumers' choices to some kinds of businesses, such as fast food industry, or for public transportation tool choice case example, one time poor passenger feels need to go to the destination in short time. The time poor passenger will prefer to choose taxi in preference, then it is possible train or underground train, next it is tram, tain, it is bus or ferry public transportation tool choices. Otherwise, for one time rich passenger, he has more time to go to the destination. The time rich passenger will prefer to choose the cheap public transportation tool , such as bus, ferry, underground train, ferry, train. The final choice is taxi. So, passenger's time pressure will influence whose public transportation tool choice.

● Time pressure dominates consumer psychological factor

What are the factors of time pressure dominate consumer purchase psychological behaviors? How any why do this time pressure psychological factors dominate consumer behaviors? It is possible that time pressure can dominate consumer mind and behavior either choose to buy the product/consume the service or not buy the product/consume the service. Every consumer's final purchase decision, he/she is influenced how to make by himself/herself personal psychological limited time pressure . It means that he/she will have one time maximum standard to demand himself/herself to make the final purchase decision in whose individual psychological time standard (the consumer's individual psychological limited consumption time). So, it seems that ever consumer's final decision how he/she chooses to buy the product or consume the service, his/her consumption behavior will be dominated by whose psychological time limited consumption pressure.

So, time pressure issue seems evolutionary psychology, it looks at how consumer behavior has been affected by psychological adjustments during time pressure . It seeks to identify which consumer psychological traits are evolved through adaptations, e.g. time pressure consumption adaptations to choose the final purchase decision in the final time limited consumption pressure environment, e.g. the consumer expects this day is the final day to choose to buy what kinds of the product. If he/she can't make final purchase decision on the day, he/she will choose to buy the kind of product later, even he/she does not choose to buy the kind of product in the first or again, that is the products of natural selection, or the supermarket visitor case, he expects to choose which kind of food to eat within final 15 minutes, if he/she can't make the final decision to buy what kind of food to eat within final 15 minutes in this supermarket , or the restaurant eating consumer case, he is queueing to wait to enter the restaurant to eat. He/she expects the final queue waiting time is 15 minutes maximum. If after this 15 minutes, he/she can not be permitted to enter this restaurant, then he/she will choose to leave this restaurant and he/she will find another restaurant to replace it. So, it seems that any consumer will have himself/herself consumption limited standard time to decide whether he/she ought choose to buy any products or consume any services in any consumption environment.

Hence, the cause of consumption time pressure dominates consumer behavior, it is based on these hypothesis: Every consumer has demand characteristic and time pressure can dominate how he/she make final decision to buy or not buy any product or consume any service as well as any consumer needs have time pressure consumption demand because he/she does not expect to spend more time to choose what kinds of products to buy or what kinds of services to consume. He/she expects to make purchase or consumption final decision in short time.

IN fact, consumers will be encoded to influence how they make final purchase decision. There are three main ways in which product information can be encoded. They include: Visual (product picture) ; for example, the consumer stores the memory by visualizing it as on product image. Aconstic (sound); here the consumer stores the information as a sound , this explains why some consumers sometimes get the brand name(words) that sound the same mixed up when they try to remember them. Semantic (meaning); here the object is stored in terms of what it means rather than as an image or sound, e.g. when the brand of toys can let many children feel fun to play. Then, when many parents feel familiar to the toy brand, they must remember this toy brand company is selling any kinds of toys to let children to play. So, famous brand can let consumers familiarize what products that it is selling. Such as the toy brand company can let parents feel its toys are fun to let their children to play. All these sensory information can dominate consumers make final choice purchase behavior to buy its product or consume its service in preference in any time limited pressure environment, if the brand can give positive information memory to let many customers to remember.

So, it seems that consumers are dominated to choose which kinds of products to buy or which kinds of services to consume by positive or negative emotion, time pressure in any consumption environment immediately. It is one time pressure consumption environment theory factor, it can influence consumer behavior is changed in any consumption environment time. Consequently, it explains that why time pressure can dominate consumer behaviors in possible. Also, any product seller or service provider needs to consider how to manage consumption time process to be longer to cause its consumers doe not choose to buy its product or consume its service consequently.

Methods avoid consumers
feel time pressure

In business society, it seems that any consumers will feel time pressure to cause their purchase decision making process changes in any consumption situations, when they feel time pressure either by themselves or third parties influence, e.g. not buying any thing, not consuming any service, irrational making consumption final decision etc. consumption behaviors. How to reduce their time pressure to avoid they do above consumption behaviors. I shall indicate some consumption situtations to explain how to avoid their reducing consumption , due to time pressure factor influences as below:

Firstly, I shall indicate supermarket consumption environment example. In general, supermarket visitors will expect to spend less time to visit any supermarkets to make choice to any foods. They will stay short time when they expect to buy less foods, even, they will stay more short time when they expect to buy more less foods in any supermarkets. So, any supermarkets will need to calculate their clients' limited time pressure how to influence their foods consumption number. If the supermarket visitor expects to spend maximum 20 minutes to buy any foods in the supermarket. Then, he may choose some different kinds of foods to buy, e.g. ice cream, fruit, bread, jam, fish etc. different kinds of foods, Otherwise, if the another supermarket visitor expects to spend maximum 10 minutes to buy any foods in the supermarket. Then, he may choose less different kinds of foods to compare the first one, e.g. fish, jam, ice cream only or bread, fruit , jam only. So, the second one supermarket visitor will buy less different kinds of foods, because he expects to spend 10 minutes maximum , his shopping spending time is less 10 minutes to compare the first one supermarket visitor. Because different supermarket visitor personal time pressure will limit him/her to choose more or less different kinds of foods to buy. However, time pressure will not influence every kind of foods number because every kind of food purchase number will not be influenced to buy more or less , due to the supermarket visitor personal time pressure variable factor influences his/her foods purchase number. Otherwise, the different kinds of food choice will be influenced to choose to either buy or not buy , due to every supermarket visitor personal time pressure is different.

Hence, supermarkets can focus on how to avoid any kinds of food purchase choice loses , due to supermarket consumer personal time pressure influences. In fact, in supermarket every shelf, it usually has many different brands of every kind of foods to let supermarket visitors to choose to buy. For example, the kind of jam food number has many brands are placed on shelf to let them to choose, e.g. there are more than 10 different brands of jam food are placed on one shelf. It will bring one choice problem. IF one supermarket visitor expects to choose one brand of jam within 5 minute, then he finds the shelf has more than 10 different brands of jam are placed on the shelf. Then he will feel time pressure to cause difficulty to choose the best brand of jam to buy from these 10 brands of jam. It will bring the negative emotion if he feels that all of these 10 brands of jam taste and price has no more difference. Consequently, these 10 brands of jam choice will cause he can not make the final jam purchase decision within this 5 minutes individual time limited. Anyway, if there are only 5 brands of jam are placed on this shelf, then the 5 minutes time limited consumer will has less brands of jam choices, it will influence him to do more easy choice to buy one kind of brand jam food from the shelf. It is one limited time pressure of psychological choice factor to influence any consumers feel to do any brand of food choice more easy in short time. Hence, I recommend supermarket shelf ought place every kind of food brand maximum to 5 brands , it is the best food brand number to every supermarket's shelves to let any consumers to choose different kinds of foods to make the easy food choice way in supermarket food market.

So, in super store market, it is similar to supermarket market. Super stores' main products are cloths, shoes, bags, stationaries, electronic products, e.g. fans, air conditions, televisions, radios, warmers, washing machines, dry machines, computers etc. However, super store visitors will like to spend more time to stay in any super stores, due to they feel to need more time to make purchase decision in order to make the most right choice to buy these any products. They usually expect to stay half hour , even one hour or more time in super stores. Their time pressures are depended on whether what kinds of products that they expect to buy in the super store. For example, if the super store visitor expects to buy one laptop computer. He will expect to make purchase choice decision within half hour, even more time. Otherwise, if the super store visitor expects to buy stationery, e.g. pen and rubber and pencil, he will expect to make purchase choice decision within 10 minutes. So, when the super store visitor expects to buy the product is more expensive, then his time pressure time will be longer than the super store visitor expects to buy the product is cheap, such as stationery and laptop two kinds of products.

However , due to super store 's expensive and cheap product consumers whose time pressures are different. So, brands choice number will have much different between them. For laptop example, due to superstore visitors can accept to spend longer time to make laptop purchase choice. So, one shelf can place 5 to 10 different brands of laptops , another shelf can place 5 to 10 different brands of laptops to let them to choose. Otherwise, for stationery example, due to superstore visitors can not accept to spend longer time to make stationery purchase choice. so, one shelf can place less than 5 brands of pens, the another shelf can place less than 5 brands of pencils or another shelf can place less than 5 brands of rubbers , another shelf can place less than 5 brands of rulers to let them to make purchase choice in short time.

Secondly, for restaurant eaters example, when one restaurant has many eaters choose to enter this restaurant to eat its food, then it only chooses to let some eaters to enquire ticket number to queue to wait. Of course, some eaters will not like to wait too long time, so they will leave the queue to choose another restaurant to replace it in possible. For example, in afternoon eating time, these are two busy eaters, the student feels hurry to go to school or the working person feels hurry to go to office after lunch, although the restaurant service staff had given him one ticket to let them to queue to wait. However, their expected queue waiting time is within 15 maximum, but there are many eaters are queuing and their ticket numbers are small numbers. So, they feel that they must not enter this restaurant within 15 minutes themselves limited queue time. Consequently, their late entering this restaurant after 15 minutes issue will influence that they will choose another restaurant in possible. So, the restaurant long time queue will cause some eaters choose another restaurant in busy time. I recommend that the restaurant can limit every eater's eating time, e.g. it calculate every eater's restaurant entering time and it limits every must leave the restaurant within half hour in busy eating time. It can post notice to let them to know in the front door, e.g. Every eater needs to leave our restaurant within half hour, otherwise, you will need to bring your food to leave please. So, every eater know that they need to eat all food within half hour, otherwise, they need to bring their food to leave this restaurant. Then, this restaurant can increase more seats to let many queue waiting eaters , they do not queue to spend long time to wait to enter this restaurant. Consequently, many queue waiting eaters will choose to enter this restaurant, due to their queue waiting times are not exceed their time pressure limited time.

The final case is cinema queue . In general, any cinemas will have many audiences need to wait to buy tickets to watch movies. However, if the cinema has many audiences , they need to spend one hour, or two hours , even more than two hours to queue to wait to buy the ticket to watch any movies in the cinema. If some audiences' expected queue waiting times are within one hour. So, if these audiences' expected queue waiting time are more than one hour. Then, they will choose to leave this cinema and choose other cinemas to replace it in possible. How to avoid these time pressure audiences losing number increases in cinema busy time? I recommend that this cinema ought increase ticket purchase counter service staffs number , e.g. opening more three to five ticket purchase counters number in order to let these one hour time queue time waiting audiences can purchase ticket to watch their movies within one hour. So, opening urgent ticket purchsase service counters number issue is depended on whether there are how many audiences are waiting to buy ticket in the cinema in the time. However, it is only one best way to avoid the cinema audiences number loses in cinema busy time.

Time press how influences video playing game consumer purchase behavior

I shall explain that why it has relationship between the video game student consumer individual learning time and the working people individual working time both can influence video game playing consumer individual video game choice behavior. I shall assume that the different kinds of video game content difficult or easy win competition and entertainment spending on playing time factor will have more influence how the student or working person individual choice of what kind of video game purchase. Otherwise, every video game price and brand and video game entertainment design content will have less influence to every video game consumer individual purchase choice.

Why do the every video game's learning playing time and the playing time is spent to satisfy the feeling of winning game both factors will be the main factors to influence the feeling busy learning student or feeling rest working personal target video game playing consumer individual kind of which video game software purchase choice? Why do feeling busy learning students or feeling rest working people will be prefer to choose to buy the kinds of need spending little time to learn to play to achieve the easy winning of the video game content aim in short time?

Nowadays, the different brands of video game products have different prices, various entertainment design contents and the easy or difficult win content feeling to be promoted to sell to satisfy the students or working people video game players' entertainment needs. However, time pressure will be one important factor to influence students of working peoples' video games choices. I shall explain that the time pressure factor how will influence the feeling busy learning or feeling rest working video game players or video game content software consumers to choose to buy the kinds of video games software which can let them to feel to spend little playing and learning time and they can feel easy to win the video game competition in short time preference in this electronic entertainment video game industry.

Nowadays, video game target customers, they are young students and adult working people in common. When , the student does not need to go to school and he/she stays at home, he /she will like to play video game after he/she finishes to learn just a moment usually or the adult working person finishes jobs on the day, after he/she ate dinner, he/she will also like to play video game at home. So , video game can be one kind of entertainment product to let they feel enjoy to play when they re staying at homes.

Video game can be one kind of entertainment culture or entertainment behavior at home to them in popular. A player's ability to perform within a game entertainment is important, and players tend to knowledgeable about their achievements and failures within any game world. So, when one student hopes to get pass grade in school examination. He will choose to spend little time to attempt to win the video game content competition in short time because it can let him to feel that may increase his confidence to pass the grade in the school examination later in possible when he ensures that he had won the video game content competition. He believes that he can be trained to raise whose judgement and mind and analysis ability in his playing video game proceed. Instead of playing video game can increase student learning confidence, it can also increase the working people's confidence, when the working person hopes to be promoted or increased salary later from his supervisor's appreciation. He will attempt to spend little time to win the kind of video game content competition in short time. He will have more confident to achieve to raise his working performance to let his supervisor appreciation if he can learn how to win the kind of video game competition in short time.

It seems that whether the player needs to spend how much time to learn how to win any kind of video content game competition , this " spending learning time of winning any video content game competition in time pressure playing environment feeling factor will influence the student or working person 's video game content purchase choice. If the video game design is more complex or difficult to let the player to feel to learn to win the game competition as well as it also needs them to spend more long time to learn to play and win the kind of video content game competition. Then, it has possible to influence the hard learning students or hard working people video game consumers, they do not choose to buy any kinds of need spending long learning and playing time to win the kinds of video content game competitive software products. So, it seems that the spend how much playing and learning time to win the video game content competition factor will bring time pressure to let the hard working people or hard learning student video game consumers choose to buy the video content game software products are easy to learn to play in preference because they expect to pass grade or appreciate easy, if they feel that they can learn how to win the video game content competition in short time as well as they do not spend much playing time to win the kind of video game content competition and they will reduce their learning time at homes.

I shall explain why price won't be the main factor to influence video game players' purchase choices in preference. Some video game software sellers feel reduced sale price can attract many video game buyers' choice in preference. It is one wrong mind, due to video game software price is not too much high, it is one kind popular cheap entertainment software product. So , the kinds of similar entertainment content design video game products , their sale price difference between the kind of most expensive , the highest price video game software and the kind of the cheapest , the lowest price video game software won't be difference very much. Their price difference level may be US 410 to US$50 or even less than US$50 level. So,, one video fame entertainment player won't feel that the kind of similar content design of video game software's higher price which will influence he chooses to buy another cheaper similar of kind video game content design software product to replace to the prior higher price one. Because their price difference are not too much or video game software entertainment product is not on kind of expensive product to let them to feel. So, it seems what video game software price won't influence the video game players' prior one of preference choice, it is not easy to be replaced from later cheaper one, when the video game player feels like to play the kind of high price of video game content software before.

Can the video game content influence player individual purchase motivation in preference? In fact, there are many different kinds of video game contents to let players to choose. This free-to -play business model that has rapidly speed to achieve games services to general . So, some students or working people players can free download some kinds of video game software to play from online channel. It will be attractive to the no paid video game players. Hence, free download video game content will influence the paid video game players' purchase decisions for in -game content are not only affected by people's existing general attitudes, consumption values, and motivation , but also by the design decisions and the needs built into the game by the developers. Because the paid video game players won't like to buy the similar content video games, which can be free download to play from online or internet channel. They will feel unfair or not worth or loss if they choose to pay to buy the similar video game content entertainment software, after they discovered that they may be free download this kind of similar video game content to play from internet.

It will bring this question: Why will time pressure influence video game player chooses to download free video game to play in preference? When one student feels that he has no enough time to study, he won't choose to to any video game shops to do video game software comparative behavior to compare which one's price is lower, game playing content is more attractive, brand is familiar in order to make final purchase decision in preference. If he discovered that there has one kind of video game content, which can be free download to play from internet or online channel . So, when the student feels that he needs have much time to study on the day. How will choose to attempt to find some kind of video game contents from computer tool which has the attractive entertainment content , it can let he to feel enjoy to play and it is free download from mobile or computer. Then, he won't choose to spend non predictive time to visit any video game shops to make purchase decision on that day. So, time pressure will be one factor to influence some video game software consumers to feel whether they ought either visit any video game shops to make purchase choice or download some free video game contents at homes for the feeling no enough learning time student players. Even time pressure will also influence adult working people video game players, when the working person feels tries after his full day busy working on that day. Then, he will want to stay at home to rest . Although, he expects to visit any video game shops to choose which video game software product(s) to buy on that day, but when he discovered that there are some video game contents which are attractive to influence him to do free download behavior from internet at home. Also, he feels very tried and he will choose to stay at home on that day. If he can find some free video game contents are attractive to influence he chooses to do free download video game contents behavior and replace visiting video game stores behavior on that day. So, free download video game content entertainment activity will be one attractive promotion video game software method to assist the video game sellers' new video game products to let many feeling time pressure learning or working video game players to know from internet channel. Consequently, online free entertainment video game content download playing choice will influence many video game shops will lose many feeling time pressure video game players number every day in possible. Also, it means that the lazy students or disliking learning students or no job people or (less working hours) part time working people, they will be the main target video game customers, due to they accept to spend much time to visit their video game shops to choose any kinds of video game software to buy in preference.

● How can video game advertisement method influence feeling time pressure and feeling without time pressure video game software consumer purchase ?

In fact, video game sellers can choose new media channel to advertise their new video game software products, e.g. computer online advertisement channel, instead of video game pictures in shops, magazine, newspapers, television, radio ,cinema, public transportation tools poster traditional advertisement channels. However, computer online advertisement channel can attract many feeling learning time pressure of students consumers and feeling lack of enough rest time working people consumers to let them to choose to view their video game software advertisements from online websites at homes conveniently.

It is easy to understand , due to these feeling lack of enough learning time student video game players and feeling lack enough rest time working people video game players, they go back home after they finished learning in schools or they finished jobs in workplaces on that video game purchase planning day. After they eat their dinners, they may turn on computers to search information from internet. Suddenly, they discover some attractive video game contents photos or images are advertised from the video game seller's website or public yahoo website , even they can choose to buy any one of these video game software from online shopping channel. Then, they will feel convenient to buy any one of these video game software from internet channel. SO, online video game advertisement will be the feeling time pressure video game players' first time contact channel at homes or the fastest advertisement contact channel to compare visiting video game store post advertisement, television , radio , magazine contact advertisement channels, when they are staying at homes.

Due to internet is popular to be used to search any information for consumers. So, the traditional magazine, newspapers, television, radio and visiting video game stores advertisement channels won't be more attractive to the feeling time pressure video game consumers . They will choose to find any information from internet at homes in preference , when they have at least one computer to use at home, they can click website to search any information from internet easily.

The most important factor is that they can feel to spend little time to search information from internet to compare spending more time to find anywhere places whether they has magazines or book stores to sell video game magazine and newspapers publishers, radios and television won't inform them when they have video game advertisements to let they know whether what new video game software will promote to sell as soon as possible when they buy newspapers or turn on radios or televisions at home.

Otherwise, internet will be easy to let the feeling pressure video game software consumers to know when whose liking new video content game software(s) will be promoted to sell from internet advertisement easily. Also, the feeling time pressure video software consumers can choose to buy their liking video game software (s) from online shopping channel in possible if the video game seller can provide one website to let him/her to pay visa to buy and then it can deliver the video game software(s) to his/her home immediately or tomorrow or later time when the buyer's home located in overseas or far away from the video game seller's warehouse and their software are needed to be delivered by air plane transportation.

So, the feeling time pressure video game players won't need to leave their homes to spend more time to visit any video game stores to make final video game purchase decision any time. Hence, online advertisement and shopping channel will be one good sale promotion method to any feeling time pressure video game players nowadays. It will influence the traditional visiting video game stores' video game consumers' purchase behaviors to change to online purchase behaviors at homes conveniently, because they avoid to waste much time to visit video game stores as well as avoid to waste much time to choose any video game products in different video game stores, when they are staying in different video game stores. Visiting video game purchase behavior will need they spend whole day time to make final purchase choice, even it is possible that they can not make any video game software purchase decision after they visit many video game stores on that day.

Otherwise , online game advertisement channel can let them to feel to spend little time to search any new video game contents from every web page as well as every web page can show the new video game content images or photos or pictures to let every online users to see clearly when he/she sits down to turn on computer to search any kinds of video game content information to view at home in short time.

In conclusion, online video game advertisement and online shopping channel can attract many feeling time pressure video game players' consideration when they need to search any kinds of new or old video game contents information and it also changes their purchase decision to online shopping from traditional visiting video game store shopping behavior. Video game industry's advertisement method , sale method is the kind of video game playing content's easy or difficult feeling degree , spending how much playing time to win the competition in the game entertainment environment factors will influence the feeling time pressure video game players' final purchase decision making choice behavior to any video game software publishers nowadays.

Time pressure consumption or production situation explanation

Will one consumer feel difficult to make consumption choice or one employee feel pressure to work when the worker works in the company's high pressure productive environment or the consumer makes difficult purchase choice in high pressure consumption environment? Will time pressure bring motivation to the consumer purchase decision or the employee working efficiency? It depends on some factors to either cause time pressure working environment or raise the employee individual efficiency , or time pressure consumption environment can either encourage the consumer purchase decision or discourage the consumer purchase decision . I shall explain as below: What does efficiency mean? Due to economic problem is a scarcity of resource, efficiency is concerns with the optimal production, consumption environment. For time pressure consumption situation example, e.g. supermarket shopping counter check out purchase queue waiting time pressure, cinema purchase ticket queue waiting time pressure, restaurant queue waiting booking table time pressure etc. different consumption pressure time waiting situation. For time pressure working situation example, e.g. supervisor's demand tasks finishing on time before the employee leaves the office on the day, then the supervisor's demand will cause the employee feels time pressure to do all tasks on time, otherwise, he needs to work overtime, even no extra allowance compensation to his extra time loss, or the employee needs to do another employee's tasks , due to he is absent on the day. However, this situation can be called economically efficient production or consumption if: no one can be worse off, no additional output can be obtained, without increasing the amount of inputs, production proceeds at the lowest possible per unit cost. For these economic efficient consumption situation example, the consumer has much time to wait, the shop has less different styles of products to let them to spend time to choose in the shop's shelf.

However, these definitions of efficiency are not exactly equivalent, but all they are caused by the idea that a system is efficient if nothing more than be achieved given the resources available. On time pressure working environment influence aspect, Time pressure working environment may bring efficiency, but time pressure working environment may also bring inefficiency, e.g. employing workers who are not necessary for the productive process. For example, a firm may be more concerned about the political implications of making people redundant than getting rid of surplus workers, or lack of management control, if a firm does not have supervision of workers, then productivity may tall as workers talk it easy, not finding cheapest suppliers, a firm may continue to source raw materials from a high cost supplier rather than look for cheaper raw materials to be supplied to let workers to work in one short time task finishing environment. Then, they may feel short time task finishing pressure to bring inefficiency production result. I shall indicate efficient production and efficient consumption situations as below:

For building a new airport working time pressure situation example, how to evaluate that it is one efficient productive situation. When a new airport may lead a greater increase in social benefit than social cost. It seems that an efficient productive situation in time pressure working environment. The time pressure can excite or encourage workers hard to work and the won't feel pressure to work to cause inefficient performance. Therefore, these is a net gain to society. However, those people living near the new building airport will lost out. Therefore, this is not an improvement.

However , if the people living nearby were compensated for extra noise, when the workers need to use equipment build the new airport in the pressure building time when they feel lack of enough equipment supplies or lack of enough workers to cooperate to work. Then, it is possible to have a negative improvement inefficient production. So, how to evaluate whether the new airport builders feel time pressure to finish this new airport building project before the due date or not. It can depend on whether the people living near the new airport often listen noise or not. In a without time pressure working situation, the workers do not need often to cause noise in their airport production process. If they feel no time pressure to finish this new airport building project before the finishing due date. Their working behaviors ought not often cause noise to influence themselves nervous or emotion to be poor to work, or feeling workload to bring the inefficient performance consequence to finish this new airport after the due date in possible. It ought seem that they won't feel time pressure and they have confidence to finish to build this new airport before the due date. If the employer has enough workers number and equipment supplies number to let them to do this new airport building task. Otherwise, if they need to often cause noise. It implies that it has no enough workers number and equipment number to let them to build this new airport before the due date. They feel time pressure to finish this new airport building project. So , the employer ought increase workers and equipment to reduce their worry about on building this new airport project before or one due date finishing, if the employer hoped that they can perform efficiently.

For avoiding feeling time pressure on consumption situation example, when the product can be allocated efficiency, then consumers will feel less time pressure consumption psychological influence. This occurs when products and services are distributed according to consumer choice preferences. It means that the seller can make more accurate preferable choice prediction whether consumers will choose to buy what kinds of styles of products or characteristics of services provision in preference. So, they won't need to spend more time to do choices to decide whether which styles of products or characteristics of service provisions whom hope to buy or consume in preference.

In one allocative efficient occurs when the price of the product or service is same to the marginal cost. A more precise definition of allocation efficiency is at an output level where the price equals the marginal cost of production . This is because the price that consumers are willing to pay is equal to the marginal utility that they get. Therefore, the optimal distribution is achieved when the marginal utility of products equals the marginal cost. For example , when firms in perfect competition are said to product at an allocative efficient level, monopolies can increase price above the marginal cost of production and are allocative inefficient. So, if the product is sold in the monopolies market environment. Many the similar product sellers raise sale price to sell similar styles of products to let consumers to choose to make purchase decision. Then, will influence them to feel their choices to the kinds of similar styles of products in the time pressure product choice consumption situation. Otherwise, firms are in the perfect competitive consumption environment. Consumers can feel their similar product prices are not difference too much. Then, they will feel less time pressure to make which kinds of product choice of purchase decision in preference. They will spend less time to make final purchase decision. So, whether the kind of product market is monopolies or perfect competition which will influence consumers feel more or less time pressure consumption generally. Consequently, consumer time pressure feeling and the kind of product 's market environment, they have close relationship to influence consumer purchase decision making behavior.

What is dynamic efficient production environment? This refers to efficient over time. Dynamic efficiency involves the introduction of new technology and working methods to reduce costs over time, e.g. letting workers feel that productive time can be reduce to produce the same level of tasks. Then, they can avoid long time pressure to influence their working performance. With this mind, we can define dynamic efficiency as an aspect of economic efficiency that measures the speed or the rate at which the production possibility curve moves from one static equilibrium point to another within a given period. For Ford Motor company efficient production predictive method case example, in the 1920 year, the Ford Motor factor were very efficient for that particular year. However, compared to later decades, we can not say that the production methods of the 1920 year were efficient. On other words, it is important for firms to make best use of given resources. But, they also need to develop greater use of resources over time. Hence, Ford Motor can let workers to avoid time pressure feeling to produce its any motor vehicles i their productive process in 1920 year. When its new productive technology is adopted to be used to manufacture any kinds of its more vehicles in factory. Also, it can raise their productive efficiency to manufacture any motor vehicles in 1920 year. However, although Ford Motor can make best use of given resources to assist workers to produce any kinds of motor vehicles efficiently. The vehicle buyers' driving needs or new design motor demands are increasing. They need new different kinds of Ford Motor design to be provided to let them to choose. So, Ford Motor also needs to develop greater use of more resources over time, due to the more different styles of new design motor vehicles are needed. So, the new kinds of productive resources are needed to be develop in order to adopt to vehicle buyers' needs. If Ford Motor can not find or discover any new productive material and it can not innovate any new kinds of productive methods to be taught to let workers to learn how to manufacture the future new designs of Ford Motor vehicles efficiently. Then, they wil be possible to feel time pressure to work, due to they can not adopt how to manufacture the future new design motor vehicles, when they are not proficient to apply the future new productive technology to manufacture any new design of motor vehicles.

This is one good example to explain high technological manufacturing resources and techniques and method can let workers to reduce time pressure to manufacture in their manufacturing process, but if the manufacturer can not improve its manufacturing technology to let its workers can continue adapt how to apply the new different manufacturing method to manufacture the future new design or innovative products. Then, they will be possible that they feel time manufacturing pressure and raising inefficient manufacturing performance, due to the manufacturing technology or productive technique can not be improved and training to them to raise skillful proficiency. So, these productive workers will onle reduce time pressure to manufacture in short time, if the manufacturer can not improve any new kinds of manufacturing techniques and teach them how to apply the future new manufacturing techniques to work efficiently. .Then, their performance will be ppor in possible when they feel long time pressure o work in the long time pressure working environment. Hence, it has relationship between new technique improvement and long or short time working pressure and performance.

Distributive efficiency can raise consumption desire and it can reduce consumer individual choice time to make purchase decision in short time. Concerned with allocating products and services provision according to who needs them most . Therefore, requires an equitable distribution . Distributive efficiency occurs when products sale and service provision are consumed by those who need them most. Distributive efficiency is concerned with an equitable distribution of resources because of the law of diminishing marginal returns .

The law of diminishing marginal returns states that as consumption of product increase the product users tend to get diminishing marginal utility. For example, if a family already has three cars, but gets a fourth car, this fourth car will only increase this family net utility by a small amount. If by constrast someone on a low income is able to get their first car, the marginal utility will be much higher. Therefore, to be distributive efficient, society will need to ensure an equitable distribution of resources. For car sale case example, if the car seller has distribution of resource, such as different styles of car kinds sale number efficiently, e.g. the high quality expensive car number manufacturing number is less than the low quality cheap car number. Then, there are many low income people may have enough time too pay to buy the cheap car in the car sale market. Then, it is possible that the car company can sell more cheap cars in short time, due to many low income people do not need to spend long time to consider whether they ought buy or not buy any first car, even another car or other cars for their family to drive. They will not feel purchase time pressure to make final car purchase choice, due to there are many common low quality cheap cars number are supplied to be sold in the country's car market immediately. So, when the car company can concentrate on manufacturing many low quality cheap cars to prepare to sell. Although, its high quality expensive car number reduces, and it will increase its high profit earn in possible in short time only. Otherwise, in long time benefit aspect, many low quality cheap cars sale number will increase many low income car buyers nu,bers when they find the car manufacturer can have many different style design of low quality cheap cars to let them to choose more than other car competitors in the country's car sale market.

In long time, it will reduce time purchase choice pressure to its car consumers, when many car buyers believe this car company only it has many different styles of design low quality and cheap price cars to let them to choose to buy to compare other brands of car companies in whose country. Then, they won't feel need to spend extra much time to choose other brands of cars to compare this car company's cars. It implies that the country car buyers only consider to spend less time to choose this brand of any cars to make car purchase decision in preference. They won't feel time pressure to consider other brands of any kinds of style cars purchase choices often habitually.

So, this brand cars have built choice habit to many low quality and cheap car buyers in this country. So, when the seller can build long time brand of any this car company's any car products choice habit to let many buyers this brand cars are preferable choice, then they will prefer to spend short time to make purchase decision for this company's any cars . Then it can sell any low quality and cheap cars to compare other brands of car companies more easily.